QUELLING INSURRECTION

This book re-examines the origins and development of the laws of war and human rights law and exposes an over-looked provision of the European Convention on Human Rights which permits the use of lethal force where absolutely necessary to quell an insurrection.

When civilian casualties occur in internal armed conflicts, questions are asked about how civilians can be better protected against the use of force by armed insurgents and state security forces. The laws of war include protection against the targeting of civilians but permit the use of force based on 'military necessity' and allow 'proportionate' civilian casualties. Where those laws do not apply, the use of force is generally seen as being limited to self-defence. This creates paradigms of armed conflict and law-enforcement with very different rules. The paradigms are then treated by governments and other actors as being separate and divided by a threshold of violence, when, in practice, they overlap, both in the conduct of military operations and, this book argues, as a matter of law.

Revisiting the law provides the opportunity to reassess the benefits and risks of the existing paradigms and consider how applying the provision permitting the use of lethal force in quelling an insurrection would affect them. The book concludes that it offers a middle way based on the existing law, but it requires wider recognition and development in order to achieve a more appropriate balance between human rights and collective security.

Quelling Insurrection

Lethal Force, Human Rights and the Laws of War

David Bicknell

•HART•

OXFORD • LONDON • NEW YORK • NEW DELHI • SYDNEY

HART PUBLISHING

Bloomsbury Publishing Plc

Kemp House, Chawley Park, Cumnor Hill, Oxford, OX2 9PH, UK

1385 Broadway, New York, NY 10018, USA

Bloomsbury Publishing Ireland Limited, 29 Earlsfort Terrace, Dublin 2, D02 AY28, Ireland

HART PUBLISHING, the Hart/Stag logo, BLOOMSBURY and the Diana logo are trademarks of Bloomsbury Publishing Plc

First published in Great Britain 2026

1

A catalogue record for this book is available from the British Library.

A catalogue record for this book is available from the Library of Congress.

Library of Congress Control Number: 2025949142

ISBN: HB: 978-1-50999-222-5
ePDF: 978-1-50999-224-9
ePub: 978-1-50999-223-2

Typeset by Compuscript Ltd, Shannon

ACKNOWLEDGEMENTS

This book is a revised and expanded version of the thesis for my PhD which was based on research at King's College London from 2017–21. I have been greatly helped and encouraged by the staff at all levels at King's College London but most of all I should like to thank my Supervisor, Professor Rachel Kerr, my Second Supervisor, Lord Verdirame KC, and my upgrade examiner, Professor James Gow, for their advice throughout my PhD and afterwards; and, from King's and elsewhere, Dr Henry Lovat, Dr Jack McDonald and Dr Henry Redwood for their time and encouragement as I grappled with the process of turning a PhD into a book. Perhaps the most significant part of that process began in the viva for my PhD when my examiners, Professor David Armitage and Professor Noëlle Quénivet, challenged me to think about the wider implications and importance of my thesis on the use of lethal force in British military operations and I am very grateful to them for conducting the viva so generously and for setting me on the path to this book. I should also like to acknowledge and thank the Huntington Library, San Marino, California and the Milton Eisenhower Library, John Hopkins University, Baltimore for giving me access to their collections of the papers of Francis Lieber. Along with access, I was given excellent support by the archivists and librarians at the archives and libraries that I visited during the period of researching my PhD and then extending the research afterwards, in particular: Steve Hindle at the Huntington Library and James Stimpert at the Milton Eisenhower Library and their colleagues for making me so welcome on my research visits to the United States as well as those who helped me at the Library of Congress, the National Archives, the British Library, the Imperial War Museum, the London School of Economics, Queen's University, Belfast, and the Maughan Library at King's College London. I am very grateful too for the support I have received, especially from my wife, Deborah, my friend and former colleague, Professor Sarah Paterson, and my other friends and colleagues that has kept me going throughout. Finally, I should like to thank Sinead Moloney, Sasha Jawed, Tom Adams, the readers and the others in the editorial team at Hart Publishing for their guidance through the publication of this book from start to finish. If after all that assistance there are still errors, I am responsible.

Dr David Bicknell
Visiting Research Fellow
King's College London

CONTENTS

ABBREVIATIONS

AG	Attorney General.
AP(I)	1977 Additional Protocol I to the 1949 Geneva conventions.
AP(II)	1977 Additional Protocol II to the 1949 Geneva conventions.
British Manual	The *Manual of Military Law* published by the War Office in successive editions from 1884 to 1957 and the *UK Manual* of 2004.
CA	Court of Appeal.
CD	Chancery Division.
Common Article 3	Article 3 of the four 1949 Geneva conventions.
DORA	Defence of the Realm Act 1914.
ECHR or European Convention	1950 European Convention on Human Rights.
ECtHR	European Court of Human Rights.
General Order 100 or the Lieber Code	US War Department, Adjutant General's Office, *General Orders, No. 100: Instructions for the Government of Armies of the United States in the Field* (Washington: GPO, 1863).
HCJ	High Court of Judiciary (Scotland).
HEH	Huntington Library, San Marino, California, USA.
HL	Appellate Committee of the House of Lords.
ICC	International Criminal Court.
ICCPR or International Covenant	1966 International Covenant for Civil and Political Rights.
ICJ	International Court of Justice.
ICRC	International Committee of the Red Cross.

ICTR	International Criminal Tribunal for Rwanda.
ICTY	International Criminal Tribunal for former Yugoslavia.
IRA	Irish Republican Army.
IWM	Imperial War Museum, Lambeth, London.
JAG	Judge Advocate General.
KBD	King's Bench Division.
ME	Milton Eisenhower Library, John Hopkins University, Baltimore, Maryland, USA.
PC	Judicial Committee of the Privy Council.
PKK	Kurdish Workers' Party.
QBD	Queen's Bench Division.
ROIA	Restoration of Order in Ireland Act 1920.
Rome Statute	1998 Rome Statute of the International Criminal Court.
SC	Supreme Court.
TNA	The National Archives, Kew, London.
UK	United Kingdom.
UN	United Nations.
UN HRC	United Nations Human Rights Committee.
Universal Declaration	1948 Universal Declaration of Human Rights
US Manual	*The Rules of Land Warfare* published by the United States War Department/Department of the Army in successive editions from 1914 to 1976 and *The Law of War Manual* published by the United States' Department of Defense in 2015.

TABLE OF CASES

International Court of Justice (*ICJ*)

International Criminal Tribunal for the former Yugoslavia (*ICTY*)

European Court of Human Rights (*ECtHR*)

English, Scottish and Irish (pre-partition) cases

Other courts

Introduction

Quelling Insurrection: Lethal Force, Human Rights and the Laws of War

At the end of June 2004, the occupation of Iraq by United States', British and other coalition forces was officially ended. The Coalition Provisional Authority relinquished power and the Iraqi Interim Government was formed. To mark the change, the British forces which were mainly located in the south of Iraq around Basra changed their rules of engagement from rules based on the laws of war – international humanitarian law as they are also known – to peace-time rules based in self-defence.[1] The US forces did not change their rules of engagement. Three months later though, in the face of increasing violence that the British forces could not contain under the rules based in self-defence, they changed them back again to permit the war-like use of force.[2] The fact that the British army changed its rules of engagement from one basis to the other and back again in the middle of its operations in Iraq has received little attention but it was problematic in a number of ways, such as the way that the rules could restrict pre-planned operations and impede the army's ability to take the initiative against the insurgents as the conflict worsened, as it did. Later operations were conducted with rules made under the laws of war that permitted planned offensive operations but, nonetheless, killings continued to be justified in self-defence. This led to considerable legal difficulties as it set a peace-time standard by which the British government had to defend allegations of unlawful killing and embroiled it in litigation. In broad terms, soldiers who act in self-defence have to establish that they thought that there was an immediate threat to their life, or to other soldiers or civilians, and that their use of lethal force was necessary and proportionate, whereas in an armed conflict it is only necessary to establish that the person targeted and killed was an enemy combatant or a civilian directly participating in hostilities who was not *hors de combat*, for example, not having surrendered or been wounded and no longer able to fight. An example of the British government's approach can be seen in one of the cases considered by the Iraq Fatalities Investigations (IFI) which was set up by the British government in 2014 to examine the circumstances of the deaths of Iraqi civilians who were allegedly killed by British soldiers. One of the cases it examined concerned the death of Ali Salam Naser who was said to be an unarmed civilian shot dead by British troops in an operation in Basra

[1] Report of the Iraq Inquiry, 6 July 2016, section 9.2 (May 2003 to June 2004) §1145.
[2] ibid, section 9.3, §278.

in 2007.[3] Naser was killed during a 'strike' operation carried out by three infantry companies mounted in armoured fighting vehicles and supported by tanks. The 'strike' operation was, in effect, a battle to regain control of an area of Basra from Iraqi insurgents who were reported to be armed with automatic rifles, rocket propelled grenades and a 12.7mm heavy machine gun. An American newspaper reporter, Michael Yon, who was with the British troops on the operation reported that 26 to 27 'enemy' were killed and that the main infantry platoon engaged on the ground fired some 4,000 rounds of ammunition. Nonetheless, the shootings were all justified as being made in self-defence and the cases were investigated by IFI on that basis.[4]

This book helps to fill a gap about what happened in Iraq during the period 2004–09 but it is not about British military operations in Iraq as such. The operations serve as an illustration of a much larger issue over how international law governs the use of lethal force in military operations in internal armed conflicts that might also be described as insurrections or rebellions and what is the appropriate basis for the use of force to quell them. In principle, the law does this by separating the issue into questions arising under two separate bodies of law – the laws of war and international human rights law – but in practice this separation operates in a way that is remote from the conduct of military operations. In order to understand how this separation arises and what are its consequences, rather than starting with the minutiae of the law it helps to begin by taking a step back to see the context in which the law operates, to see how this modern framework was created through the development of international and municipal law over two centuries and why this creates a problem. Having done that, it is then possible to look into deeper issues concerning the way that the law is seen as being divided into separate legal paradigms of law-enforcement (in which human rights law applies) and armed conflict (in which the laws of war apply) which then provide the legal basis for the use of force, including the setting of rules of engagement, conducting operations against insurgents and defending claims of unlawful killing by state security forces.

Rules of engagement are directives issued for military operations 'which specify the circumstances and limitations under which forces will initiate and/or continue combat engagement with other forces encountered'.[5] They are not themselves rules of law and may be shaped by political and diplomatic policies as well as by the constraints of law in order to support political, military or legal objectives. They are also usually classified as confidential or secret and states refuse to discuss them on

[3] The Iraq Fatalities Investigations, 'Investigation into the Death of Ali Naser' 8 February 2017.

[4] ibid. For completeness, the IFI Inspector's report into the death of Ali Salam Naser concluded that he was shot in the head by a single bullet at a time that UK forces were engaged in a large-scale counter-insurgency operation resulting in intense fighting. However, the Inspector found that it is not possible to determine by whom Naser was shot.

[5] There are various definitions of rules of engagement but this one was taken from NATO doctrine and is typical of the concept as applied in British military operations. See, eg, G Solis, *The Law of Armed Conflict: International Humanitarian Law in War* (New York, Cambridge University Press, 2016) 479.

the grounds that it may jeopardize their military operations. Nonetheless, where the rules have been disclosed, they show that they have a close connection to states' perceptions of the law that applies within the legal paradigms of armed conflict and law-enforcement. Under the paradigm of armed conflict, military forces may use the full spectrum of armed force permitted by the laws of war in the conduct of hostilities whilst under the law-enforcement paradigm international human rights law is generally seen as permitting only a limited use of force in self-defence, for example as set out in the United Nations' 'Basic Principles on the Use of Force and Firearms by Law Enforcement Officials'.[6] The rules of engagement reflect the underlying paradigms as, although as a matter of policy the rules may be more restrictive than the law allows, they cannot be more permissive. As a matter of international human rights law, the European Court of Human Rights (ECtHR) has confirmed that, in relation to the right to an investigation following a killing by British forces in Iraq, the investigation was required to determine 'whether in each case the soldier fired in conformity with the Rules of Engagement'.[7] However, the court did not say what would be the consequences of finding that there was a breach of those rules. As a matter of English law, the House of Lords has said that rules of engagement have no legal force.[8] What it meant by that is that compliance with the rules of engagement, in the form usually set out for soldiers in a small coloured card, does not of itself provide a legal defence to a charge of unlawful killing. They have also said that killing or seriously wounding another person by shooting outside of an armed conflict is prima facie unlawful.[9] Furthermore, they have not accepted that where a killing was made in compliance with the rules of engagement, there is a defence against it having been unlawful based on the act having been carried out in accordance with superior orders.[10] Each killing has, therefore, to be justified according to the law. However, as a matter of military law, rules of engagement may be binding on soldiers as either standing orders or a lawful command. As a matter of policy, in operational theatres the British army's Royal Military Police, Special Investigation Branch, investigates shooting incidents 'to ensure that, where rules of engagement have been breached, these offences are investigated'.[11] So it appears that the breach is prima facie an offence under military law. In Northern Ireland, the courts have found that a police officer who fired a baton round (a baton round is a large plastic bullet which is used in crowd control and intended to be a less lethal weapon) in breach of the police internal rules and killed a man was not guilty of manslaughter on the basis of a 'residual

[6] United Nations, 'Basic Principles on the Use of Force and Firearms by Law Enforcement Officials' (New York, 1990).

[7] *Al-Skeini v United Kingdom* App no 55721/07 (2011) ECHR 1093, §170.

[8] *R v Clegg* [1995] 1 AC 482, HL at 491.

[9] *Attorney General of Northern Ireland's Reference (No 1 of 1975) (Re House of Lords (Northern Ireland))* [1977] AC 105, HL at 136.

[10] *R v Clegg* (n 8) 498.

[11] Her Majesty's Inspectorate of Constabulary, 'Royal Military Police Special Investigation Branch inspection' (August 2006) 8.

discretion to decide when to use force notwithstanding the police regulations'.[12] This suggests that, as a matter of municipal law, a breach of rules of engagement would not be conclusive evidence of the use of unlawful force.

The events in Iraq in 2004 provide a starting point because, although the rules of engagement are usually classified, the rules during the period of military occupation were considered in an important case on the conduct of British military operations known as the *Al-Skeini* case that was brought before the English courts and the European Court of Human Rights. In it, a copy of the card issued to British forces giving guidance on the rules, known as 'Card Alpha', was disclosed to the court.[13] Card Alpha was essentially the same as the 'Yellow Card' that set out the rules of engagement applied by the British army in the Troubles in Northern Ireland during law-enforcement operations during the 1970s to 1990s. Nonetheless, the apparently strict terms of the guidance given by Card Alpha, based as it was on the earlier Yellow Card which allowed the use of force only in self-defence, can be contrasted with the actual use of force in operations in Iraq during the period of occupation and afterwards which included the use of automatic weapons, armoured vehicles, tanks, artillery, helicopter gunships and strike aircraft. From that starting point, this book includes an examination of the legal paradigms of armed conflict and law-enforcement under which rules of engagement are set. It examines how the legal paradigms came to be constructed and understood as they currently are, and why the modern framework of the law has apparently resulted in a choice between the two paradigms that have such different rules. The separation of the paradigms and the devising of the different rules that result from them is, to some extent, something which states may decide but it has consequences for the conduct of military operations and gives rise to issues of legitimacy and accountability, as the litigation and investigations into Iraq show. What these choices were and on what basis they were decided is then an issue for investigation both from legal and policy perspectives and because of the impact they have had on those involved in military operations or otherwise caught up in their effects.

This book focuses on the UK not only because of the example that Iraq provides of the problems encountered in the use of military force in quelling insurrections and its domestic relevance, but also because focusing on the UK provides the opportunity to study in detail a state that has been actively involved in military operations and purports to recognize the importance of complying with international law. The UK is subject to an active human rights regime including an international court – the ECtHR – with jurisdiction to hear applications by individuals. By comparison, the United States is not subject to an international human rights court, and other European states that are parties to the 1950 European Convention on Human

[12] S Skinner, 'Citizens in Uniform: Public Defence, Reasonableness and Human Rights' *Public Law* (2000), 270 citing *R v Hegarty* [1986] 12 NIJB 25; R J Spjut [1987] PL 35 at 37.

[13] *Al-Skeini v United Kingdom* App no 55721/07 (2011) ECHR 1093, §24.

Rights[14] (the ECHR), and so subject to the ECtHR, are in general not as militarily active. As a consequence, they have also been less involved in international human rights litigation in relation to armed conflict.[15] Furthermore, the UK was one of the main participants in the drafting of the first two international human rights instruments – the ECHR and the 1966 International Covenant on Civil and Political Rights (the International Covenant) at the United Nations where the UK also worked closely with Commonwealth countries. As will be seen, the UK was the main drafter of the provisions on the right to life in article 2 of the ECHR and based the exceptions in it to the right to life on the provisions for killings which would be justified or excusable homicide under English law. Furthermore, the exceptions were part of a legal framework grounded in English law that was used as the basis for the use of force in British military operations in Ireland (1916–22) and the colonies of the British Empire prior to the drafting of the ECHR and continued to be applied in colonial conflicts through the 1950s and 60s. Looking at the UK also raises other issues of municipal law as its armed forces are subject to municipal law as well as international law when operating at home or abroad. Technically, the United Kingdom has four national jurisdictions – England, Scotland, Wales, and Northern Ireland – and the local municipal law will apply to military operations in each jurisdiction, for example cases were (and are) brought under Northern Irish law in relation to the Troubles. However, by legislation British military operations abroad are made subject to English criminal law.[16] Examining the law governing the use of force to quell insurrections is then a multi-faceted inquiry which draws in the different regimes of international law and their historical development – initially the laws of war and later international human rights law – and the development of English municipal law. It also includes the history of some of the British military operations over the period from the mid-nineteenth century, where it will be seen the modern bodies of municipal and international law began to take shape, up to the most recent experience of the British army in Iraq. Together, these rather disparate areas of inquiry can be likened to the pieces of a jigsaw which, when put together, reveal the complete picture.

Regulating the Use of Lethal Force in Internal Armed Conflicts

The international law that regulates military operations was traditionally known as 'the laws of war'. Different writers may now use the expression 'the laws of

[14] Convention for the Protection of Human Rights and Fundamental Freedoms (Rome, 4 November 1950).

[15] It could be argued that, other than domestic relevance, Turkey and Russia (until it ceased to be a party to the ECHR in 2022) also fulfil the criteria mentioned as supporting the choice of the UK and they are included in the discussion of decisions of the ECtHR in ch 7.

[16] Armed Forces Act 2006, ss 42–48.

war' or the more modern expression 'the law of armed conflict' to mean either or both of *jus ad bellum* and *jus in bello. Jus ad bellum* is the legal regime that deals with the lawfulness of the decision to use armed force in international relations whilst *jus in bello* governs the conduct of military operations in armed conflict. The term 'international humanitarian law' (IHL) is usually synonymous with *jus in bello.*[17] However, the use of different terminology does indicate a shift in priority after 1945 away from an approach based on mutual obligations between states who are at war to a focus on the suffering of the victims of war.[18] In this book, the term 'the laws of war' is preferred to 'international humanitarian law' as it is both historically more accurate for the greater part of the period being explored here and indicates the continuity of core rules on the conduct of hostilities which form an important part of the argument.

International law can be made through a number of sources but here the most important sources are treaties made between states (which include, amongst other things, international conventions, such as the 1949 Geneva conventions) and international customary law which arises from the practice of states. The customary laws of war developed over centuries but were brought together in the later part of the nineteenth century into a general set of rules that applied to wars as 'the contention between two or more States through their armed forces', as wars were then understood to be.[19] The laws of war did not regulate military operations within states, such as those to put down riots, insurrections and revolutions, that was left to the municipal law of states, at least so long as the violence did not spill over borders or occur on the high seas.[20] After 1945 this distinction began to be eroded. The laws of war were revised so that they covered 'all cases of declared war or of any other armed conflict' between states party to the 1949 Geneva conventions – commonly called 'international armed conflicts' – but were also extended to 'armed conflict not of an international character' occurring in the territory of a state – commonly known as 'non-international armed conflicts'.[21] The conventions set out a large and expanded set of the rules of war that applied to international armed conflicts and a discrete set of rules that applied to non-international armed conflicts, the so-called 'Convention in miniature' as it contained within one article

[17] Some writers make a technical distinction between the laws of war (or the law of armed conflict) and international humanitarian law on the basis that the latter excludes the law of neutrality – eg D Fleck (ed), *The Handbook of International Humanitarian Law* (Oxford, Oxford University Press, 2013) 11, but this is not an important distinction here.

[18] SC Neff, *War and the Law of Nations, A General History* (Cambridge, Cambridge University Press, 2005) 315.

[19] L Oppenheim, *International Law, A Treatise, Vol II, War and Neutrality* (London, Longmans, Green, and Co, 1912) §54.

[20] The issue of whether a state whose territory, shipping, trade or other interests were affected by an armed conflict in another state could or should have treated the conflict as a belligerency, that is a conflict to which the laws of war and neutrality applied, was, and in some writers' opinions still is, a central issue in the classification of armed conflicts. The state of belligerency is discussed further in ch 1.

[21] Articles 2 and 3 common to the 1949 Geneva conventions.

all of the provisions of the treaty applicable to non-international armed conflicts. What was meant by the phrase 'armed conflict not of an international character' was a 'burning question' at the diplomatic conference at which the conventions were negotiated but it received no clear answer.[22] Although not mentioned in the conventions, whether or not they applied to a particular conflict was understood to be based on the notion of a threshold of violence which was described by the International Committee of the Red Cross (ICRC) – the non-governmental, humanitarian organization that assisted in the creation of the Geneva conventions – as 'distinguishing a genuine armed conflict from a mere act of banditry or an unorganized and short-lived insurrection' but, as will be seen, the level at which the threshold applied was contested.[23] Where the conflict fell below the threshold, the use of force was still to be governed by the municipal laws of states. The threshold was to be determined as a matter of fact which meant that states gave up their 'sovereign right' to treat a rebellion only as an issue of law-enforcement under municipal law and conceded that international law applied on an objective test.[24] Some saw this as also meaning that the rebels were granted 'belligerent rights' as a matter of international law. Belligerent rights are the 'rights that are available to states and persons only in a state of war, such as killing and capturing enemy troops or the occupation of enemy territory', but the granting of them was contested and, whether or not the rights were granted, the rebels remained subject to municipal law and could be tried for offences such as treason or murder.[25] Unless the issue of whether particular circumstances of organized armed violence may or may not be classified as an armed conflict as a matter of law is on point in the discussion that follows, these circumstances will be referred to as 'internal armed conflicts'. This emphasizes that no particular legal classification has been given but, as a matter of fact, the non-state groups involved are organized and armed and carrying out violence to an extent that, in order to maintain or restore public order, they must be opposed by the use of military force.

In the aftermath of wide-scale abuses of individuals and their rights before and during the Second World War, there was also a separate expansion of international law as states agreed with each other to respect certain human rights. The process began with the Universal Declaration of Human Rights made by the General Assembly of the United Nations (the Universal Declaration) in 1948.[26] It was quickly followed in Europe in 1950 by the ECHR. Among the rights created

[22] ICRC, *Commentary on the First Geneva Convention: Convention (I) for the Amelioration of the Condition of the Wounded and Sick in Armed Forces in the Field* (ICRC, 1952), 'Commentary of 1952. Article 3: Conflicts not of an international character' 49.

[23] ibid 50.

[24] Neff, *War and the Law of Nations* (2005) (n 18) 251.

[25] SC Neff, *Justice in Blue and Gray: A Legal History of the Civil War* (Harvard, Harvard University Press, 2010) 260.

[26] The Universal Declaration is not binding as it was made in the form of a resolution of the General Assembly of the United Nations and its resolutions are not binding on states. There are scholars who argue that some or all of its provisions have become binding as a matter of customary international law but there is little consensus on the rights that should be regarded as customary. If there is a customary

by the convention was the right to life – the right directly challenged by the use of lethal force in military operations.[27] The right to life was recognized as not being absolute, meaning that there were exceptions to it, such as the taking of another life in self-defence and the death penalty, which were enumerated in the ECHR in what was drafted to be an exhaustive list. The list also included an exception for the use of lethal force to quell a riot or an insurrection and it is this that provides a focal point for the examination of the application of international law to military operations in internal armed conflicts. Although there were negotiations taking place at the United Nations in relation to a binding instrument on human rights to supplement the Universal Declaration at the same time as the negotiations on the ECHR, the International Covenant was not agreed until 1966 and it came into force in 1976. Other than the death penalty, instead of including specific exceptions to the right to life, it provides more simply 'No one shall be arbitrarily deprived of his life'.[28]

The development of international human rights at the United Nations after the Second World War was based on a general consensus that human rights applied in peace and the laws of war applied in war.[29] Although the negotiations on laws of war prior to the making of the 1949 Geneva conventions occurred over the same period, they were conducted separately and there was little regard given to how the two bodies of law would relate to each other in a potential area of overlap caused by the extension of the laws of war to non-international armed conflicts. Even if the parameters of what was or was not 'armed conflict' were unclear at the time of the 1949 Geneva conventions, further developments in international law and the use of force since the period following the Second World War have increasingly blurred the fact-based and legal distinctions around which the paradigms were formed. Modern armed conflicts rarely take place between armed forces on the battlefield in the traditional sense, although there are notable exceptions such as the conflict in Ukraine. As a result, the relationship between these paradigms now appears to be more difficult to determine. On the one hand, the paradigms are said to be exclusive in that where the laws of war do not apply, the law-enforcement paradigm will apply.[30] On the other hand, although the two paradigms are separate in that sense, they overlap in that thirty years ago it was established by the International Court of Justice (ICJ) – the court established at the same time as the United Nations to adjudicate disputes between states – that international human rights law applies in war as well as in peace.[31] The existence of

right to life, the main issues arising from it are likely to be its form, interpretation and interaction with the treaty-based rights to life.

[27] Article 2 of the ECHR.

[28] Article 6.1 of the 1966 International Covenant for Civil and Political Rights.

[29] R Kolb, 'The Relationship between International Humanitarian Law and Human Rights Law: A Brief History of the 1948 Universal Declaration of Human Rights and the 1949 Geneva Conventions' (1998) 38 *International Review of the Red Cross* 324, 409.

[30] C Greenwood, *Essays on War in International Law* (London, Cameron May, 2006) 432.

[31] *Legality of the Threat or Use of Nuclear Weapons, Advisory Opinion* [1996] ICJ 226, §25. The point was also considered by the ICJ in *Legal Consequences of the Construction of a Wall in the Occupied Palestinian Territory, Advisory Opinion* [2004] ICJ 136, §105–06; and *Armed Activities on the Territory of the Congo (Democratic Republic of the Congo v Uganda), Judgment* [2005] ICJ 168, §216.

two regimes of law that may apply to military operations creates great uncertainty for states and their armed forces both when making life and death decisions and afterwards when being held accountable for the choice that was made, particularly under human rights law which allows for individuals to make claims against states. It may also arise through international criminal law which makes individuals accountable for the violations of the laws of war that constitute war crimes. This uncertainty has been seen in the conduct of military operations in the so-called 'War on Terror' against groups such as Al-Qaeda or so-called Islamic State which led to a debate on whether the US-led military operations fell outside the existing paradigms and required a new one.[32] As the War on Terror continued, the international reaction to the conduct of military operations and, in particular, the denial of rights to detainees from the conflicts in Afghanistan, Iraq and elsewhere led to a number of different responses based around applying the existing paradigms to the circumstances.[33] New approaches also emerged that sought to combine the laws of war and human rights law in a 'mixed approach' or, more ambitiously, sought to combine them with international criminal law in a 'law of humanity'.[34] However, it should be seen that these are matters of approach not status and the traditional view persists that in international law there is no third, mixed status between war and peace.[35] I am not seeking to argue that there is a need for a third paradigm in international law to be placed between the existing paradigms of armed conflict and law-enforcement but to question the consequences of choosing one paradigm over another and to explore an alternative approach based on the recognition that the paradigm of law-enforcement includes the right to use lethal force to quell an insurrection.

War and Armed Conflict

When considering the law that applies to military operations, the concept of 'war' should be distinguished from the legal concept of 'armed conflict'. 'War' is not a term

[32] C Greenwood, 'International Law and the "War on Terrorism"', *International Affairs* (2002) 78, 301. For the debate see, eg, Greenwood, *Essays on War*, 432 who argues against a third category; Neff, *War and the Law of Nations* (n 18) 397 who argues against an over-arching concentration on terrorism; and E Wilmshurst (ed), *International Law and the Classification of Conflicts* (Oxford, Oxford University Press, 2012) 484, who noted that none of the contributors to the book argued for a new category. For an earlier reflection on the issue, see PC Jessup, 'Should International Law Recognize an Intermediate Status between Peace and War?' (1954) 48 *American Journal of International Law* 98–103.

[33] See eg, A Roberts, 'Counter-Terrorism, Armed Force and the Laws of War' (2002) 44: 1 *Survival* 7–32 which takes a practical approach to adapting the law; and ME O'Connell, 'The prohibition on the use of force' in ND White and C Henderson (eds), *Research Handbook on International Conflict and Security Law* (Cheltenham, Edward Elgar, 2013) 109, which took a more principled approach insisting that the use of lethal military force is unlawful outside armed conflict.

[34] D Kretzmer, 'Targeted Killing of Suspected Terrorists: Extra-Judicial Executions or Legitimate Means of Defence' (2005) 16: 5 *European Journal of International Law* 203; and R Teitel, *Humanity's Law* (Oxford, Oxford University Press, 2011) 6, respectively.

[35] Y Dinstein, *War, Aggression and Self-Defence* (Cambridge, Cambridge University Press, 2017) 18.

of art in international law: it is not defined in a treaty and its possible customary nature predates the development of the legal concept of 'armed conflict' in international law after the Second World War.[36] In Western military and academic writing, war was increasing defined in terms described by Carl von Clausewitz (1780–1831), the nineteenth century Prussian military strategist, as 'an act of force to compel our enemy to do our will' and, more famously, 'war is not merely an act of policy but a true political instrument, a continuation of political intercourse, carried on with other means'.[37] This conception of war as politicized and instrumental armed violence is known as the 'nature' of war and never changes but wars may have a different 'character' as they are adapted to the particular circumstances in which they occur; for example, in the way that war on the battlefields of Europe in the Second World War was different from the Vietnam War during the 1960s.[38] This understanding of war is broader than the traditional legal usage as it is not solely identified with conflict between states and would include guerrilla warfare between insurgents and state forces.[39] The modern legal concept of 'armed conflict' is something of a fusion of these ideas as it requires there to be at least two opposing armed groups and a certain level of violence.[40] For a non-international armed conflict to occur, the violence has to be sustained: in the widely-accepted definition given by the Appeals Chamber of the International Criminal Tribunal for former Yugoslavia (ICTY) in *Prosecutor v Tadić*, there has to be 'protracted armed violence between governmental authorities and organized armed groups within a State'.[41] The definition is then linked to a de minimis threshold of violence borrowed from the 1977 Additional Protocol II to the 1949 Geneva conventions.[42] It excludes 'internal disturbances and tensions, such as riots, isolated and sporadic acts of violence and other acts of a similar nature'.[43] These parameters create the threshold of violence which divides the paradigms of armed conflict and law-enforcement and may mean that situations that are not 'armed conflict' may still be 'war' in the sense described above. In particular, it will be argued that an 'insurrection' involves the use of armed force for a political purpose and may amount to war.

[36] ibid 3–21. Dinstein also describes how a state of war may exist between states and makes a case for a legal status of war for the purposes of *jus ad bellum*.

[37] C von Clausewitz, *On War*, edited and translated by M Howard and P Paret (Princeton, Princeton University Press, 1989) 75 and 87.

[38] The concept of the 'character' of war was introduced by Clausewitz in *On War* in a passage in which he wrote that '[w]ar is more than a true chameleon that slightly adapts its characteristics to the given case'. He went on to explain the practical importance of the concepts of the nature and character of war as being that 'the first, … the most far-reaching act of judgment that the statesman and commander have to make is to establish … the kind of war on which they are embarking; neither mistaking it for, nor trying to turn it into, something that is alien to its nature'. (Clausewitz, *On War* ibid 88).

[39] H Strachan and S Scheipers (eds), *The Changing Character of War* (Oxford, Oxford University Press, 2011) 6.

[40] International Law Association, 'Final Report on the Meaning of Armed Conflict in International Law' (2010) 2.

[41] *Prosecutor v Dusko Tadić* (Decision on Jurisdiction), Case no IT-94-1-AR72, Appeals Chamber, (1996) 35 ILM 32, 2 October 1995, §70.

[42] APV Rogers, *Law on the Battlefield* (Manchester, Manchester University Press, 2004) 219.

[43] 1977 Additional Protocol II to the 1949 Geneva Conventions (AP (II)), Art 1(2).

My argument starts from the proposition that the British government's approach to the use of lethal force in military operations is based on the concept of legal paradigms of armed conflict and law-enforcement separated by a threshold of violence which was a product of the revision of the laws of war and the creation of a body of human rights law after the Second World War. In practice, the British government has treated the paradigms as separate or, at least, it has said it did and justified its actions accordingly. Treating the paradigms as separate creates an artificial distinction that does not reflect how force is used in military operations in practice nor, it is argued, in all circumstances as a matter of law. Rather than seeing the legal paradigms as separated by a threshold of violence, the application of international human rights law in a law-enforcement environment and, in principle, in armed conflict means that the paradigms may be seen as overlapping so that both may apply to particular circumstances of armed violence.[44] The idea that they overlap gives rise to legal argument as to how to resolve the consequences of the overlap between the two bodies of law. One approach has been to see it as a matter of 'complementarity' – such that the bodies of law are seen as mutually reinforcing so as, in any given situation, to prioritize the law that gives the greatest protection to civilians and other persons in the power of a party to the conflict. Another approach is to give priority to one of the bodies of law as the *lex specialis* to resolve any conflict between them. *Lex specialis* is a shortened form of the Latin legal phrase *lex specialis derogat legi generali*. It is used in legal interpretation and means in substance that, in relation to a particular legal question, any more specific rules relating to the question will prevail over more general rules of law. In relation to armed conflict, however, the nature of the relationship between the laws of war and international human rights law itself is contested. In determining which law is the *lex specialis*, it is controversial whether or not international human rights law applies on the battlefield itself and, if it does, whether the laws of war trump human rights law on the basis that the doctrine of *lex specialis* would give priority to the specific rules of the laws of war.[45] Alternatively, some argue that human rights are 'trumps' on the basis of their importance.[46] Despite extensive literature on this issue, there is no consensus on which approach to take although it is easier in the case of the right to life under the International Covenant as there is a well-established argument on applying the laws of war as *lex specialis* in armed conflict.[47] This argument

[44] C Droege, 'The Interplay between International Humanitarian Law and International Human Rights Law in Situations of Armed Conflict' (2007) 40: 2 *Israel Law Review* 312. Droege, among others, identifies an area of legal 'overlap' based on the development of international human rights law from the late 1960s but I argue that it is a much deeper and more historical phenomenon.

[45] Solis, *The Law of Armed Conflict* (2016) (n 5) 26.

[46] Christopher Greenwood, 'Human Rights and Humanitarian Law – Conflict or Convergence' (2010–11) 43: 1 *Case Western Reserve Journal of International Law* 500. Greenwood rejects this argument as too extreme.

[47] See, eg, UN HRC, 'General comment No 36 (2018) on article 6 of the International Covenant on Civil and Political Rights, on the right to life', dated 30 October 2018, §64; and ICRC, *How does Law Protect in War?* (2012) Chapter 14, II 1 'Rights protected by both branches: the *lex specialis* principle'.

has, however, certain consequences. It allows the permissive rules that were developed for international armed conflicts to apply to conflicts that are classified as non-international armed conflicts as a matter of law but applies the much narrower rules of self-defence to those that are not. Whether or not a conflict is a non-international armed conflict is often uncertain and may be known only in retrospect, which, amongst other things, makes it very difficult to set rules of engagement. Issues over the powers of courts established under the laws of war or international human rights law to apply other bodies of international law have complicated this further in practice, particularly in the case of the ECtHR which has heard a large number of cases relating to armed conflict. It has adopted a version of complementarity which it calls 'harmonization' but, until recently, it rarely mentioned the laws of war in cases relating to armed conflict and it was (and is) unclear whether it applies them or not.[48] However, when considering the issue, inadequate attention has been given to how the ECHR makes provision for the use of lethal force in military operations as can be seen through the separate exceptions to the right to life for the use of force in self-defence and to quell an insurrection and its provision for derogation for deaths resulting from lawful acts of war.[49] It is this potential latitude to establish a defence for the use of force in insurrection that Britain and other states have forgone by relying only on self-defence for reasons they have not explained. The underlying policy was, nonetheless, manifested in rules of engagement such as those used in Iraq and Afghanistan. Primarily, states have appeared to be unwilling to acknowledge the fact of an insurrection or the armed violence of the insurgents as anything but criminality or terrorism as they feared that it would impinge on their sovereignty, in order not to appear weak, or because they feared that it amounted to political or legal recognition of the rebels.[50] However, the explanation also goes deeper into the legal framework as states and other actors have sought to shape the law on which the paradigms rest to support their views or interests at a particular

[48] See, eg, N Quénivet, 'The History of the Relationship between International Humanitarian Law and Human Rights Law' in R Arnold and N Quénivet (eds), *International Humanitarian Law and Human Rights Law: Towards a New Merger in International Law* (Leiden, Martinus Nijhoff Publishers, 2008) 332 who argues that the ECtHR has applied the laws of war *sub silentio*; and W Schabas, 'The Right to Life' in A Clapham and P Gaeta (eds), *The Oxford Handbook of International Law in Armed Conflict* (Oxford, Oxford University Press, 2014) 383–84 who argues that the court has avoided applying the laws of war.

[49] Articles 2(2) and 15(2) of the ECHR respectively. There has been only one instance of a state pleading the exception for the use of lethal force in an insurrection in a case before the ECtHR, although the court has itself referred to arts 2.2(a) to (c) collectively on many occasions. The case is *Cangöz v Turkey* App no 7469/06 (2016) ECHR 377 in which Turkey sought to justify its actions under art 2(a), (b) and (c) in relation to the killing of 17 people whom it said were members of an armed group but the court found against it without addressing the grounds separately. In relation to more general references made by the ECtHR see, eg, *McCann v United Kingdom* App no 18984/91 (1995) ECHR 3, §149 and *Isayeva, Yusupova, Bazayeva v Russia* App nos 57947/00, 57948/00 and 57949/00 (2005) ECHR 129, §169–81. These cases are discussed more fully in later chapters.

[50] N Zamir, *Classification of Conflicts in International Humanitarian Law: The Legal Impact of Foreign Intervention in Civil Wars* (Cheltenham, Edward Elgar, 2017) 20; and S Sivakumaran, *The Law of Non-International Armed Conflict* (Oxford, Oxford University Press, 2012) 16.

time in both the international and municipal spheres but with contingent and unanticipated results that affect the use of force in internal armed conflicts.

This book sets out to explore how the two legal paradigms were formed, how states – primarily the UK – understood the new laws that were being made at the time that they were made, how the paradigms have changed over time, and how states have sought to apply them. By proposing a different understanding of the two paradigms as overlapping rather than being divided by a threshold of violence, it can help to identify the common elements in the use of lethal force and some of the consequences of the distinction that has been made in practice. A better understanding of the two legal paradigms is important for a number of reasons. First, and most obviously, it is important because the right to life is one of the most important, if not the most important, of human rights and identifying the standards governing human rights in situations of emergency is one of the most difficult issues within international human rights law. Yet in relation to what is often recognized as the most developed of the international human rights regimes, there is little mention in textbooks or other literature of the provisions of the ECHR in relation to insurrection. Although states have appeared to be reluctant to admit to an insurrection on their own territory, the implications of the UK's reluctance to argue the exceptions for insurrection or war have been a significant factor in litigation and should be better understood. Second, it is important in the context of a concern about how the laws of war and international human rights law influence each other and whether it has, in either case, a positive or negative effect. In particular, there is a concern that bringing the principles and rules of the laws of war into human rights law may widen the scope of the exceptions that may be applied to human rights in peacetime. Applying human rights law in armed conflicts may also 'water-down' the protection that human rights law affords more generally and compromise the distinction between it and the laws of war.[51] In the case of the ECHR, this concern is particularly relevant in circumstances where states such as the UK, Russia and Turkey have argued before the ECtHR that they have used military force only in self-defence. Third, the scope of the application of the ECHR has gradually been expanding from its original, narrow territorial approach to include its application outside of the territory of state parties, including military operations in Afghanistan and Iraq, at least to the extent of those held in detention, and cases continue to be brought to test the position on the right to life.[52] Given this expansion, some practitioners have begun to think that one way to

[51] M Milanovic, *Extraterritorial Application of Human Rights Treaties: Law, Principles, and Policy* (Oxford, Oxford University Press, 2011) 231.

[52] The ECtHR decided against extra-territorial application of the right to life (other than whilst a person was under the physical control of a state's agents) in *Banković v Belgium* App no 52207/99 (2001) ECHR 890. However, the issue was raised again in the *Al-Skeini* case but left unresolved in a number of important respects. The most recent cases have been *Georgia v Russia (II)* App no 38263/08 (2021) ECHR 58 and *Hanan v Germany* App no 4871/16 (2021) ECHR 131 which supported some limited, extra-territorial extensions of the procedural right under art 2 to the investigation of killings by state agents but did not explore the substantive right to life.

address the issues that this brings would be through refining rules of engagement. This, however, raises further concern over their lack of transparency and uncertain legal status. Even if there is no further expansion of the territorial application of article 2, an understanding of the exceptions in it may assist in determining policy in relation to the use of lethal force in military operations.

The argument that this book makes is a legal argument on the appropriate type and level of lethal force that may be used by state forces to quell insurrections. It builds the argument by exploring the historical basis of the modern law and its continuing relevance. There are two separate aspects of this which may appear to be in tension but, nonetheless, form part of the argument. The first is that law that was made in the past and has become lost from view in modern cases and textbooks may still be current law. Although laws may be repealed or superseded and treaties may be revoked, neither international law nor English common law has a concept of desuetude which makes law that has fallen into disuse inapplicable as a basis for arguing and deciding new cases. The second is that law and war have a mutual context and, as one changes, so may the other. Some of the military–legal framework that is explored in the chapters below was developed in colonial wars and other conflicts and used to justify actions which were seen at the time or are now regarded as unnecessary or disproportionate, for example, through indiscriminate firing by troops. The argument made here is not an apologia for those actions nor is it intended to make a moral judgment on historical events. It addresses what has been described as a 'norm–conflict' between the laws of war and human rights law in relation to the right to life of combatants and civilians in armed conflict,[53] and it extends the analysis to what could also be said to be a norm–conflict in relation to the right to life of soldiers, armed insurgents and civilians in insurrections. One of the features of making a legal argument is that it requires the use of terminology which has political or moral connotations but is used in a specifically legal sense. This raises the issue of what to call those who take up arms against the State and the armed conflict that ensues. As has been explained, I use the term 'internal armed conflict' as it covers situations that would fall within the legal definition of a 'non-international armed conflict' and conflicts that are similar but would not fall within the definition. In addition, there are different terms used to describe internal armed conflicts when looked at from the perspective of international and municipal law up to the formation of the paradigm of armed conflict in 1949 and afterwards, including insurgency, insurrection, rebellion and civil war. For those, I prefer the term 'insurrection' both for simplicity and, unlike the others, it has a specific source in international law – the ECHR – and various sources of English law that are relevant to the argument. As regards the non-state participants, states often refer to them as terrorists to deny them any political legitimacy whilst others may call them 'freedom fighters' or just 'fighters' in order to lend support to their cause. I use the term 'insurgent' primarily as it is

[53] Milanovic, *Extraterritorial Application of Human Rights Treaties* (n 51) 255–56.

the legal term to describe a person who takes part in an insurrection but it is also helpful that it has been recognized as a more neutral term for such contentious debate.[54] By drawing on these and other legal sources, the argument separates a narrow application of the use of lethal force in engagements between state forces and insurgents – in military terminology, where troops are in 'contact' – from the wider uses of force under martial or emergency law, such as in the detention of insurgents or the forced resettlement of civilians. In doing so, it identifies which laws within that framework are *lex latis* – the law as it is (as distinct from the law as it was in the past (*lex prior*) or is desired to be in the future (*lex ferenda*)) – and might be applied in modern conditions. Importantly, the modern conditions include, on the military side, more heavily armed insurgents but, on the legal side, higher standards of accountability through the courts for unlawful killings and the excessive use of force. Accountability was part of what is sometimes called the 'soldier's dilemma' in the use of force in support of public order: the dilemma being that using too little force and thereby failing to quell a riot or insurrection could result in a soldier being held in dereliction of his or her duty to maintain or restore public order, whilst using too much force could result in the soldier being charged with murder; and both used to be capital crimes punishable by death. In practice though, soldiers were seldom held accountable to the courts. However, recourse to the courts is now a much more accessible remedy, rather than a mostly theoretical possibility, as can be seen through the multiple actions that have been brought under article 2 of the ECHR through the municipal courts and the ECtHR. This increased accountability when combined with a reassessment of the law applicable in internal armed conflicts provides the opportunity for a new approach to the use of force based on the existing law rather than requiring a new treaty or legislative changes which are unlikely to be made.

Structure of the Book

Chapters one and two trace the historical roots of the legal paradigms from the 1860s as the spheres of the laws of war and municipal law were developed as separate responses to internal armed conflict during the American Civil War (1861–1865) and a rebellion in Jamaica in 1865. The American Civil War saw the first modern codification of the laws of war under *General Order 100* – also known as the Lieber Code after its main author, Dr Francis Lieber (1798–1872). It was issued to the Union army in 1863 with detailed rules on the conduct of hostilities and martial law and, although issued in a civil war, it was conceived as reflecting the existing laws and customs of war. However, the code had also been shaped by

[54] D French, *The British Way in Counter-insurgency, 1945–1967* (Oxford, Oxford University Press, 2011) 9. French also cites the earlier British practice of calling its opponents 'thugs', 'bandits' or 'gangsters' in order to deny them political legitimacy. Later, the term 'terrorist' began to be used.

Lieber and the US government in significant ways to apply the rules of the laws of war to support the Union's position in the conflict and, shaped as it was, it was to have a significant influence on the future development of the laws of war which still resonates today. The Jamaica Rebellion brought different actors and interests to the issue of regulating military force. Following a public outcry over the severe measures taken under martial law to repress the rebellion, the British government appointed a Royal Commission to conduct a public inquiry into the events and the Jamaica Committee was formed in London as an interest group opposed to the violence. It supported the bringing of three court cases in Britain that sought to hold the governor of Jamaica and two military officers to account for their actions in the rebellion. In the course of these proceedings and subsequently, the rebellion also led to the writing of what became foundational works setting out the legal arguments on the limits on the use of lethal force to restore or maintain public order.

Chapter three describes how the regulation of internal armed conflicts continued to develop under the municipal law in the first half of the twentieth century. This is seen through the court cases and military literature arising from British military operations in South Africa during the Boer War (1899–1903), Ireland (1916–22), Palestine (1928–38), and elsewhere. The development was shaped to support the State's interests but also involved institutional actors and individuals within the government and the judiciary. It included judicial confirmation of the State's right to repel force with force which was distinct from the wider powers arising under martial law and the beginnings of a military–legal framework containing recognizable principles of distinction and proportionality and rules of engagement.

Chapters four and five examine the second half of the twentieth century and explain how the sphere of the laws of war between states became the paradigm of armed conflict and included both international and non-international armed conflicts – that is armed conflict both between and within states. The sphere of municipal law that governed internal armed conflicts became the paradigm of law-enforcement and included both international and municipal law. The paradigms, like the spheres, were initially seen as separate but gradually they developed and overlapped over time, like a Venn diagram.[55] As the two paradigms developed and their subject matter and rules began to overlap, the laws of war and human rights law also each began to be applied to a larger spectrum of internal armed conflicts. Chapter four traces the development of the laws of war from the 1899 Hague conventions to the 1949 Geneva conventions, laws that prior to the 1949 Geneva conventions were agreed to apply only to wars between

[55] Zamir refers to the law of non-international armed conflict moving from the 'internal sphere' of municipal law to the 'external sphere' of international law under the Geneva conventions in 1949 (Zamir, *Classification of Conflicts* (n 50) 46), whereas I use the image of separate spheres of municipal law and international law but overlapping international law paradigms of armed conflict and law-enforcement.

states that were party to the various conventions. The 1949 Geneva conventions were mostly concerned with what were termed 'armed conflicts' between states instead of 'war' but also included the landmark step to extend the laws of war to 'armed conflicts not of an international character' under article 3 of the each of the four Geneva conventions ('Common Article 3'). The chapter looks in particular at the differing views on how Common Article 3 was conceived to apply in non-international armed conflicts and suggests that it should be seen as a limited provision protecting those not, or no longer, involved in hostilities that was uncoupled from the laws of war on the conduct of hostilities. Chapter five describes the formation of the law-enforcement paradigm in the second half of the twentieth century out of municipal law and the addition of an international dimension in the foundation of modern human rights law to regulate the conduct of states. The chapter looks in detail at the drafting of the right to life in the ECHR and the International Covenant and also considers the initial development of the jurisprudence of the ECtHR in relation to it.

Chapter six deals with the further expansion of the armed conflict paradigm through the lowering in practice of the threshold at which Common Article 3 was said to apply and the supplementing of the 1949 Geneva conventions by the 1977 additional protocols. It explores issues that arose on the application (or non-application) of Common Article 3 in colonial conflicts and the way in which British forces continued to develop and apply a military–legal framework for the use of force under municipal law. The 1977 additional protocols were the last treaties to be made on the conduct of hostilities but they were followed by the further development of customary international law and influenced by international criminal justice instruments and decisions. In 2005 the ICRC produced the Customary International Humanitarian Law Study (the Customary Law Study) which identified 161 customary rules of the laws of war, most of which it found applied in both international and non-international armed conflict.[56] The study did not receive universal acceptance and it was criticized particularly for its methodology and for merging the rules applying to international and non-international armed conflict. It is treated throughout the book as a resource for identifying customary law rather than a definitive statement of it. There is no equivalent study of customary law in relation to human rights. International criminal law was developed principally through the statutes and jurisprudence of the international criminal tribunals created by the United Nations' Security Council in the 1990s and the founding of the International Criminal Court under the 1998 Rome Statute. The chapter also examines the further development of the principle of military

[56] JM Henckaerts and L Doswald-Beck, *Customary International Humanitarian Law*, Vols I and II (Cambridge, Cambridge University Press, 2005). Put generically, the rules that do not apply to non-international armed conflicts are those derived from the principle of distinction or the status of occupation in international armed conflicts. There are two rules that are unique to non-international armed conflicts that cover reprisals and amnesties (rules 148 and 159). The rules contained within Common Article 3 of the 1949 Geneva conventions have been separated and applied to all armed conflicts.

necessity under the laws of war and the linking of it with Common Article 3 of the 1949 Geneva conventions to provide a regime for the conduct of hostilities that fall below the threshold set by the 1977 Additional Protocol II.

In chapter seven the paradigms are seen to overlap with the extension of human rights law into situations of armed conflict through the development of case law from international courts and opinions of other bodies. Although the overlap began with the International Court of Justice, the extension has principally been made through the jurisprudence of the ECtHR and the development of its approach which mostly relies on a particular conception of necessity and proportionality in self-defence in peacetime law-enforcement operations. The court has then considered the use of military force in internal armed conflicts predominantly within that framework and has avoided deciding when and how much force may be used in circumstances of insurrection and armed conflict. The chapter examines the case law of the court in detail and the elements of the exceptions to the right to life for self-defence, the making of an arrest, and the quelling of a riot or insurrection. It also considers how self-defence operates as a defence to murder under English law and the defence of necessity that may apply to a killing made in the quelling of an insurrection.

Chapter eight draws together the issues that go towards explaining the problem that is created by the overlap between the paradigms of armed conflict and law-enforcement and the application of the exception to the right to life for quelling an insurrection. At one level, this explains how and why the British government got itself into a position of such uncertainty about the use of lethal force in the conduct of British military operations in Iraq through its application of a narrow understanding of the use of force in law-enforcement that is limited to self-defence. However, this leads into the more complex reason in that the British approach was based on legal paradigms of armed conflict and law-enforcement that were treated as separate by the British government and other actors even though in practice there they can be seen as overlapping both in terms of military operations and legal paradigms so as to accommodate different levels of violence. The chapter sums up the current state of the law in relation to the exception to the right to life for the use of force to quell an insurrection and then goes on to consider the potential consequences of making use of the exception. One consequence is that it may facilitate a reduction in the types and levels of force that are permitted under the laws of war and the exclusion of the use of force based on the principle of proportionality that can justify collateral civilian deaths and destruction of property. There would, however, need to be development of the concepts of necessity and proportionality in the use of force to quell an insurrection under the ECHR which provide a balance between the lawful purpose of the use of force and the competing (and sometimes conflicting) rights of civilians, insurgents and state security forces. The historical precedents suggest that the use of force in such circumstances was intended to be limited to armed insurgents but this raises a number of questions about how it should apply to others who participate in an armed insurrection (such as bomb makers), or are drawn into it (such as civilians used as human shields). Another consequence is the potential justification of shoot-to-kill policies and targeted killings of insurgents but, to the extent that this did occur, killings would still have to be justified as being absolutely necessary and proportionate to the purpose of quelling the insurrection. The book concludes that the use of force remains a political choice of governments but that, in internal armed conflicts that fall short of civil war, use of the exception to the right to life for the use of force that is necessary to quell an insurrection and is accountable as such to the courts offers an alternative approach which may provide a better balance for the protection of civilians and the security forces in maintaining public order in conditions of armed insurrection than the existing practice of applying either the laws of war or the law of self-defence.[57]

[57] In more precise legal terms, as used here the reference to a civil war means an armed conflict that would meet the requirements for the application of Additional Protocol II to the 1949 Geneva conventions.

1

The Lieber Code

The term 'non-international armed conflict' has become the basis of the modern legal classification for non-state armed conflicts in place of four terms that were commonly used (and continue to be used): insurrection; rebellion; insurgency; and civil war. A participant in an armed group in these types of conflicts is then called a 'rebel' or an 'insurgent'. However, of these terms, only 'insurrection' appears in the main treaties on the laws of war or international human rights law, which might imply that the terms ought to be given their ordinary meaning.[1] Nonetheless, there is a traditional legal context which places them in a hierarchy of violence. The terminology is not standardized but it may comprise (in ascending order) rebellion, insurgency and belligerency.[2] Alternatively, the hierarchy has been described as insurrection, rebellion and civil war.[3] In order to understand these terms, they have to be seen in their particular context and their use by individual writers. This becomes clearer when, on closer examination of the sources used by the leading modern writers, it can be seen that there are two which underlie much of the writing. One is *International Law, A Treatise* by Professor Lassa Oppenheim (1858–1919) which uses the hierarchy of 'rebellion, insurgency and belligerency'.[4] The other is *General Order 100* – the Lieber Code – which uses the

[1] In the *Concise Oxford English Dictionary* 'insurgent' means 'a rebel or revolutionary', and (adj) 'rising in active revolt'; 'insurgency' is defined by reference to 'insurgent'; 'insurrection' is defined as 'a violent uprising against authority'; 'rebellion' means 'armed resistance to an established government or ruler'; and 'civil war' means 'a war between citizens of the same country' – *The Concise Oxford English Dictionary* (Oxford, Oxford University Press, 2011). 'Insurrection' is referred to in article 2 of the ECHR.

[2] A Cullen, 'Key Developments Affecting the Scope of Internal Armed Conflict in International Humanitarian Law' (2005) 183 *Military Law Review* 66.

[3] SC Neff, *War and the Law of Nations, A General History* (Cambridge, Cambridge University Press, 2005) 250; and D Armitage, *Civil Wars A History in Ideas* (New Haven, Yale University Press, 2017) 193.

[4] L Oppenheim, *International Law, A Treatise, Vol II War and Neutrality* (London, Longmans, Green, and Co, 1912) §54–60. This approach was continued by Sir Hersch Lauterpacht (1897–1960) as editor of the revised edition of the work: H Lauterpacht (ed), *International Law, A Treatise by L Oppenheim*, Vol II (London, Longmans, Green & Co, 1940). See, eg, A Cassese, *International Law* (Oxford, Oxford University Press, 2005), 124–30; M Milanovic and V Hadzi-Vidanovic, 'A Taxonomy of Armed Conflict' in White and Henderson (eds), *Research Handbook on International Conflict and Security Law* 256–313; L Moir, 'The Historical Development of the Application of Humanitarian Law in Non-International Armed Conflicts to 1949' (1998) 47: 2 *International and Comparative Law Quarterly*, 337–61; S Sivakumaran, *The Law of Non-International Armed Conflict* (Oxford, Oxford University Press, 2012) 9–10; and N Zamir, *Classification of Conflicts in International Humanitarian Law: The Legal Impact of Foreign Intervention in Civil Wars* (Cheltenham, Edward Elgar, 2017) 16.

terms 'insurrection, rebellion and civil war'.[5] The nomenclature of this typology is taken from the writings of Emer de Vattel (1714–67) who had first introduced the idea that 'rebels against a sovereign or "public power" could legitimately be recognized as belligerents'.[6] The two hierarchies share the conception that internal disorder was a matter of municipal law until the fighting reached such a scale that the conflict became subject to the laws and usages of war. In Oppenheim's scheme, this was at belligerency and it was the term given to the legal qualification to make war.[7] Since, as a matter of fact, armed groups within a state could make war, these groups could under certain conditions become 'belligerent powers' and subject to the laws of war.[8] However, it was more controversial whether the insurgents were accorded belligerent rights automatically in such circumstances. Whilst some argued that they were, in practice they were not.[9] The issue concerned third-party states in that recognition of belligerency invoked neutrality and, as the consequences of recognition were so far-reaching, an interim state known as 'recognition of insurgency' arose.[10] This allowed states to decide what rights they would grant to the insurgents, whether as a third-party or the state involved in the insurgency, and, as Professor Hersch Lauterpacht (1897–1960), one of the leading international lawyers of the mid-twentieth century, argued, it was not possible to define the legal status of an insurgency in general.[11] The concept of belligerency as a status is now thought to have become largely redundant in international law as it is used so rarely.[12] In international armed conflict, the decline in use of 'belligerency' followed from the development of international law which is reflected in the use of the term 'war' giving way to 'armed conflict'.[13] For non-international armed conflicts, the term had largely fallen into disuse by 1945 and was superseded by the development of objective criteria for determining that a non-international armed conflict exists without the need for state recognition.[14] However, the two hierarchies of armed conflict have an important legacy in the creation and development of the modern paradigm of armed conflict which is complex and interlinked.

[5] In *War and the Law of Nations* (2005) (n 3) 250, Neff refers to Vattel and Lieber as the sources of the formulation 'insurrection, rebellion and civil war' but I argue that Lieber reconceptualized the hierarchy from Vattel's work. Another leading modern work, E Castrén, *Civil War* (Helsinki, Suómalainen Tiedeakatemia, 1966) 28, uses a simpler typology of insurrection and civil war.

[6] D Armitage, 'Cosmopolitanism and Civil War' (2016) 19.

[7] Oppenheim, *International Law* Vol II (1912) (n 4) §54. Most writers seem to infer from *General Order 100* that this applied to civil war although their views on how this arose differ or are unclear and this point is explored in more detail in the light of research on Lieber's manuscripts and letters below.

[8] ibid §76.

[9] Neff, *War and the Law of Nations* (n 3) 265.

[10] ibid 251.

[11] H Lauterpacht, *Recognition in International Law* (Cambridge, Cambridge University Press, 1947) §79.

[12] Zamir, *Classification of Conflicts* (2017) (n 4) 22.

[13] Nonetheless, the term 'belligerents' is still in use, for example, it is used in the 1949 Geneva conventions in the context of states (or the armed forces of states) party to a conflict.

[14] D Akande and L Hill-Cawthorne, 'The Lieber Code and the Regulation of Civil War in International Law' (2015) *Columbia, Lieber Series* 643.

This chapter begins by looking at *General Order 100* and examines its place in the development of the laws of war. *General Order 100* has been described as 'the quarry from which all subsequent codes were cut' and can be traced as the source for the first international conventions on the laws of war agreed at the Hague in 1899 and 1907.[15] As such, *General Order 100* is said to represent the laws and usages of war between states even though it was introduced by the Union army in 1863 in the midst of the American Civil War.[16] Some see the introduction of the code in the civil war as implicit recognition by the United States that the international rules applied in civil war whilst others think that the code had no force under international law.[17] This chapter argues that these narratives have obscured the place of the Lieber Code as an original source and, in particular, its contingent influence on the armed conflict paradigm in relation to internal armed conflicts. Drawing on the collections of Lieber's papers held at the Huntington Library in San Marino, California and the Milton Eisenhower Library at John Hopkins University in Baltimore, Maryland and other sources, it shows how the Lieber Code influenced the development of the law and obscured other approaches to the use of force in internal armed conflicts.[18] It also shows that the main motivation behind some important distinctions made in the code was political and a peculiar product of the American Civil War. In particular, these included the conceptualisation of a principle of military necessity and its application to a monolithic conception of internal armed conflict encompassing insurrection, rebellion and civil war to justify the fullest use of military force permitted under the laws of war but without recognition of the rebels as lawful combatants. This supported the Union's policy of waging war whilst denying belligerent rights to the Confederacy.[19]

[15] G Best, *Humanity in Warfare: The Modern History of the International Law of Armed Conflict* (London, Weidenfeld and Nicholson, 1980) 171. For a critique of the idea of a progressive development of the laws of war see, eg: R Liivoja, 'Technological Change and the Evolution of the Law of War' (Winter 2015) 97: 900 *International Review of the Red Cross*, 'The Evolution of Warfare' 1157–78; and A Alexander, 'A Short History of International Humanitarian Law' (2015) 26: 1 *European Journal of International Law* 109–38.

[16] An address by Elihu Root (1845–1937), the president of the American Society of International Law and a former US Secretary for War and Secretary of State, on Lieber on the fiftieth anniversary of the code is perhaps the most influential source of the view that the code was of general application and led directly to the development of the laws of war between states – E Root, 'Francis Lieber' (July 1913) 7: 3 *American Journal of International Law* 453–69. Root's view was then adopted in another widely quoted article by T Meron, 'Francis Lieber's Code and the Principles of Humanity (1997) 36 *Columbia Journal of Transnational Law* 269.

[17] For a view that *General Order 100* applied to the American Civil War, see Akande and Hill-Cawthorne, 'The Lieber Code' (2015) (n 14) 640. Solis argues that it applied only to the Union army and was binding by virtue of being a military order, G Solis, *The Law of Armed Conflict: International Humanitarian Law in War* (Cambridge, Cambridge University Press, 2016) 45. A leading article written in 1963 by RR Baxter seems to suggest that Lieber intended the code to apply both to war between states and civil war, RR Baxter, 'First Codification of the Law of War: Francis Lieber and General Orders No 100' (April 1963) 3: 25 *International Review of the Red Cross* 170–89.

[18] In the footnotes in this chapter, references to letters and manuscripts at the Huntington Library are prefaced 'HEH' and those at the Milton Eisenhower Library, 'ME'.

[19] SC Neff, *Justice in Blue and Gray: A Legal History of The Civil War* (Harvard, Harvard University Press, 2010) 260.

The extension of the laws of war to conditions of civil war was not adopted by states when they agreed the Hague regulations in 1899 and 1907 but it would provide a foundation for the later development of the laws of war and their application to non-international armed conflicts which brought together versions of the concept of military necessity and the monolithic conception of internal armed conflicts which had originated in the Lieber Code. These two concepts are important as they would come to underpin the use of force in modern military operations in internal armed conflicts in circumstances where the conflict satisfied the legal test for an 'armed conflict'. This means that there are now within the category of 'non-international armed conflict' circumstances that may previously have been seen as an insurrection or rebellion and not subject to the laws of war. In effect, this moved the applicable law governing the use of force in insurrection and rebellion from the sphere of municipal law to the sphere of international law and the paradigm of armed conflict. This, in turn, would provide the legal basis for rules of engagement in military operations in internal armed conflicts that were based on the laws of war and, in particular, the permissiveness of the use of force justified through military necessity rather than the more limited municipal law concept of necessity.

The Lieber Code and the American Civil War

As is generally acknowledged, Dr Francis Lieber, Professor of History and Political Science at Columbia College, New York, was the initiator and main author of *General Order 100*. Lieber wrote to General Henry Halleck (1815–72), the Commanding General of the Army, in November 1862 proposing that 'the President ought to issue a set of rules and definitions providing for the most urgent issues occurring under the Law and Usages of War' and that a committee might be appointed to draw up a code.[20] After some hesitation, Halleck took up the suggestion and Lieber was appointed to a board constituted 'to propose amendments and changes in the Rules and Articles of War, and a code of regulations for the government of armies in the field, as authorized by the laws and usages of war'.[21] Although the basis for the code was customary law and usage, the issue of the law's application to the civil war was not specifically addressed. Lieber had written to the US Attorney General earlier in November 1862 on another issue of much debate in the civil war, the status of a naval blockade, and had admitted:

> I have searched in the books at my disposal, for authorities, I find none; for Civil war is little treated by the authors on the Law of War. Nor has there ever been a Civil war with the peculiar characteristics which signatize [sic] ours. But I have a better authority than authors – the authority of Common Sense – the directness of reasonableness and the simplicity of truth.[22]

[20] Lieber to Halleck, 13 November 1862 (HEH LI 1764).
[21] US War Department, Special Orders No 399 dated 17 December 1862.
[22] Lieber to Bates, 9 November 1862 (HEH LI 852).

Among Lieber's papers there are in effect four drafts of the code prior to its publication as *General Order 100*: an initial looseleaf draft; a more developed draft in a notebook; a printed draft entitled 'A Code for the Government of Armies in the Field' containing 97 articles that Lieber sent to the board and a number of individuals, including Halleck, in February 1863 as the draft code; and several copies of the printed draft annotated with proposed amendments. The final form issued as *General Order No 100* was a further development from the annotated drafts. It had 157 articles, including a new final section X 'Insurrection, Rebellion and Civil War', and was issued on 24 April 1863.[23]

When Lieber sent a printed draft of the code to the board in February 1863, he had already drafted three paragraphs on 'Rebellion and Invasion of our country with reference to the treatment of our own citizens by the command genl [sic]' but omitted them from the draft on the basis that their subject was not within the remit of the board.[24] This is unconvincing as Lieber himself had conceived the idea and content of the code for use in the conflict and Halleck asked for the paragraphs to be included.[25] In response, Lieber drafted a new six page section for the code entitled 'Insurrection Rebellion Civil War Foreign Invasion of the United States' and sent it to Halleck and the board.[26] Halleck edited it severely to less than three pages and the edited section became 'Section X' of *General Order 100*.[27] There is no record of the finalisation of the draft code but, based on the correspondence, my view is that Lieber left the final section alone after Halleck's editing.[28]

Lieber had begun his draft of the new final section with a definition of war as 'an armed contest between sovereign, that is independent nations'. He then acknowledged that

> § There are great contests, however, with all the grave intrinsic characteristics of war, and exceeding at time in magnitude and intensity, many wars between sovereign nations … the wars of revolution, of rebellion, and of insurrection; and Civil War … All the rules, therefore, that are devised from the intrinsic character of war, and especially those rules and usages … for the mitigation of the calamities of war ought to be observed likewise.

He then gave a revised definition of war: 'War according to its intrinsic characteristics is to be defined as a protracted state of armed hostility between the multitudes organized as armies or at least massed together in large contending

[23] Although dated 24 April, the final version does not appear to have been distributed until May 1863 as *General Orders No 100*, 'Instructions for the Government of Armies of the United States, in the Field' (Washington, GPO, 1863) which is here referred to as either the 'code' or *General Order 100*.

[24] Lieber to Halleck, 20 February 1863 (HEH LI 1774).

[25] Halleck to Lieber, 28 February 1863 (HEH LI 1654).

[26] Manuscript 'Insurrection Rebellion Civil War Foreign Invasion of the United States', undated (HEH LI 1829).

[27] Halleck to Lieber, 8 April 1863 (HEH LI 1658) and Lieber to Halleck, 10 April 1863 (HEH LI 1786).

[28] Halleck sent his comments on the new section to Lieber in a letter of 8 April 1863 and, although Lieber sent further comments to the board before the draft was finalized, there is no record of them. In his subsequent letters, Lieber expresses a sense of frustration and pique at not being involved in the finalization of the code.

bodies'. The draft also defined insurrection, rebellion, revolution and civil war and linked them to the laws of war by stating that 'Humanity and the force of circumstances have induced many modern governments of the civilized nations to adopt the rules of regular war towards the insurgents and rebels'. However, '[t]he adoption of the rules of regular war, towards insurgents or rebels, whether the adoption is partial or entire, does in no way imply a partial or complete acknowledgement of them as public belligerents'. Of this scheme, only the definitions of insurrection and rebellion, a modified definition of civil war, and the non-acknowledgment of recognition were carried into *General Order 100*.

Lieber's Conception of the Laws of War in Internal Armed Conflicts

Lieber's approach to the application of the laws of war to internal armed conflicts in the draft code was based on two key principles: that the duty to apply rules and usages of war in internal armed conflicts was a moral, and not a legal, duty that arose out of humanity; and, where they were applied, their application did not amount to recognition of the rebels. However, an analysis of the changes made during drafting, the correspondence between Lieber and Halleck, and Lieber's earlier work show some revealing aspects of how the code was developed and how it was specifically designed to apply to the civil war. There are five points that become apparent from this analysis in relation to what Lieber called the 'new structure' provided by the new final section.

First, as Lieber explained in a letter to Halleck, he had deliberately set out an argument 'giving the reasons' for the new section to the code but Halleck removed the explanatory passages on grounds of brevity.[29] Looking at the argument that Lieber set out, there is some similarity in the style of argument to that used by Clausewitz in *On War*. Lieber began with an initial definition of war and then, after recognizing that there are other war-like contests, there was a modified definition that led to a conclusion that the laws of war 'ought to be observed likewise' in these conflicts but that this did not amount to recognition.[30] This was a contested view of the law at that time and took a position that was somewhere between those who argued that the laws of war did not apply to internal armed conflicts and those who applied them as part of the concept of belligerency. The final code took a step back from this position and confined itself to assertions that the application of the laws of war did not amount to recognition.

[29] Halleck to Lieber, 8 April 1863 (HEH LI 1658) and Lieber to Halleck, 10 April 1863 (HEH LI 1786).

[30] To illustrate the stylistic similarities, in chapter one of book one of *On War*, Clausewitz defines war as 'an act of force to compel our enemy to do our will' and then, after discussing the theoretical and practical aspects of war, he arrives at the famous conclusion that 'war … is a continuation of political intercourse, carried on with other means'. References and text from C von Clausewitz, *On War*, translated and edited by M Howard and P Paret (Princeton, Princeton University Press, 1989) 75 and 87.

Second, both Lieber's draft and *General Order 100* treated rebellion as an amplified form of insurrection, the draft then implied that civil war was an extension of rebellion but the order omitted this.[31] In his detailed study of Lieber's influence on the idea of civil war, Professor David Armitage notes that Lieber provided two distinct definitions of civil war. The first defined it as a contention between two parts of a state for mastery of the whole and the second provided: 'The term is also sometimes applied to war of rebellion, when the rebellious provinces or portions of the states are contiguous to those containing the seat of government'. This, Armitage points out, was a novel idea drafted specifically for the American Civil War.[32] However, this second definition did not appear in Lieber's draft manuscript and, given that Halleck redrafted the section, it is likely that it was added by him. Both the draft and the final code then referred to the application of the laws of war to insurrection, rebellion and civil war without distinction in a monolithic approach. One of the reasons for this may have been that under the US constitution, congress had the power to levy taxes '[t]o provide for calling forth the Militia to execute the Laws of the Union, suppress Insurrections and repel Invasions' and the constitution also provided that '[t]he Privilege of the Writ of Habeas Corpus shall not be suspended, unless when in Cases of Rebellion or Invasion the public Safety may require it'.[33] There were, therefore, good reasons for being able to classify the civil war as both an insurrection and a rebellion.

Third, Lieber's draft had stated that

> the adoption by the legitimate government, of the common rules of regular war in insurrections and rebellions, is necessarily subject to great modification regarding the treatment of the inhabitants of the revolted provinces, by the commander of the legitimate army, in all cases for which the distinct law of his country or the positive orders of his government does not provide.

In his earlier notes Lieber had gone further than this and developed some principles as to how the rules would differ between international war, which he sometimes referred to as 'regular war', and civil war but he did not put them in his draft and the general qualification he had included was omitted from *General Order 100*. This had the effect of applying the rules of war to insurrection, rebellion and civil war at the discretion of the legitimate government and without modification.[34]

Fourth, Lieber had created a classification of internal armed conflicts that was both different from that in his previously published work and lectures, and from Halleck's. In his 1839 work, *Political Ethics*, Lieber had critiqued various classifications of war given by the leading modern writers on war and the laws of war, including Hugo Grotius (1583–1645), Vattel, Samuel von Pufendorf

[31] The draft states 'Civil war, *if this term has a definite meaning different from rebellion*, designates a war between two portions of a country or a state …', *General Order 100*, article 150 (italics added).

[32] Armitage, *Civil Wars* (2017) (n 3) 189.

[33] The US Constitution (1787), article I, sections 8 and 9 respectively.

[34] The principles are contained in Lieber's note 'Civil War', undated (ME Box 2 Folder 18).

(1632–94), Cornelius von Bynkershoek (1673–1743) and Clausewitz, finding all their theories inadequate in one way or another. He had then proposed a variant of just war theory that included both external wars, such as wars of self-defence or 'chastisement' where a wrong had been committed by one state on another, and internal wars, such as wars of insurrection to gain or regain liberty, wars of independence or wars to quell armed factions.[35] At the beginning of the civil war, Lieber also gave a series of lectures at Columbia College, New York on 'the Law and Usages of War', some of which were published in the New York press.[36] In notes written in 1861–62 for the lectures, he defined war for the purposes of the lectures in general terms as 'a protracted physical contest between large numbers'.[37] He then went on to give more precise definitions:

> 21. In international law we mean, as a matter of course, by war the contest between nations or independent governments, acknowledged as such by the family of nations. By civil war we mean the protracted state of active hostility of one portion of a political society against another portion.
>
> 22. Insurrection is the rising of one portion of a political society against another; by revolution we mean the successful rising or the change of a government or some of its [essentials] by violent means.[38]

Lieber was also aware of Halleck's book, *International Law*, which was published in 1861 and he quotes from it in the 1862 'Guerrilla Parties' paper he wrote for Halleck, at Halleck's request, on the status of guerrillas and other irregular participants under the laws of war.[39] Halleck's book is mostly a compendium of other authors' works on international law and in it he covers the classification of wars from many different perspectives but does not guide the reader to a conclusion or attempt to deal with the contradictions between the various classifications. He describes civil wars as 'those which result from hostile operations, carried on between different parts of the same state' but thinks the term is 'more usually applied to those contests which are waged between rival families and factions, for party ascendency in a state, rather than for its dismemberment, or for radical change in its government'.[40] If one applies his classification to the American Civil War, it seems it would have been a civil war, although it was not fought between families or factions for control of the state, and, being more than a 'mere rebellion', it could also have been a war of insurrection or revolution and

[35] F Lieber, *Political Ethics* (Boston, CC Little and J Brown, 1839) 654–55.

[36] RS Hartigan, *Lieber's Code and the Law of War* (Chicago, Precedent, 1983) 13. Notebooks containing copies of Lieber's lecture notes are in the Milton Eisenhower Library (ME Box 2, Folders 16 and 17).

[37] Lieber, 'Law and Usages of War, No II', 29 October 1861 (ME Box 2, Folder 16).

[38] Lieber, 'Twenty-Seven Definitions and Elementary Positions Concerning the Law and Usages of War' (ME Box 2, Folder 15). Parenthesis added as the word 'essentials' is unclear in the manuscript notes. Although the document is entitled 'Twenty-Seven Definitions', there are only 23 and it appears that a final page is missing.

[39] F Lieber, 'Guerrilla Parties Considered in Reference to the Laws and Usages of War', 17 August 1862. Copy in Hartigan, *Lieber's Code* (1983) (n 36) 33–44.

[40] H Halleck, *International Law: Or, Rules Regulating the Intercourse of States in Peace* (New York, D Van Nostrand, 1861) 332–33.

the participants would have been entitled to be treated as belligerents by the state. This suggests that the editing of the draft code so that it conceived of a war that could at the same time be an insurrection, a rebellion and a civil war (but not a revolution) was the product of what Lieber had called the 'ticklish work' of preparing the new section and Halleck's editing of it.[41] It illustrates the difficulty both writers had in classifying wars but, more specifically, the extent to which they were tailoring the section to fit the Union's particular political cause, not only through the bespoke definition of civil war that Armitage highlights but also by dropping references to revolutionary war as it was an argument being used in support of the Confederacy. It is notable, however, that both Lieber and Halleck referred to 'wars' of insurrection and rebellion which presupposes the type and scale of the conflict and focuses on purpose rather than the approach of placing insurrection and rebellion in a hierarchy of violence subordinate to civil war.

Fifth, not only was the classification different, so was the application of the laws of war for in his lectures Lieber had made an important distinction:

> 23. All these states of war, other than international war, carry along with them the moral obligations between the warfarers which have been alluded to, although they stand in different relations. In international war the idea of punishment of the individual combatant would be illogical; in rebellion it is not.[42]

Here Lieber clearly distinguished rebellion and insurrectional wars from 'regular war' between states. The reference to 'moral obligations' in relation to 'all states of war, other than international war' would also seem to include civil wars and exclude them from the application of the law and usages of war. Professor Johann Bluntschli (1808–81), a professor of law at the University of Heidelberg in Germany and a friend of Lieber's who used the code as a source for his own works on the laws of war, noted Lieber's tendency to refer to moral and legal justifications saying that Lieber's 'legal injunctions rest upon the foundation of moral precepts. The former are not always sharply distinguished from moral injunctions, but nevertheless through a union with the same are ennobled and exalted'.[43] This is special pleading by Bluntschli on behalf of his friend but the references to morality can also be seen as special pleading by Lieber when he does not wish to be clear about the nature of a right or an obligation. There is another particular example of this use of legal 'injunctions' based in morality in the 'Twenty-Seven Definitions' in which Lieber creates a relationship that links morality with the limits on the use of force:

> 14. War being a physical contest, yet man remaining for ever a moral and a rational being, and peace being the ultimate object of war, the following conclusions result:
>
> a. War is a physical contest but not an exclusively physical contest

[41] Lieber to Halleck, 4 March 1863 (HEH LI 1778 and 1779).
[42] Lieber, 'Twenty-Seven Definitions' (n 38).
[43] JC Bluntschli, 'The Service of Francis Lieber to Political Science and International Law' (1880) XIII *International Review* 54.

b. All means to injure the enemy so far as to deprive him of power to injure us or to force him to submit to the conditions desired by us are allowed to be resorted to, but
c. only so far as necessary for this object and
d. We must abstain from everything that will make the ulterior peace the normal state unnecessarily difficult or unsubstantial[44]

Here Lieber started to develop the idea of the permissibility of the use of force as well as its limitation and it is possible to see in it the beginning of Lieber's development of the principle of military necessity, a term that he did not use in the definitions and rarely used in the lecture notes but was developed in the drafting of the code and is one of its lasting influences.

War and 'Military Necessity'

Several authors have noted that *General Order 100* appears to be the origin of the term 'military necessity' in the law of war and that there is a correlation between the adoption of the doctrine of military necessity and a Clausewitzian approach to war. In *Lincoln's Code*, John Fabian Witt portrays military necessity as Lieber's development of President Abraham Lincoln's (1809–65) distinction between his presidential war powers, grounded in necessity in war and within the president's prerogative, and domestic powers grounded in and subject to the constitution of the United States.[45] Whilst he presents some evidence for Lincoln's use of the phrase 'military necessity' as the basis for the emancipation of slaves in the Confederate states, the linkage between the two is superficial. An alternative explanation is that the concept of military necessity reflects a development of Lieber's own thought as can be seen in his papers. Following on from its beginnings in his lectures, the principle of military necessity is developed through each of the drafts of the code. In the first draft Lieber introduced a concept of '*martial* necessity' (emphasis added):

> Martial Necessity consists in the necessity of those measures which are requisite and unavoidable for the obtaining of the ends of the war, and are lawful according to the Law and Usages of war by civilized nations.[46]

In the second draft, he added a caveat to the principle in that it was martial necessity 'as understood by modern nations' and changed the word 'unavoidable' to 'indispensable'. He also added a new sentence that 'Martial Necessity allows of all destruction and obliteration, requisite for the speedy obtaining of the ends of the war, short of

[44] Lieber, 'Twenty-Seven Definitions' (n 38) – emphasis in the original.
[45] JF Witt, *Lincoln's Code: The Laws of War in American History* (New York, Free Press, 2012) 211–12.
[46] Lieber, Manuscript (untitled) (HEH LI 183 A).

cruelty'.[47] This definition is further developed in the printed draft of the code as 'Military Necessity' in three articles. In the first, it is defined as 'the necessity of those measures which are indispensable for the obtaining of the ends of the war, and are lawful according to the modern law and usages of war'. In the second, its parameters are established, it 'admits of all direct destruction of life or limb of the armed enemies, and of those whose destruction is incidentally unavoidable in the armed contests of the war' and further illustrations are given. In the third, its limitations are stated in that it 'does not admit of cruelty – that is, the infliction of suffering for the sake of suffering or for revenge' and specific exclusions are given, such as poisoning. It ends with a characterization that 'in general, Military Necessity does not include any act of hostility which makes the return to peace unnecessarily difficult'. This is essentially the form appearing in *General Order 100* although a specific exclusion for perfidy was added at Halleck's suggestion.[48]

The principle of military necessity can be seen to establish the means that may be applied in war as it referred to those measures that are requisite for obtaining the ends of war and it was complemented by the development of Lieber's thought on the ends of war. This developed over a longer period than the development of the principle of military necessity and can be seen in his published works and manuscript notes. In his lecture notes, Lieber had continued to follow the just war approach that he had argued in *Political Ethics*:

> 13. The object of all civilized war is either defence or the intention of forcing of the enemy to conditions which we think necessary and just. It lies beyond the war and beyond the battle. Distruction [sic] of the hostile army is rarely the object of a land battle, but even when it is, it is only a means to obtain the ulterior end of the war.[49]

However, in an undated note written about the time of the code and entitled 'War and Peace' he reflected more widely on war and peace in the then modern world in a way that begins to show a change from *jus ad bellum* just war theory towards *jus in bello* and the more equal treatment of belligerents.[50] He characterized peace as the normal state and wars as the exception that both caused and permitted the destruction of property, but 'is lawful only as a means to obtain the great end for which it was undertaken, and not for its own sake'. The views set out in the note are largely encapsulated in article 29 of *General Order 100*:

> Modern times are distinguished from earlier ages by the existence at one and the same time of many nations and great governments related to one another in close intercourse.
>
> Peace is their normal condition; war is the exception. The ultimate object of all modern war is a renewed state of peace.
>
> The more vigorously wars are pursued the better it is for humanity. Sharp wars are brief.

[47] Lieber, Manuscript 'Code of War on Land' (HEH LI 183 B). There remains a reference to 'unavoidable?' in a marginal note alongside 'indispensable'.

[48] Copy of the printed draft code annotated with manuscript comments by Gen Halleck (HEH LI 243077).

[49] Lieber, 'Twenty-Seven Definitions' (n 38).

[50] Francis Lieber, 'War and Peace' (HEH LI 391).

Witt describes the inclusion of the idea that the 'more vigorously wars are pursued, the better it is for humanity' in the code as giving it a Clauswitzian perspective.[51] Although Clausewitz's *On War* was not well known in the United States until after the Second World War,[52] Lieber was familiar with Clausewitz, as he explained in his 1839 work, *Political Ethics*:

> General Clausewitz, in his work On War (Vom Krieg) Berlin, 2 vols 1835, – a work which bears the imprint of a powerful mind, says, 'War is the act of compelling an opponent to submit to one's will. Thus force is the medium, and submission the object, and the latter can only be obtained by the development of the former. In order to effect this, the enemy must be rendered powerless. This is the grand aim of all hostilities.'[53]

The translation would have been his own as he wrote this only four years after *On War* was first published and an English translation was not published until 1870.[54] Military necessity is one of the main themes of Witt's argument that the 'American way of war' combines humane restrictions with a permissive destructiveness and that both are grounded in the laws of war that the United States has helped to develop. However, I think it is possible to see Lieber as the originator of a concept of military necessity that was novel for its time both in its scope and its application to internal 'wars' as well as international wars but which has been changed in substantial ways by others from Lieber's conception of it.

Three further manuscript notes in Lieber's collections of papers help to show the development of his wider thinking on war, particularly with regard to internal 'wars' around the time that he was producing his lecture notes and then drafting the code.[55] In the notes, he addressed the justification for revolutionary wars and cited passages from his own book *Political Ethics* and other writers such as de Vattel, Bluntschli and Professor William Whewell (1794–1866). The common theme in the references is that they considered when citizens or subjects – 'the People' – would be justified in rebelling against their sovereign. Lieber had dealt with this in a discussion on just war in *Political Ethics* and he clearly saw an event such as the American Revolutionary War against Great Britain (1775–83) as a just war.[56] Vattel had made a quite different distinction between insurrection, rebellion and civil war in that insurrection and rebellion are to be dealt with by the sovereign according to municipal law but, once the sovereign faced 'effectual opposition', the conflict became a civil war and the rules of war

[51] Witt, *Lincoln's Code* (2012) (n 45) 236.

[52] C Coker, *Rebooting Clausewitz: On War in the 21st Century* (London, Hurst & Company, 2017) xvii.

[53] Lieber, *Political Ethics* (1839) (n 35) 631.

[54] Witt, *Lincoln's Code* (n 45) 185.

[55] F Lieber, Note on 'Case of Revolution' and two notes on 'War' (HEH LI 183).

[56] See, eg, The Loyal Publication Society Pamphlet No 77, 1865 Reprint of 'An Address on Secession' delivered in South Carolina in 1851 by Francis Lieber (ME Box 2, Folder 3) which rejects any comparison between the justification for the American Revolutionary War and secession by South Carolina.

applied to it.[57] In the longer term, it was Vattel's argument that the separation of a nation into two separate societies in a civil war brought the conduct of the hostilities under the law of nations that was to prevail in international law over the Lieber Code's approach.[58] However, in a sentiment that is partially echoed by Lieber in the draft section X, Vattel went on to suggest that a sovereign ought to apply the rules of war in rebellion, by detaining captured rebels and avoiding retaliation, even though the rebels have no claim to them, in order to avoid the conflict becoming more cruel and destructive, at least until order is restored.[59]

All the writers listed in Lieber's note use the principle of 'necessity' to justify acts of war. The principle of necessity derives from the medieval theory of just war and 'functioned as a license to States enforcing their just rights to take whatever steps were necessary – including, as a last resort, the use of force' and went so far as to justify the killing of hostages or other innocent civilians.[60] Lieber had been very interested in the development of the doctrine of necessity in the *Caroline* incident.[61] It involved the burning of a ship in American inland waters in 1837 by forces loyal to the British Crown in anticipation that it was about to be used to supply arms to rebels in Canada. It led to correspondence between the British and US governments that became the basis of the doctrine of anticipatory self-defence in international law. In the now famous words of the US Secretary of State, Daniel Webster (1782–1852), the doctrine requires 'a necessity of self-defence, instant, overwhelming, leaving no choice of means, and no moment of deliberation'.[62] It was during the nineteenth century, however, the concept of war moved away from just war to be seen as a clash of national self-interests.[63] The code can be seen as an important step in this regard as it marks the making of the distinction between *jus ad bellum* and *jus in bello* and demonstrates a change in thinking from Lieber's earlier writing. As the concept of *jus ad bellum* developed, it retained the concept of necessity in the doctrine of self-defence and the classic formulation taken from the *Caroline* case. However, the development of *jus in bello* through *General Order 100* takes a separate route based on the principle of military necessity as laid down by Lieber. Although the law of necessity has been described as 'a highly unexplored area of law', a contemporary reaction to Lieber's development of the law can be seen in the Confederate response to *General Order 100* which referred both to

[57] *The Law of Nations; or Principles of the Law of Nature, Applied to the Conduct and Affairs of Nations and Sovereigns*. From the French of Monsieur de Vattel, Sixth American edition, from a new edition, by J Chitty (Philadelphia, T & JW Johnson, 1844) Book III, Ch VIII, §292–93.

[58] Armitage, *Civil Wars* (n 3) 131.

[59] Vattel, *The Law of Nations* (1844) (n 57) Book III, Ch XVIII, §295.

[60] SC Neff, 'The Prerogatives of Violence – In Search of the Conceptual Foundations of Belligerents' Rights' (1995) *German Yearbook of International Law* 38, 43.

[61] There are excerpts from various letters from Lieber about the incident in TS Perry (ed), *The Life and Letters of Francis Lieber* (Boston, James Osgood and Company, 1882) 149–61.

[62] See E Wilmshurst, 'The Chatham House Principles of International Law on the Use of Force in Self-Defence' (2006) 55: 4 *International and Comparative Law Quarterly* 963.

[63] Neff, *War and the Law of Nations* (2005) (n 3) 4.

the traditional concept of necessity and Lieber's new military necessity.[64] After delivery of a copy of *General Order 100* to the Confederate forces through their agent, Judge Ould (1820–82) who conducted a cartel with the Union army for the exchange of prisoners of war, Ould sent copies of it to the Confederate leaders.[65] In response, the Confederate Secretary for War, James Seddon (1815–80), sent a detailed review of it to Ould in which he rejected the code's doctrine of military necessity. In his view, in words that reflect Webster's formulation of necessity

> Military necessity as a legislator has a supreme authority; but the range of its jurisdiction is limited. The necessity must be present, urgent, and overruling, and the acts done under it must afford probable means of escape from an impending danger.[66]

As such, he said, it was unjustifiable to deduce from necessity a general rule of practice that prescribed the 'measures of violence' that could be applied in advance of actual circumstances. It is notable that this more traditional form of necessity may, depending on the circumstances and the interpretation of the code itself, be more extensive than Lieber's doctrine. It does not express any limitation on the acts that may be carried out which would otherwise be unlawful, or more limited, and it does not prescribe in advance what measure of force is lawful. In its context, Seddon's view is an understandable reading of the doctrine set out in the code, in particular of the sentence 'To save the country is paramount to all other considerations' which stands out both by its unqualified scope and by its positioning as a separate paragraph at the end of article 5 of *General Order 100*. Bluntschli wrote that the code authorized 'the harshest measures and most reckless exactions' against those engaged in war.[67] These views of military necessity as harsh and unlimited *in extremis* would later evolve into the doctrine of *Kriegsraison* (which is translated into English as 'military necessity' but has connotations of permitting unrestrained warfare where the situation demands). *Kriegsraison* was then used to justify the violation by the German army of many of the laws of war until it was rejected by war crimes tribunals after the Second World War.[68]

Despite the uncertainty as to its parameters and the interpretation of the principle that led to *Kriegsraison*, Lieber's conception of military necessity survived and developed in *jus in bello*, particularly though the development of military doctrine in the United States. US army officers were taught the code at West Point and *General Order 100* was reissued unchanged in 1898 during the United States war

[64] Neff, 'The Prerogatives of Violence' (1995) (n 60) 60, n 22. He referred readers to BC Rodick, *The Doctrine of Necessity in International Law* (New York, Columbia University Press, 1928).

[65] Hartigan, *Lieber's Code* (n 36) 110–11. Copy of letter from William Ludlow, Union Army Agent for Exchange of Prisoners to Robert Ould, Confederate Agent for Exchange of Prisoners, 22 May 1863 and Letter from Ould to Ludlow, 5 June 1863.

[66] Hartigan, *Lieber's Code* (n 36) 120. Copy of letter from James Seddon, Confederate Secretary of War, to Ould, dated 24 June 1863.

[67] Bluntschli, 'Francis Lieber' (1880) (n 43) 54.

[68] BM Carnahan, 'Lincoln, Lieber and the Laws of War: The Origins and Limits of the Principle of Military Necessity' (1998) 92: 2 *American Journal of International Law* 218.

with Spain and the insurrection in the Philippines.[69] Major General George Davis, who was a Judge Advocate General and a US representative at the Hague conference in 1907, is said to have preferred *General Order 100* over the 1874 Brussels Declaration that was made at the end of the first international conference on the laws of war and preceded the 1899 Hague conventions, as Davis thought that the convention favoured protecting humanitarian interests at the expense of military necessity.[70]

In 1914, following the 1907 Hague conventions, the United States produced new *Rules of Land Warfare* that, referring to *General Order 100*, gave the object of war as being 'to bring about the complete submission of the enemy as soon as possible by means of regulated violence' and then restated the principle of military necessity as 'Military necessity justifies a resort to all the measures which are indispensable for securing this object and which are not forbidden by the modern laws and customs of war'.[71] These were then combined in later versions, for example, in 1940, the *US Manual* was revised and republished with a specific principle of military necessity:

> The principle of military necessity, under which, subject to the principles of humanity and chivalry, a belligerent is justified in applying any amount and any kind of force to compel the complete submission of the enemy with the least possible expenditure of time, life, and money;[72]

Comparison of the various forms of expression of the principle of military necessity show how it has changed over time and been influenced by the writings and interpretations of Clausewitz. As has been seen, Lieber was aware of Clausewitz's idea that submission of the enemy was the object of war but there are indications that Lieber was deliberately constructing a concept of war that opposed Clausewitz's conception, for example, one of the 'Twenty-Seven Definitions' that he used in his lectures included the point that 'Wars or battles are not duels', whereas Clausewitz had written that 'War is nothing but a duel on a larger scale'.[73] His notes also show that the idea that the object of war is peace was a later one taken from a speech by the Duke of Wellington (1769–1852) in Parliament in 1852.[74] There is some evidence that Lieber was well aware of the difficulties of defining necessity in internal armed conflicts through his notes on the writings of Whewell.[75] Whewell was Professor of Moral Philosophy at the University of Cambridge and one of the most important and influential figures in nineteenth-century Britain, a polymath

[69] US Government Printing Office, *Instructions for the Government of Armies of the United States in the Field, prepared by Francis Lieber, LLD, Originally Issued as General Orders No 100, Adjutant General's Office, 1863* (Washington, GPO, 1898).

[70] TL Dowdeswell, 'The Brussels Peace Conference of 1874 and the Modern Laws of Belligerent Qualification' (2017) 54: 3 *Osgoode Hall Law Journal* 846.

[71] US War Department, *Rules of Land Warfare* (Washington, GPO, 1914) 14.

[72] US War Department, *Rules of Land Warfare, FM27–10* (Washington, GPO, 1940) 1.

[73] Lieber, 'Twenty-Seven Definitions' (n 38), Definition 12; Clausewitz, *On War* (n 30) 75.

[74] Note to p 629 of Lieber's interleaved copy of 'Political Ethics' (ME Box 5).

[75] Lieber, Manuscript note 'War' (HEH LI 183).

who wrote works on the philosophy of science, physical science, moral philosophy and numerous other subjects. Lieber's notes refer to a passage in which Whewell argued that it is inadvisable for a moralist to attempt to define or enumerate cases of necessity as they have, by their nature, to involve 'moral anguish and afterwards regret' that the general rules 'were compelled to give way'. 'This being the case', he wrote, 'we must necessarily abstain from laying down any definition of the limits of Cases of Necessity; and any Precepts for such cases'.[76] It is not possible to tell whether Lieber agreed with this but in the code he created a concept of military necessity that was different in that it applied to war not rebellion, as Whewell had considered, but it was then extended to rebellion and insurrection when section X was added to the draft code.

The Application of the Lieber Code to Internal Armed Conflicts

After he received a copy of the published *General Order 100*, Lieber wrote Halleck a congratulatory (and self-congratulatory) letter that proclaimed 'As the order now stands, I think that No 100 will do honour to our country. It will be adopted as a basis for similar works by the English, French, and Germans'.[77] Having asked for 100 copies of the order for himself, he set about making his prediction a reality. He asked his friend, Senator Charles Sumner (1811–74), to send copies of the order to the French book reviewers and the Prussian, French and Russian governments.[78] He was also in contact with leading European intellectuals, including Blunstchli in Germany and Professor Laboulaye (1811–83), a professor of law at the Collège de France, both of whom made use of the code. Laboulaye wrote the introduction to a French edition of the code and Bluntschli is said to have done little more than translate *General Order 100* into German for his book *Das Moderne Kriegsrecht der Civilisirten Staten* ('The Modern Law of War of Civilised States').[79] Bluntschli himself said that he had used *General Order 100* as a 'model' for 'The Modern Law of War'.[80] However, although the rule sections appear to bear a close resemblance to each other, it is incorrect to

[76] W Whewell, *The Elements of Morality, Including Polity, Vol I* (New York, Harper & Brothers, 1845) 269.

[77] Lieber to Halleck, 20 May 1863 (HEH LI 1796).

[78] Lieber to Halleck, 16 May 1863 (HEH LI 1664) and Lieber to Sumner, 19 May 1863 (HEH LI 3583).

[79] On Bluntschli, see, eg, Witt, *Lincoln's Code* (n 45) 328; Hartigan, *Lieber's Code* (n 36) 22; and MR Thayer, *Life, Character and Writings of Francis Lieber* (Philadelphia, Collins, 1873) 35. On Laboulaye, see S McCurry, 'Enemy Women and the Laws of War in the American Civil War' (2017) 35: 3 *Law and History Journal* 705.

[80] Bluntschli, 'Francis Lieber' (1880) (n 43) 54. Bluntschli also included a copy of the 'Instructions' as an appendix to his *Le Droit International Codifié* (['International Law Codified']) (Paris, Guillaumin, 1870).

say that Bluntschli's book is little more than a translation of *General Order 100*, at least in relation to the section of the book that deals with the definition of war and the application of the laws of war to internal armed conflicts.[81] Bluntschli's book reorganizes the material in the code into a more logical structure and begins with a chapter setting out the definition of war and the different categories of war. His classification begins with war between states but then directly applies the laws of war to internal armed conflicts in which there are organized armed parties that operate under the rules of war. Clearly with the American Civil War in mind, he creates a special category of war within federal states which both applies the laws of war to the conflict and preserves the right of the federal forces to apply the criminal law against participants in the rebellion. Bluntschli's classification anticipates one of the key distinctions created in the law of non-international armed conflicts by the 1977 Additional Protocol II to the 1949 Geneva conventions in making compliance with the rules (or, in some interpretations of the protocol, the ability to comply with the rules) a requirement for recognition.[82] What Bluntschli appears not to do, however, is to apply the laws of war to insurrection. This suggests that Bluntschli did not adopt Lieber's monolithic approach and reverted to a more traditional classification by excluding insurrection from the definition of war and making rebellion a tipping point for the application of the laws of war. In addition, it is often asserted that Lieber's prediction of the code's adoption came true with the subsequent publication of similar works in Britain, France, Prussia and a number of other countries.[83] In particular, the code received early acclaim for having been adopted by Prussia prior to the Franco-Prussian War of 1870.[84] However, the inclusion of Britain in the list is I believe mistaken.[85] The British first published the *Manual of Military Law* (the *British Manual*) in 1884 and it is very different in form and substance to *General Order 100*.[86] In particular, it has separate chapters on 'Riot and Insurrection' and 'War' which follow a traditional distinction between internal and external

[81] JC Bluntschli, *Das Moderne Kriegsrecht der Civilisirten Staten* (Nördlingen, CH Beck, 1866). I have been unable to find an English translation of the book and the German is very difficult to translate into English as the German is somewhat obscure, probably deliberately so. Nonetheless, I think it is possible to identify the structure of the laws of war that Bluntschli creates in it and I am grateful to Professor Jan Honig for taking the time to look at it with me.

[82] AP(II), article 1(1). For differing views as to whether there is a requirement for compliance or only the ability to comply with the protocol, see Maj Gen AVP Rogers, *Law on the Battlefield* (Manchester, Manchester University Press, 2004) 221 and Y Dinstein, *Non-International Armed Conflicts in International Law* (Cambridge, Cambridge University Press, 2014) 47, respectively.

[83] See, eg, Solis, *The Law of Armed Conflict* (2016) (n 17) 44. The lists of countries varies between authors.

[84] Carnahan, 'Lincoln, Lieber and the Laws of War' (1998) (n 68) 218.

[85] Solis cites TE Holland, *The Laws of War on Land* (Oxford, Clarendon Press, 1908) 72–73 as the authority for the list of countries but in the pages cited Holland dismissed the notion that a systematic treatment had been carried out by any country and gave examples of what a number of countries had produced. His reference to Great Britain supports my own finding and, in relation to Prussia, he says that confidential instructions were issued to officers in 1870 but makes no mention of Bluntschli's *Das Moderne Kriegsrecht*.

[86] War Office, *Manual of Military Law* (London, HMSO, 1884).

military operations (internal operations including, for the purposes of the time, those by colonial governments) and which indicate the existing British framework and policy. This will be considered further in the next chapter.

General Order 100 was taken up by the Russian government as part of a proposal for an international treaty made at the Brussels conference of 1874. As part of the proposals, the Russian government drew up a draft code of the laws of land warfare, provisionally entitled the 'Draft Declaration Concerning the Laws and Customs of War' that cross-referenced *General Order 100*.[87] The conference was attended by representatives of 15 European states including the Great Powers of the time: Austro-Hungary, Britain, France, Prussia and Russia. There was considerable debate over the draft at the conference but in the end it finished with a non-binding declaration. Among the controversial aspects of the draft were the provisions on occupation that were based on *General Order 100* and widely regarded as legitimizing the harsh methods used by the Prussian army in France in the Franco-Prussian War of 1870, to the extent that it was referred to in diplomatic circles as the 'The Code of Conquest'.[88] Although the draft regulations were not adopted as binding at Brussels, they were adopted with some modifications by the Hague conference of 1899 and again with minor amendment in 1907. Under their terms, the conventions only apply to wars between the Contracting Powers, and then only if all the belligerents are parties to the particular convention.[89] Among other things, the regulations annexed to the conventions setting out the rules of war formally established the principle of distinction as a matter of the laws of war and limited belligerents to state parties and *levees en masse*.[90]

Although there are very differing views on whether *General Order 100* should be regarded as applying only to wars between states or civil wars, or both, it is possible to gain more understanding of the law that applies in internal armed conflicts from the analysis of Lieber's papers. As has been seen, Lieber had previously applied the laws of war to certain categories of internal armed conflict but he omitted any mention of the issue in the printed draft that he sent to the Union army board. There may be a number of reasons for this. One possible explanation is that he thought that the American Civil War actually was a 'regular war' between states with the Confederate states on one side and the Union states on the other. However, this conflicts with his firm belief that the Union could not be severed and his rejection of the 'States Rights' doctrine that held that, when the individual states had approved the US constitution, they had retained the individual power

[87] Dowdeswell, 'The Brussels Peace Conference' (2017) (n 70) 823.

[88] K Nabulsi, *Traditions of War, Occupation, Resistance and the Law* (Oxford, Oxford University Press, 1999) 6.

[89] See article II of the Hague Convention II, 1899 and Hague Convention IV, 1907, the wording is different between the two conventions.

[90] The principle of distinction is set out in article 1 of the Hague regulations. It is now supplemented by the extended definitions of state armed forces contained in 1949 Geneva Convention III, article 4 and AP(I), article 43. The ICRC *Customary Law Study* takes a different approach and treats state armed forces as combatants in both international and non-international armed conflicts.

to secede.[91] Although his views on secession had a legal underpinning, they were also highly political. Lieber was actively involved in union politics and a passionate supporter of the North writing a number of pamphlets and articles that strongly supported the Union cause using a mixture of legal and political arguments.[92] In his legal advice to the US government and the US army, however, he adopted a more formal approach and style but beneath the formal approach there is a strong awareness of the interaction of law and politics.

In his formal advice, Lieber seems to be reluctant to become involved in the issue of how to approach the problem of civil war and take refuge in, and to some extent hide behind, his position as a lawyer. This can be seen in his 'Guerrilla Parties' pamphlet. In the pamphlet he discussed the application of the laws of war to guerrillas and set out what we would now recognize as the criteria for recognition of a combatant under the principle of distinction in the laws of war.[93] However, he concluded it by stating that the pamphlet did not apply to the American Civil War.[94] His reticence was shown again in the drafting of the code until requested by Halleck to include a section on civil war. He then set out to provide legal definitions of insurrection, rebellion, revolution and civil war, which we would now recognize as issues of classification, but once again he did not tie their legal status into the rules. He also did not include the principles that he had developed to distinguish the rules that applied in civil war or the exception for wars of insurrection and offered only the advice, which was not included in *General Order 100*, that the rules of war in insurrections and rebellions would be subject to great modification regarding the treatment of civilians. Once section X was included in the code without that qualification, it implied that the rules it contained applied equally in insurrection and rebellion as well as civil war.

Although Lieber adopted a formal approach to giving legal advice, he was not greatly concerned about the philosophical or theoretical justification for the application of the code to the civil war and he makes his arguments at different times on different, expedient grounds. When the issue of the treatment of captured Confederate soldiers was a political controversy, Lieber had argued that the civil war or rebellion in which they were engaged was 'to all intents and purposes war … and allow the laws and usages of war to regulate their conduct with each other'.[95] He then opined that if the Confederacy took the benefit of the laws of war through the treatment of its captured soldiers as prisoners of war, 'they must accept their own logic. The negro is free'. Here Lieber was tenuously trying to connect two issues in the code – prisoners of war and emancipation – when the 'logical' point

[91] Lieber to Halleck, 25 November 1862 (HEH LI 1766).

[92] See, eg, Loyal Publication Society Pamphlet, 'Dr Lieber's Remarks on the Final Adjournment of The Loyal Publication Society' (ME Box 2, Folder 35) and F Lieber, 'The Civil Status of Paroled Rebels', published in the *Army and Navy Journal*, New York on 27 May 1865 (ME Box 2, Folder 30).

[93] Witt, *Lincoln's Code* (n 45) 195.

[94] Armitage, *Civil Wars* (n 3) 186. See Lieber, 'Guerrilla Parties' in Hartigan, *Lieber's Code* (n 36) 43–44.

[95] Lieber to Bates, 8 June 1862 (HEH LI 832).

was surely that if the Confederate states wanted to benefit from the code, they should also undertake to obey it. Lieber had a theory of law which he encapsulated in the phrase 'No right without its duties, no duty without its rights'.[96] He had it printed on his stationery and thought that it might be his only lasting contribution to jurisprudence.[97] He did not, however, apply it to the code. As has been seen, in his lectures he applied the rules to civil war and rebellion as well as 'regular' wars and in the 'Guerrilla Parties' pamphlet he used the terms 'civil war' and 'wars of insurrection or rebellion' as if they are interchangeable and argued that the application of the laws of war to them was 'always undefined'. In the draft code, he first ignored the issue and then, when directed to include something, his explanation is opaque but suggested that the application of the laws of war in internal conflicts was at the discretion of the government. After *General Order 100* was published, he wrote to Sumner that he thought that section X 'has been too much cut-down' but does not make much of it and he was far more indignant about a trivial point on the editing of an article that he thought was inappropriate.[98] Some writers put his apparent lack of interest in the application of the code to civil war down to his own ambition to produce a work of general scope for which he would be feted.[99] There does seem to be something in this but it also seems that it was a political choice made in the realisation that the competing principles of classification and recognition were irreconcilable and that the Union was picking and choosing from the law to best suit in its own interests. However, there is one further qualification to this. There is, I think, an argument that, when the modern laws of war were first codified, the use of force in internal armed conflicts was intended to be more limited. The argument is based on the printed version of *General Order 100* which contains an unusual typographical feature that has disappeared in modern reprints. In article 15, one of the articles that set out the principle of military necessity, it states:

> Military necessity admits of all destruction of life and limb of *armed* enemies, and of all persons whose destruction is incidentally *unavoidable* in the armed contests of the war …

The italicized emphasis is in the first printed version of *General Order 100* and continued to be shown in this way when the order was reprinted in 1863 and 1898.[100] These are the only words italicized in the order and they were not

[96] F Lieber, 'Report of a Lecture on the Inter-Relation of Rights and Duties, belonging to a Course on Political Philosophy, now delivering in the Law-School of Columbia College', undated (ME Box 2, Folder 11).

[97] JF Childress, 'Francis Lieber's Interpretation of the Laws of War: General Orders No 100 in the Context of His Life and Thought' (1976) 21: 1 *American Journal of Jurisprudence* 47.

[98] Lieber to Sumner, 19 May 1863 (HEH LI 3583) and Lieber to Halleck, 20 May 1863 (HEH LI 1796).

[99] See, eg, J Garner, 'General Orders 100 Revisited' (1964) 27 *Military Law Review* 42.

[100] Eg, there is a copy of the first print of *General Order 100* by the US Government Printing Office in the Huntington Library (HEH 238598) and a copy of the reprint by D van Norstrand (New York) in 1863 (HEH 137049), which is also available as a facsimile book published by Leopold Classic Library. A copy of the 1898 reprint is enclosed with a letter from the US Secretary of War to Congress 'Orders and Instructions Issued to Military Officers in The Philippines', dated 7 May 1902 (HEH 119953).

italicized in the draft code that Lieber had printed in February 1863 to send to the US army board or in Lieber's own manuscript drafts. He would underline words in the manuscripts for emphasis but did not do so in this context. This suggests that the italicization was inserted by the board that oversaw the completion of the order for use in the civil war. This then may be a more limited conception of military necessity and proportionality that was to be applied to internal armed conflicts than the principles that were developed for international armed conflicts and, as will be seen in chapter six, subsequently applied to non-international armed conflicts.

Conclusion

The Lieber papers show that, although much of *General Order 100* was based in existing customary law, it was also a source in itself which contained a bespoke classification of war to which the measures of war applied and developed a particular conception of what those measures were. Lieber adopted a novel, monolithic approach in treating hostilities in insurrection, rebellion and civil war as all being subject to the laws of war at the discretion of the state and without recognition of the rebels' rights as belligerents. He also laid the foundations for the modern understanding of the laws of war as a balance between military necessity and humanity in a way that specifically identified the measures permitted by military necessity with the concept of war as a contest between states. Articles 14 to 16 and 29 of *General Order 100*, which set the parameters of military necessity, establish a close connection between means and ends in public wars between states, the means are determined by military necessity and the end is the return to peace and the resumption of what Lieber saw as the 'normal' relations between states. Lieber did not then revisit it when adding section X on 'Insurrection – Civil war – Rebellion'. In drawing up the definitions of insurrection, rebellion and civil war, Lieber moulded the definitions to serve the political purposes of the Union cause and it was probably Halleck who took the further step of producing a definition specific to the American Civil War. Whilst Lieber certainly considered the application of military necessity to the American Civil War to be justified, he did not consider whether the ends in an internal conflict were different from those of war between states or how the different ends of the protagonists might affect military necessity. However, his conception of military necessity was not what it has become for it can be seen that the 'end' of military necessity has changed over time into a more Clausewitzian conception of the submission of the enemy. The association of Lieber with the modern conception of military necessity should, therefore, be qualified. The part of the narrative that leads from *General Order 100* to the modern laws of war as applied to non-international armed conflicts should also be qualified by recognizing its contingency. In particular, it was drafted by Lieber as a code of the laws of war between states and then adapted only in part for a civil war that was in a state of belligerency by making changes that supported the Union's policy of waging war whilst denying belligerent rights to the Confederacy. Furthermore, it treated conditions of civil war, rebellion and insurrection as war for the purposes of the laws of war. The use of military force was justified through the development of the principle of military necessity and drew no distinction between the different levels of violence embodied by types of armed conflict. That distinction was, however, made through the subtle qualification to military necessity made by the italicized text in the original copies of the code, probably by the board that approved the code rather than Lieber. The effect of Lieber's approach to internal armed conflicts outside of the context of the American Civil War was largely contained by international reluctance to discuss the application of the laws of war to them. The development of the laws of war in the late nineteenth century and early twentieth century at the Brussels and Hague conventions was limited to the formal status of war between states but it would provide a foundation for the later development of the laws of war and their application to non-international armed conflicts after the Second World War. This extension would bring together the versions of the two concepts originated in the Lieber Code: military necessity and the monolithic conception of internal armed conflicts that encompassed insurrection, rebellion and civil war, which had been developed contingently by different events and interests.

2

The Jamaica Rebellion

As the American Civil War ended in 1865, a rebellion occurred in the British colony of Jamaica that was to lead to an extensive public debate in Britain on the power of the public authority to deal with rebellion and whether its powers to do so were subject to accountability before the civil courts.[1] The debate was very different to that carried on in the United States during the American Civil War in relation to the application of the laws of war to a civil conflict. In Britain the debate revolved around the issue of martial law and what it entailed as a matter of municipal law.

This chapter considers the circumstances of the debate, the issues it raised on the nature of martial law and the uncertainties that persisted in the second half of the nineteenth century over whether the use of military force to suppress insurrection and rebellion was a matter of law-enforcement or war. At the time of the Jamaica Rebellion, martial law was generally seen as justified where a state of war existed which made it impossible for the ordinary courts to function and, as such, was contingent upon the breakdown of law.[2] The public debate in England over the powers that arose under martial law was based on two opposing concepts of martial law.[3] The first permitted the use of military force where there was an 'immediate local necessity' but it excluded deterrent actions or summary justice and, at least in principle, the military could be held accountable for their actions by the courts once the crisis had passed. The other permitted the military forces to use repressive, aggressive, or deterrent measures in the field and summary powers of punishment over which the civil courts had no jurisdiction.[4] This debate continued well into the twentieth century but Professor Charles Townshend, who is one of the leading modern historians of British internal security operations in the nineteenth and twentieth centuries, argues that there was a general consensus among nineteenth century commentators that 'the

[1] The public disorder in Jamaica in 1865 is commonly referred to as a rebellion and this chapter follows that usage whilst acknowledging that there are different views, eg: it is argued to be a riot in VJ Marsala, *Sir John Peter Grant, Governor of Jamaica, 1866–1874: An Administrative History* (Louisiana State University, LSU Historical Dissertations and Theses, 1967). The Report of the Jamaica Royal Commission, 1866 described it as both a rebellion and an insurrection.

[2] C Townshend, 'Martial Law: Legal and Administrative Problems of Civil Emergency in Britain and the Empire, 1800–1940' (1982) 25: 1 *Historical Journal* 171.

[3] AWB Simpson, *Human Rights and the End of Empire: Britain and the Genesis of the European Convention* (Oxford, Oxford University Press, 2010) 54–90.

[4] ibid 60 and 63.

Crown (and indeed all lawful citizens) had the common law right and the duty to repel force with force'.[5] This chapter draws out the distinction between martial law and the right to repel force with force in order to establish an alternative conception for the use of force in insurrection and rebellion. The conception represents the core of a legal–military framework that was developed over that period and included elements of British constitutional theory, policy and practice. The constitutional theory developed out of the debate over martial law and the excessive use of force in the Jamaica Rebellion and was formalized in Dicey's *An Introduction to the Study of the Law of the Constitution*, the leading constitutional law textbook of the period which was first published in 1885 (*The Law of the Constitution*). AV Dicey (1835–1922) was a professor of jurisprudence at Oxford University and had earlier been involved in the public debate over the Jamaica Rebellion. *The Law of the Constitution* contained a limited conception of the military's power to use force to quell an insurrection based on a common law right to repel force with force and made it subject to the rule of law. As the use of martial law became increasingly controversial in Britain, the British army developed a practice that permitted the use of lethal force where necessary to suppress an insurrection under a limited set of rules drawn from the law on the conduct of hostilities in war. The use of force by the military in these circumstances was subject, in theory at least, to accountability under the municipal law but it also carried with it the expectation of exoneration under an act of indemnity for actions carried out in good faith. This conception was formalized in the first edition of the *Manual of Military Law* and then remained in successive editions for over 50 years. It contained a detailed consideration of the meaning of insurrection and distinguished it from riot by its public purpose. This provides the basis for understanding the British approach to the development of the paradigms of armed conflict and law-enforcement after the Second World War which acknowledged a threshold at a state of belligerency – in effect civil war. It then treated politically-motivated violence below the threshold as insurrection within a law-enforcement paradigm that included the concept of the use of military force subject to municipal law but never resolved the tensions between them that gave rise to the debate over the Jamaica Rebellion. This framework is then the foundation of an approach to the use of lethal force under both municipal law and international human rights law that overlaps with the circumstances in which laws of war may also apply in internal armed conflicts.

The Jamaica Rebellion (1865)

The facts of the Jamaica Rebellion received renewed interest during the United States 'War on Terror' and there now exists a discrete but deep literature of the

[5] Townshend, 'Martial Law' (1982) (n 2) 171. Townshend argues that it is a common law right rather than a prerogative right of the Crown but there is no clear answer as to which it is – see *Halsbury's Laws of England* (5th edn, 2011) vol 3, para 185. The issue is discussed further in subsequent chapters.

rebellion.[6] In brief summary, Jamaica had been conquered by Britain in a war with Spain and was officially ceded to Great Britain by the Treaty of Madrid in 1670. It was subsequently settled by British emigrants who established and maintained sugar plantations through slavery until its abolition in the British empire in the early nineteenth century. Following abolition, labour was mainly supplied as 'task work' – work made available when required by the plantation owner or overseer and paid by reference to the product rather than time.[7] Violent disturbances were common and there were rebellions in 1757 and 1832. In 1865 the colony was also suffering economic hardship partly as a result of the interruption of trade during the American Civil War. The abolition of slavery had left a large, formerly enslaved population without land of their own to cultivate and dependent on seasonal labour whilst at the same time the plantation owners sought to expand their own land holdings. Disputes arising over rights to unsettled land were brought before the civil courts and then led to the outbreak of violence in October 1865.

The Jamaica Rebellion lasted about a month but had two distinct phases. The first phase began with disturbances arising from court cases over land ownership and culminated in a confrontation at a courthouse in a small community at Morant Bay. The confrontation began with the arrival of a large crowd in the town square intending to interrupt a council meeting in the courthouse. The crowd was armed with various weapons, including firearms looted from the local police station, and was confronted in the square by a small force of local militia who had been called to protect the local magistrate and a number of others attending the council meeting. In the ensuing violence the courthouse was burned and some 22 soldiers and civilians were killed and 34 wounded by the mob.[8] When news of the attack reached the island capital at Kingston, the governor, Edward Eyre (1815–1901), convened a meeting of the legislature to declare martial law in the local area and troops were sent to Morant Bay by naval vessel to restore order. By the time that the troops arrived at Morant Bay on the day following the attack, the mob had left and dispersed in groups into the surrounding countryside and plantations. The second phase consisted of operations by the troops supported by local hillmen known as Maroons to suppress the rebellion. During the following four weeks some 439 people were killed, including 354 executed by order of courts martial; at least 600 were flogged, including a number of women; and 1000 properties were burned.[9] No troops were reported as killed or injured in suppressing the rebellion.[10] Among those executed by order of a court martial was

[6] See, eg, D Dyzenhaus, 'The Puzzle of Martial Law' (2009) 59: 1 *University of Toronto Law Journal* 1–64; RW Kostal, *A Jurisprudence of Power: Victorian Empire and the Rule of Law* (Oxford, Oxford University Press, 2005); JF Witt, 'Anglo-American Empire and the Crisis of the Legal Frame (Will the Real British Empire Please Stand Up?)' (2007) 120: 3 *Harvard Law Review* 754–96; and N Hussain, *The Jurisprudence of Emergency: Colonialism and the Rule of Law* (Ann Arbor, The University of Michigan Press, 2003).

[7] Report of the Jamaica Royal Commission 1866 (London, Eyre and Spottiswoode, 1866) 44 and 48.

[8] ibid 1081.

[9] ibid 25–26.

[10] Marsala, *Sir John Peter Grant* (1967) (n 1) 23.

the Hon GW Gordon (1820–65), a prominent politician and former member of the legislature who was accused of inciting the rebellion. Having heard that he was to be arrested, Gordon had surrendered himself to the authorities in Kingston, which was outside the martial law area, but was transported to Morant Bay, tried by court martial and hanged for high treason.

News of the rebellion and its violent suppression 'precipitated a legal and moral crisis in Britain'.[11] A royal commission was quickly established and sent to Jamaica to inquire into 'the origin, nature, and circumstances of the … Disturbances'. It heard evidence from some 730 witnesses and produced a report. The report contained a number of conclusions including that 'the disturbances … had their immediate origin in planned resistance to lawful authority', the principle object of which was 'the obtaining of land free from the payment of rent'. The report then characterized the disturbances as an 'insurrection' and the participants in it as 'insurgents'. The royal commission praised Governor Eyre, 'for the skill, promptitude and vigour' which he exhibited in the early stages of the insurrection that led to 'its speedy termination' and found that the military operations had been 'prompt and judicious'. Nonetheless, they found that martial law had continued for longer than 'the necessary period' and 'the punishments inflicted were excessive'. It made a particular note of the number of those executed, the 'reckless' and 'positively barbarous' floggings, and the 'wanton and cruel' burning of houses.[12]

The suppression of the rebellion became something of 'an English *cause célèbre*' resulting in the formation of a group called the Jamaica Committee.[13] It included a number of prominent politicians and public figures and attempted to bring criminal and civil proceedings against the governor and some of the military officers. It also led to the publication of a series of books on martial law by WF Finlason (1818–95), a barrister and law reporter for *The Times* newspaper. The first, which was entitled *A Treatise on Martial Law*, was published in 1866 and contained 'the most comprehensive discussion of martial law that had ever been written in English'.[14] It is through the works published in connection with the Jamaica Rebellion that one can see the first modern concerted effort to analyse what was the lawful response to internal conflict in Britain and its empire.

The Attempt to Create Legal Accountability for Actions under Martial Law

The Jamaica Committee instructed two leading barristers, Edward James QC and Fitzjames Stephen QC, to advise them on a number of issues in relation to the

[11] Townshend, 'Martial Law' (n 2) 169.
[12] Report of the Jamaica Royal Commission (n 7) 40–41.
[13] D Lino, 'The Rule of Law and the Rule of Empire: AV Dicey in Imperial Context' (2018) 81: 5 *Modern Law Review* 739–64.
[14] Kostal, *A Jurisprudence of Power* (2005) (n 6) 229.

suppression of the rebellion. The request for advice contained a mixture of questions on the legal nature of martial law and leading questions on the possibility of prosecuting Eyre, in particular for the treatment of Gordon.[15] The opinion that James and Stephen provided in response followed a formal legal style and contained a detailed review of the existing authorities on the nature of martial law. It concluded:

> The legality of the conduct pursued towards Mr Gordon depends … on the question whether it was necessary for the suppression of open force, and the restoration of legal authority, to put him to death. We see nothing whatever in Governor Eyre's despatch which affords any ground for thinking that such could have been the case.[16]

When it became clear that the British government would not prosecute Governor Eyre or any of the military officers, the Jamaica Committee began its own attempts to do so.[17] Three cases were brought: a private prosecution of Colonel Nelson and Lieutenant Brand RN for the murder of Gordon – they had been members of the board at his court martial – which resulted in a Charge to a Grand Jury by the Lord Chief Justice of England, Sir Alexander Cockburn;[18] a private prosecution of Governor Eyre as an accessory before the fact in the murder of Gordon which was refused at its initial stages and then a subsequent prosecution for 21 misdemeanours under the Colonial Governors' Act 1700, an Act extending the English courts' jurisdiction to actions by government officials 'beyond the seas';[19] and a civil action against Eyre for £10,000 each in damages for trespass including assault, battery and false imprisonment of two British subjects resident in Jamaica, Alexander Phillips and Dr Robert Bruce.[20] All three attempts failed. In the two criminal prosecutions, the cases went to a grand jury but it did not find a 'true bill' – meaning that there was no case to answer. The civil action was defeated on a procedural basis that the cause of action arose in Jamaica and had been removed as a matter of law by an act of indemnity passed by the Jamaica legislature. A subject that will be considered further below.

In his monograph on the Jamaica Rebellion, *The Jurisprudence of Power*, Rande Kostal describes the breadth and depth of the national debate conducted in parliament, in the press, through the publication of books on the suppression of the

[15] A copy is appended to W Forsyth, *Cases and Opinions on Constitutional Law, And Various Points of English Jurisprudence, Collected and Digested from Official Documents and Other Sources; with Notes* (London, Stevens and Haynes, 1869).

[16] ibid 561.

[17] Kostal, *A Jurisprudence of Power* (n 6) 259.

[18] *Frederick Cockburn's Special Report of the Charge of the Lord Chief Justice of England to the Grand Jury at the Central Criminal Court in the Case of The Queen Against Nelson and Brand* (2nd edn, 1867) ('Frederick Cockburn's Special Report') – cited in C Moore, *Crown and Sword: Executive Power and the Use of Force by the Australian Defence Force* (Canberra, ANU Press, 2017) 135.

[19] WF Finlason, *Report of the Case of The Queen v Edward Eyre on his Prosecution in the Court of Queen's Bench containing the Charge of Mr Justice Blackburn* (London, Stevens, 1868) – cited in Moore, *Crown and Sword* (2017) (n 18) 135. The charge is specified in Townshend, 'Martial Law' (n 2) 172.

[20] *Phillips v Eyre* (1870) LR 6 QB 1. The details are given in Kostal, *The Jurisprudence of Power* (n 6) 432.

Jamaica Rebellion and embodied in the cases brought against Eyre, Nelson and Brand. His book is the foundation of a discrete literature that took the Jamaica Rebellion as an historical example that could be used to examine issues arising out of the War on Terror and a common theme of the literature is the lack of clarity on what the law of martial law is or was. The overall impression given by the literature is that the concept of martial law is very confused and encompasses a number of very different, and probably irreconcilable, views.[21] Rather than be drawn into that debate, it is possible to extract points from the literature that are important for any contemporary consideration of the lawfulness of the use of force and see how they can be separated from the controversy surrounding martial law. The points that can be made are that: first, the circumstances of the Jamaica Rebellion drove the legal framework within which the debate was conducted. Second, despite the substantial differences of view in the debate over martial law conducted in the aftermath of the Jamaica Rebellion, there is a common core on the use of military force that is not disputed. Third, one side of the debate as represented by the legal opinion given to the Jamaica Committee is the source of the main constitutional theory in English law on martial law falling within the rule of law. Fourth, once the common core is identified and associated with the constitutional theory of the rule of law, it becomes apparent how little it has been explored. Fifth, once framed as a constitutional law issue, the debate excluded consideration of sources of municipal and international law that may significantly affect the legal analysis.

Theories of Martial Law

The revival of interest in the Jamaica Rebellion as part of the scrutiny of the United States' use of exceptional powers in the War on Terror brought with it a methodological debate on the conduct of the arguments over martial law in Britain in the late 1860s. Researchers struggled with the conflicting nature of the sources and their chosen methodology and critiqued the approach taken by others. Taken together, the modern debate and critique reveal a number of points which provide an insight into the study of the subject itself.

In an extensive article based around a book review of *The Jurisprudence of Power*, Michael Taggart was critical of Kostal's historical approach as failing to provide a legal, as opposed to an historical, assessment of the arguments raised in the debate and being 'too quick to accept that "[t]he legal discourse on martial law was politics by other means"'.[22] The comment that Taggart identifies comes at the

[21] See, eg, Simpson, *Human Rights and the End of Empire* (2010) (n 3) 60–61 and Townshend, 'Martial Law'(n 2) 170.

[22] M Taggart, Book Review: 'Ruled by Law?: A Jurisprudence of Power: Victorian Empire and the Rule of Law by RW Kostal' (2006) 69: 6 *Modern Law Review* 1024.

end of a passage in Kostal's book that is worthy of noting in full. Kostal wrote of the legal debate over the Jamaica Rebellion:

> For anyone wanting to construct a coherent picture of martial law, there was nothing to do but to excavate and assemble shards from a myriad of case reports, national histories, treatises, official opinions, military dicta, and parliamentary utterances. Martial law was not something that was to be *found* in the sources; it was something that had to be *made* from them. Every account of the subject plainly was the result of numberless choices as between competing authorities. Inevitably these choices were not random, but were determined by a political predisposition. Arguments about the law of martial law turned on the writer's *a priori* commitments of one of two general kinds: to individual liberty in England or public security in the empire. The legal discourse on martial law was politics by other means.[23]

The initial point on the novelty of the exercise is well made and it is the motivation behind Kostal's inquiry into why this debate took place in Britain at that time. The point on the great variety of sources also underlies one of Kostal's main points expressed though the title of his book that the debate was over the relationship between law and power but the reference to power may be a little misleading if is not recognized that power in this context includes the ideas of governance and order originating not only from government but also from civic interest groups. Taggart frames the Jamaica debate as part of a larger movement toward putting the use of force into a positivist, legal framework and tries to connect it to the debates that we have seen were being conducted in the United States on the laws of war in the American Civil War only a few years before, debates that he thinks Kostal overlooked.[24] However, if one reads Lieber's writing against the James and Stephen's opinion to the Jamaica Committee, it is striking how different they are. Lieber, Halleck and those others involved in the drafting of *General Order 100* sought to develop and apply the laws of war to the use of force due to issues arising from the scale and nature of the conflict. In particular, it was not possible to argue that United States federal or state law should apply to both parties to the conflict when the armies were fighting over the sovereignty of the United States itself. There was an attempt, by Lieber in particular, to frame issues as matters of the laws of war but a vagueness over the nature of the conflict and how the laws of war applied to an internal armed conflict. By contrast, the debate in Britain over Jamaica was driven by the issue of the use of force within the state where the state was able to make use of a preponderance of military power against civilians, albeit armed civilians. The law that applied to those circumstances was a municipal matter. Finlason to some extent stands in between these two approaches in his identification of martial law with war. He based his position on the inability of the civil authorities to cope, even with the

[23] Kostal, *The Jurisprudence of Power* (n 6) 255 (emphasis in original).
[24] Taggart, 'Ruled by Law?' (2006) (n 22) 1021.

army operating in aid of the civil power, and the nature of rebellion as 'levying war against the King', which was treason.[25] Both the American and Jamaican conflicts involve the use of armed force but the circumstances are essentially different and the circumstances drive the choice, whether voluntary or not, of the legal framework that is used.

The Jamaica debate is very often characterized as polarized between, on the one hand, views reflected in the legal opinion provided to the Jamaica Committee and, on the other, the writing of Finlason but, looked at closely, there was a common core that was not in dispute. The legal opinion identified four uses of the term 'martial law' and in effect dismissed them all: first, the 'law martial', a system of law that had been exercised over troops in actual service and had coexisted among other systems of law, such as ecclesiastical law, but was no longer part of English law. Second, the application of law martial by sovereigns to civilians 'in cases of foreign service or actual warfare', a system that had been declared illegal in peacetime by the Petition of Right in 1628. Third, the modern disciplinary powers exercised over the military provided for in regulations made under the annual Mutiny Acts. Fourth, 'the common law right of the Crown and its representatives to repel force with force in the case of invasion or insurrection'. Of these, the opinion stated, the first two were obsolete, the third had become a separate body of law which was more properly known as military law, and the fourth was 'we think, inaccurately and improperly' referred to as martial law when it was actually derived from the common law.[26]

There were two key aspects to this analysis: the significance of the 1628 Petition of Right and the distinction that James and Stephen sought to make between martial law and the common law right to repel force with force. The Petition of Right was in effect a constitutional compromise made between King Charles I (1600–49) and parliament prior to the English (or British) Civil War to limit the King's powers to use military practices which parliament regarded as unlawful infringements of the rights of individuals.[27] It is written in obscure language but in the debate over it following the Jamaica Rebellion there was a consensus that it excluded martial law in Britain in peacetime. However, there was no consensus on what powers were authorized by martial law or what was peacetime. The opinion to the Jamaica Committee concentrated on powers of punishment exercised by tribunals other than the regular courts and at times other than during war. In an important point of the opinion that appeared in a passage following a review of the authorities that supported their argument for a limited conception of the application of martial law, the opinion stated: 'These authorities appear to show that it is illegal for the Crown to resort to martial law

[25] WF Finlason, *A Treatise on Martial Law as Allowed by the Law of England in Time of Rebellion* (London, Stevens & Sons, 1866) xxi–xxii.

[26] Forsyth, *Cases and Opinions* (1869) (n 15) 'Case and Joint Opinion of Mr Edward James, QC, and Mr Fitzjames Stephen, QC, on Martial Law, with reference to the Jamaica Insurrection. 1866' 552.

[27] L Boynton, 'Martial Law and the Petition of Right' (1964) 79: 311 *English Historical Review* 284.

as a special mode of punishing rebellion'. Then, after a review of the authorities that put the case against their conception of martial law, James and Stephen set out their conclusions, beginning with a definition of martial law and a description of its nature:

> 1. Martial law is the assumption by the officers of the Crown of absolute power, exercised by military force, for the suppression of an insurrection, and the restoration of order and lawful authority.
> 2. The officers of the Crown are justified in any exertion of physical force, extending to the destruction of life and property to any extent, and in any manner that may be required for this purpose. They are not justified in the use of excessive or cruel means, but are liable civilly or criminally for such excess. They are not justified in inflicting punishment after resistance is suppressed, and after the ordinary courts of justice can be reopened.[28]

These conclusions were contentious, particularly on the civil and criminal accountability of the military for any 'excess' and the timing of the point at which the military could no longer inflict punishment.[29] Finlason articulated the other side of the argument in relation to the nature of martial law and his work has been described as 'often convoluted, sloppily edited, and tediously repetitive' although it did, nonetheless, contain 'some sharp observations and analysis'.[30] His arguments are set out at much greater length than the opinion to the Jamaica Committee and over several books. He argued that the military had no liability to the civil courts although they were accountable through their own internal procedures for breaches of the laws of war, and, in some of his remarks, he seems to add accountability for breaches of natural justice.[31] He saw punishment as part of the much wider scope and purpose of the powers that martial law permitted:

> In short, the true scope of martial law is not so much the resistance of actual insurrection, as its suppression and prevention by terror … a terror inspired by the stern and summary severities of martial law. So that, in this view, terror is of the very nature of martial law, and deterrent measures – that is, measures deterrent by means of terror, are of its very essence.[32]

Despite the extremity of expression of this view, if this formulation of martial law is compared with James and Stephen's, the points in issue on the nature of martial law revolve around what acts would be regarded as 'excessive and cruel' (as the opinion put it) and the extent of accountability, which is not clear in either case. It was these differences in the conception of martial law that were so contentious at the time of the debate about the Jamaica Rebellion and continue to dominate discussion of martial law but can be cut through, at least for the purposes of this

[28] Forsyth, *Cases and Opinions* (n 15) 559–60.
[29] ibid 554.
[30] Kostal, *A Jurisprudence of Power* (n 6) 228.
[31] See, eg, Finlason, *A Treatise on Martial Law* (1866) (n 25) xxxvi and xxxxvii.
[32] ibid xxxi–ii.

book, by looking at the core conception of the use of force and separating it from martial law.

The common core of the debate arises from the distinction made in accounts of martial law between the legality of the use of force against force and powers of trial and punishment. In their opinion to the Jamaica Committee, James and Stephen's referred to one use of the term 'martial law' as the name incorrectly applied to 'the common-law right of the Crown and its representatives to repel force by force in the case of invasion or insurrection' before they went on to outline the absolute powers of the military that they thought were the true expression of martial law. For all the concentration on the debate between this conception and Finlason's view of martial law, a close reading of Finlason also shows a separation of the use of force and martial law, for he wrote: 'Martial law can only be declared in time of rebellion which amounts to war, and need not be declared if there is military force adequate to the occasion'. By 'need not be declared', he means that it would be unlawful as the 'need' to do so will only arise by reason of necessity – if there is no necessity, there is no need for martial law. Furthermore, he said that since the 1688 revolution in Britain there had always been adequate military force available in aid of the civil power in England, although this had not necessarily been the case in Ireland or the colonies where military forces were smaller and the power of the 'English inhabitants' was weaker. Although the common law afforded ample legal powers for the resistance or repression of 'actual outrage or insurrection', he thought that 'where the common law is practically defective is, that it requires and implies that there shall be an actual force at its disposal, adequate to put in execution the legal powers which the common law affords – that is, to resist, and arrest, and deal with the offenders'.[33] It was where that force was not available that the need for martial law arose. The difference between the opposing views turns in part on the interpretation of the Petition of Right, whether it precluded the use of martial law (in the wider sense) in peacetime only in England or also elsewhere in the empire, and what constitutes wartime. However, it is not disputed that that there is a common law right to repel or resist insurrection at any time, anywhere in the empire. It is, therefore possible to identify a common, narrower view of the lawful use of force to suppress an insurrection and the contentious points within it in relation to the use of force.

The various authorities that James and Stephen's and Finlason referred to were largely collected together in William Forsyth's, *Cases and Opinions on Constitutional Law* which was published in 1869. The book contains copies of legal opinions given by government law officers and extensive notes by Forsyth as well as a copy of James and Stephen's opinion. The authorities were also discussed in another reference work from the period by Charles Clode, *The Administration of Justice under Military and Martial Law*.[34] Clode was a barrister and legal advisor

[33] ibid vi and xxxi.

[34] CM Clode, *The Administration of Justice Under Military and Martial Law* (London, John Murray, 1872).

at the War Office who had advised the government on martial law in relation to the Jamaica Rebellion.[35] He subsequently wrote *The Administration of Justice* as a reference work which was intended for use by army officers and discussed martial law at length.[36] By drawing on these sources, it is possible to construct some parameters for the core conception of the use of force under the common law.

First, there is the right to kill rebels whilst participating in acts of armed resistance.[37] Some of the formulations of the right amount to immediate summary execution, for example, Lord Chief Justice Cockburn included killing 'on the spot' in his speech to the grand jury on the indictment of Nelson and Brand.[38] Under martial law there is a wider right to put to death persons taking part in the rebellion but the power to execute captured rebels as punishment, the requirement for the holding of a trial following capture and the constitution and procedure of the tribunal are part of the controversy over the scope and nature of martial law.[39] Second, the right to kill must be exercised in good faith.[40] This precludes acts of malice or revenge. Third, killing is justified only by necessity.[41] There are several cases that are customarily cited on the strictness of the assessment of necessity. The usual source is *R v Pinney*:

> a party intrusted with the duty of putting down a riot, whether by virtue of an office of his own seeking (as in the ordinary case of a magistrate), or imposed upon him (as that of a constable), is bound to hit the exact line between excess and failure of duty.[42]

It should be noted that the cases overlap and potentially contradict the separate requirement for good faith for, in some cases, it is sufficient that the judgment of what is necessary was exercised in good faith.[43] Furthermore, in an important point that is not generally examined, the cases cited for strict necessity relate to riot and arguably are only a precedent for applying the test in those circumstances.

[35] Moore, *Crown and Sword* (n 18) 141.

[36] Clode, *The Administration of Justice* (1872) (n 34) iii.

[37] Forsyth, *Cases and Opinions* (n 15) 'Opinion of Mr Hargrave on an Irish case involving the question of Martial Law' [c 1800] 192; Author's notes citing Coke and Rolle (before he became Lord Chief Justice) in the debates on the Petition of Right, 212; Author's notes citing 'Lord Chief Justice Cockburn's Charge to the Grand Jury' in *R v Eyre* (1867) 25, 213; Author's notes giving his conclusion, 214; Author's notes citing Bayloy J, in *R v Burdett* 4 B & Al 323, 215; 'Case and Joint Opinion of Mr Edward James, QC, and Mr Fitzjames Stephen, QC, on Martial Law, with reference to the Jamaica Insurrection. 1866', 554 and 559. Clode, *The Administration of Justice* (n 34) 158 – citing Lord Hardwicke's Report of 1732, and other Papers, Vol II, 623.

[38] ibid Author's notes citing 'Lord Chief Justice Cockburn's Charge to the Grand Jury' 213.

[39] ibid 'Joint Opinion of the Attorney and Solicitor General, Sir John Campbell and Sir RM Rolfe, as to the power of the Governor of Canada to proclaim Martial Law. Temple, January 16, 1838' 198. Clode, *The Administration of Justice* (n 34) 158.

[40] ibid citing Lord Mansfield in *Wall v Macnamara*, (as cited in *Johnstone v Sutton*, 1 TR 536) – 'the principal inquiry to be made by a court of justice is, how the heart stood?'; Author's notes giving his conclusion 214.

[41] ibid 'Opinion of the Attorney General, Sir John S Copley, on the authority of the Military to take away life in suppression of a Riot in the Island of Barbados. Lincoln's Inn, January 18, 1824' 196; 'Joint Opinion of the Attorney and Solicitor General, Sir John Campbell and Sir RM Rolfe, 1838' 198.

[42] ibid cited in Author's notes 213.

[43] ibid 'Opinion of the Attorney General, Sir John S Copley, 1824' 196; Author's notes 213.

Beyond the idea that necessity requires a strict line to be drawn in riot at least, there is no meaningful examination of what necessity actually means. Fourth, those who have killed or authorized the killing of individuals may be held accountable before the civil courts and would be required to justify their action.[44] It was this possibility that Finlason argued generated a fear of being convicted for murder that would paralyse officials from acting when most needed.[45] Fifth, there is no definition of insurrection. Finlason cites *The Queen v Frost* (1839) as authority for the legal meaning of the term 'insurrection'.[46] The case arose out of the suppression of the Chartist uprising in Britain in 1839 but, on a reading of that case, it does not contain a definition of insurrection as such but rather deals with the offence of high treason. The headnote of the case captures the point although it is actually taken from the judge's summing up to the jury: 'To constitute the treason of levying war against her Majesty within the realm, there must be an insurrection, there must be force accompanying that insurrection, and it must be for an object of a general nature'.[47] It has been said, correctly I think, that the term 'insurrection' itself is 'a convenient shorthand for the offence of "levying war against Our Lord the King in his realm" which is declared to be treason by the Treason Act 1351'.[48] It may be shorthand but the two are distinct. The reform of the criminal offence of treason has been considered a number of times in the past 50 years and the reports prepared as part of that process give some indication of the difference between insurrection and the crime of treason through levying war against the king.

In the 1970s the Law Commission of England and Wales considered the offence of treason through levying war against the King as part of an ultimately unsuccessful project to codify the criminal law.[49] Their report is a succinct but thorough summary of the offence and cites a number of cases and textbooks from the eighteenth century onwards in support of its conclusions.[50] It recommended that the offence of treason should be updated and gave as its provisional view that there was a need for 'a specific offence applicable in peacetime to penalise conduct aimed at the overthrow, or supplanting, by force, of constitutional government'.[51] This recommendation was not acted upon and, in the most recent report on the issue, the Law Commission described the offence of treason as 'an example of an

[44] ibid Author's notes 87 – citing *Wall v Macnamara* (as cited in *Johnstone v Sutton* 1 TR 536) and 213 – citing 'The Charge to the Grand Jury of Blackburn J' in *R v Eyre* (1868); 'Opinion of the Attorney General, Sir John S Copley, 1824' 196.

[45] Finlason, *A Treatise on Martial Law* (n 25) x.

[46] Kostal, *The Jurisprudence of Power* (n 6) 198 – the full citation is *The Queen v Frost* (1839) 9 Carr & Payne Rep 129. It is also reported as *R v Frost and Eleven Others* [1839] 173 ER 771.

[47] *R v Frost* [1839] 173 ER 771, 771 and 785.

[48] G Bennett and C Ryan, 'Armed Forces, Public Order and the law in the United Kingdom', in P Rowe and C Whelan (eds), *Military Intervention in Democratic Societies* (London, Croom Helm, 1985) 170.

[49] Law Commission, *Treason, Sedition and Allied Offences* (Law Com No 72, 1977).

[50] The report draws attention in particular to *Hale's Pleas of the Crown*; *Hawkins' Pleas of the Crown* 6th edn (1788), Book 1; *Coke's Institutes*, Part III; and Sir James Stephen, *A History of the Criminal Law of England*, Vol 2, as giving interesting legal histories, and *Russell on Crime*, Vol 1 12th edn (1964), and *Kenny's Outlines of Criminal Law* 19th edn (1966) as textbooks – see ibid 6.

[51] Law Commission, *Treason, Sedition and Allied Offences* (n 49) 37.

area of the law shaped by political and social conditions that have ceased to be of contemporary relevance' and suggested that it should be reviewed.[52]

A review of the sources identified by the Law Commission and further research shows that there is a distinction between the circumstances of insurrection and the offence of treason through levying war against the King in his realm. For example: it can be seen in a leading textbook of the eighteenth and nineteenth centuries, *A Treatise on the Pleas of the Crown* by William Hawkins:

> Those also who make an insurrection in order to redress a public grievance, whether it be a real or pretended one, and of their own authority attempt with force to redress it, are said to levy war against the king

In the late nineteenth century, there had also been an unsuccessful attempt to codify the criminal law. It was based on the work of James Fitzjames Stephen (1829–94), the co-author of the legal opinion to the Jamaica Committee and by then a High Court judge and leading writer. In a book that accompanied the draft code, Stephen set out his codified definition of levying war:

> The expression 'to levy war' means:
>
> (a) Attacking in the manner usual in war the Queen herself or her military forces, acting as such by her orders, in the execution of their duty;
>
> (b) Attempting by an insurrection of whatever nature by force or constraint to compel the Queen to change her measures or counsels, or to intimidate or overawe both Houses or either House of Parliament;
>
> (c) Attempting an insurrection of whatever kind to effect any general public object.
>
> But the expression 'to levy war against the Queen' does not include any insurrection against any private person for the purpose of inflicting upon him any private wrong, even if such insurrection is conducted in a warlike manner.

Here subparagraph (c) appears to be too wide to be supported by the earlier sources but it illustrates a consistent theme of the writing that insurrection is one of the elements of the offence of levying war and, unlike riot, has not been given a particular meaning in English law. In the nineteenth century the offence of riot had both statutory and common law definitions which differed in certain respects, such as the number of persons involved and the requirement for a prescribed form of notice to be given by the authorities before taking action. The form of notice was set out in the Riot Act 1714 and the practice of giving notice became known as 'Reading the Riot Act'.[53] A leading textbook of the period summed up the term 'riot':

> A Riot seems to be a tumultuous disturbance of the peace, by three persons, or more, assembling together of their own authority, with an intent mutually to assist one another, against any who shall oppose them, in the execution of some enterprize of a private

[52] Law Commission, *Tenth Programme of Law Reform* (Law Com No 311, 2008) para 16.

[53] See 'Riot' in D Hay (ed), *Words and Phrases Legally Defined* (London, Lexis Nexis Butterworths, 2007) and in J Burke (ed), *Jowitt's Dictionary of English Law* (London, Sweet & Maxwell, 1977).

> nature, and afterwards actually executing the same in a violent and turbulent manner, to the terror of the people, whether the act intended were of itself lawful or unlawful.[54]

Although the legal parameters of what was a 'riot' were further developed under the common law in the nineteenth and early twentieth centuries, in general terms the formulation of the meaning of riot given above would continue to apply under English law until the Riot Act 1714 was abolished in 1973 and the common law offence of riot was abolished in 1986.

Dicey and the Rule of Law

The public debate over the Jamaica Rebellion and martial law can be seen to have had a direct influence on the development of the theory of the English constitution by AV Dicey. Dicey's work, *The Law of the Constitution*, was updated by Dicey in eight editions up to 1915. It was recognized at the time, and is still referred to, for setting out the principles and standards by which the English constitution may be analyzed and judged. Dicey's theory of the constitution elaborated for the first time the idea of 'the rule of law' and, despite the now ubiquitous use of the phrase, his account remains one of the most influential: 'Loved or loathed, Dicey remains a point of departure for thinking about the rule of law today'.[55] Before becoming professor of jurisprudence at Oxford University, Dicey was a barrister and had close connections to the Jamaica Committee, including providing legal advice.[56] There is also a chain of thought that can be seen as extending from the legal opinion to the Jamaica Committee through the Charge of Lord Chief Justice Cockburn to Dicey.

In *The Law of the Constitution* Dicey considered the concept of martial law and described it by reference to the narrow common law position on the use of force and public accountability for it:

> Officers, magistrates, soldiers, policemen, ordinary citizens, all occupy in the eye of the law the same position; they are, each and all of them, bound to withstand and put down breaches of the peace, such as riots and other disturbances; they are, each and all of them authorised to employ so much force, even to the taking of life, as may be necessary for that purpose, and they are none of them entitled to use more; they are, each and all of them, liable to be called to account before a jury for the use of excessive, that is, of unnecessary force.[57]

The reason for this common law rule was linked to one of the elements of the rule of law – equality of all persons before the law. As will be seen in the next chapter,

[54] J Curwood, *A Treatise on the Pleas of the Crown, by William Hawkins*, Vol I of Criminal Offences (London, S Sweet, 1824) Ch 28, Sect 1.

[55] Lino, 'The Rule of Law' (2018) (n 13) 741.

[56] ibid; and Kostal, *The Jurisprudence of Power* (n 6) 456.

[57] AV Dicey, *An Introduction to the Study of the Law of the Constitution* (London, MacMillan, 1915) republished by LibertyClassics (1982) 184.

Dicey's conception of the rights and duty of citizens to uphold the rule of law was widely adopted but its basis even at the time was questionable as one of the leading textbooks of the eighteenth and nineteenth century refers to the duty of magistrates and public officials to suppress public disorder but only a duty of citizens to assist if ordered by an official.[58] It also suggests that, although an official would be punishable for failing to take steps to put down a riot, that did not extend to insurrection or rebellion. It then cautions that it would be extremely hazardous for private persons to take part in the armed repression of a riot for they might become liable themselves although it would be warranted in the face of a rebellion.[59]

Dicey famously went on to make a comparison between English law and French law on the suspension of law involved in martial law. French law permitted the use of exceptional powers in peacetime through the proclamation of a 'state of siege' but, Dicey declared, 'this kind of martial law is in England utterly unknown to the constitution'.[60] However, the full passage from which this quotation is taken goes on:

> Soldiers may suppress a riot as they may resist an invasion, they may fight rebels just as they may fight foreign enemies, but they have no right under the law to inflict punishment for riot or rebellion. During the effort to restore peace, rebels may be lawfully killed just as enemies may be lawfully slaughtered in battle, or prisoners may be shot to prevent their escape, but any execution (independently of military law) inflicted by a Court-martial is illegal, and technically murder.

It has been noted that Dicey's comment on martial law being 'unknown' is ambiguous as it is not clear whether he is saying that it has not occurred or is precluded, although he clearly meant the reader to understand the latter.[61] However, it is striking that Dicey accepts a common law right to use force as outlined above and directs his argument against a wider conception of martial law. It is possible, therefore, once again to cut through the extensive debate on the validity of his argument on martial law and note that he also subscribes to the common core of the right to use force against rebels.

The third set of proceedings in relation to the Jamaica Rebellion were brought against Governor Eyre in a civil action in damages for trespass.[62] Trespass is a civil wrong which includes assault on a person as well as interfering with land or goods. The claim was defeated on the technical ground that the act of indemnity passed by the Jamaica legislature had the effect of barring proceedings in England.[63] Acts of indemnity were a feature of both sides' arguments in the debate over martial law and in some respects the law relating to them was less contested than martial law itself as they were generally accepted as being part of the legal powers available to the executive in connection with the suppression of rebellion. The main

[58] See Curwood, *A Treatise on the Pleas of the Crown* (n 54) 517.
[59] ibid 517 and 525.
[60] Dicey, *The Law of the Constitution* (1915) (n 57)187.
[61] Dyzenhaus, 'The Puzzle of Martial Law' (2009) (n 6) 4.
[62] Kostal, *The Jurisprudence of Power* (n 6) 432.
[63] *Phillips v Eyre* (1870) LR 6 QB 1, 28.

issue then arose over whether the particular act of indemnity passed in Jamaica was a bar to proceedings in the English courts. Governor Eyre in his evidence to the Jamaica Royal Commission had said that he did not proclaim martial law in Kingston although the situation was precarious as he preferred taking the responsibility on himself for

> [t]hose only who have seen what martial law is can tell the inconvenience and evil which it entails on any community … and I preferred taking the sole responsibility, trusting to a bill of indemnity, which was subsequently passed.[64]

Accounts of the effect of acts of indemnity usually referred to the limitation on them in *Wright v Fitzgerald*, a case arising out on the 1798 Irish rebellion against a sheriff who had a man flogged. The sheriff was an official similar to a magistrate and he was found liable to pay damages by a jury notwithstanding that an act of indemnity had been passed. The finding was made after a direction from the judge that the act had not released magistrates 'from the feelings of humanity, or permitted them wantonly to exercise power, even though it were to put down rebellion'.[65]

The technical explanation of the effect of the act of indemnity in *Phillips v Eyre* was that 'the right of action in respect of an act otherwise lawfully done by the Governor of the colony, is taken away before an action has been brought in this country, is a good defence to such action'.[66] Dicey called this the 'legalisation of illegality'.[67] To Dicey, however, the passing of acts of indemnity was an expected consequence of the use of force by the state. In a passage anticipating an argument that the constitutional restrictions on martial law that he had set out in *The Law of the Constitution* were too restrictive of government, Dicey dismissed the concern on the grounds of the importance of the protection of the individual but then added that

> whenever at a period of national danger a breach of law is demanded, if not by absolute necessity, yet by considerations of political expediency, the lawbreaker, whether he be a general, or any other servant of the Crown, who acts *bona fide* and solely with a view to the public interest, may confidently count on the protection of an Act of Indemnity.[68]

As has been pointed out, the use of acts of indemnity makes Dicey's 'claim of the unconstitutionality of martial law rather hollow'.[69] But more than that, it subordinates the use of force to political control in a manner which severely undermines his conception of the rule of law. Dicey also argued that acts of indemnity were not required where an act was carried out of necessity as necessity was a defence at common law. Although that is correct, it understates the procedural advantages of an act of indemnity. Having the benefit of an act of indemnity allows the accused

[64] Report of the Jamaica Royal Commission – Evidence of Governor Eyre (n 7) 90.
[65] Forsyth, *Cases and Opinions* (n 15) 213.
[66] ibid 84 – citing *Phillips v Eyre* (1870) LR QB 1, 225.
[67] Lino, *The Rule of Law* (2018) (n 13) 752.
[68] Dicey, *The Law of the Constitution* (n 57) 402.
[69] Dyzenhaus, 'The Puzzle of Martial Law' (n 6) 6.

to rely on the procedural bar that it provides according to its terms and, without it, the burden would be on the magistrate, officer or other person who carried out the breach to prove that they acted out of necessity.

Despite the extensive literature on the Jamaica Rebellion and the subsequent emergence of Dicey's account of the rule of law with a restricted conception of martial law, the literature does not properly take account of the development of military law in the late nineteenth century. In discussion of martial law it is common to recognize that by the late nineteenth century the use of the term 'martial law' to refer to the internal rules governing the conduct of the military had been superseded by the term 'military law'. This point does, however, then require consideration of what these rules were and whether they had any bearing on the operation of martial law.

As we have seen, when Lieber was promoting the issuance of *General Order 100* and his part in it, he had predicted that the code 'will be adopted as a basis for similar works by the English, French, and Germans' but the view that it was adopted in Britain at least is mistaken.[70] The War Office produced its first *Manual of Military Law* in 1884 and the reasons for producing it were quite different from those that had led to *General Order 100*. It has already been noted that Clode wrote *The Administration of Justice* as a reference work for army officers and he explained his reasons for the book as including 'remarks made in the Report of the Royal Commission on Courts-martial on the necessity of their being further information on the administration on Military Law' and organizational changes in the Army.[71] The second edition of Clode's work which was published in 1874 had a note on its cover that it had been 'Recommended to the Army' by General Orders in 1872 and 1873. The War Office had itself produced a work entitled 'Military Law and Discipline' around that time which was printed but not published as it was overtaken by the decision to replace the Mutiny Act and Articles of War that were the basis of military law with a new statutory code.[72] The 1884 *Manual of Military Law* included copies of the relevant statutes and rules of procedure, chapters on various aspects of service discipline such as powers of punishment and courts martial as well as separate chapters entitled 'Summary of the Law of Riot and Insurrection' and 'Customs of War'.[73] The manual was prepared by the Office of Parliamentary Counsel and the chapters on 'Riot and insurrection' and the 'Customs of War' were attributed to Sir Henry Thring (1818–1907), the first person to hold the office of Parliamentary Counsel. Parliamentary Counsel are responsible for the drafting of government bills and are respected for their knowledge of the law, intellectual ability, and command of language.[74]

[70] Lieber, Letter to Halleck, 20 May 1863 (HEH LI 1796).

[71] Clode, *The Administration of Justice* (n 34) iii.

[72] GR Rubin, 'The Legal Education of British Army Officers, 1860–1923' (1994) *Journal of Legal History* 15, 230.

[73] War Office, *Manual of Military Law* (London, HMSO, 1884).

[74] Editorial: 'Henry Thring – A Hundred Years On' (1 April 2007) 28 *Statute Law Review* 1, iii.

The 'Summary of the Law of Riot and Insurrection' was set out in language that was very different to the style of the opinions given by government officers and the opinion to the Jamaica Committee contained in Forsyth's *Cases and Opinions*. In particular, it contained a definition of insurrection based on *R v Frost*, the same case used by Finlason:

> 6 Definition of 'insurrection'. An insurrection differs from a riot in this – that a riot has some enterprise *of a private nature*, while an insurrection savours of high treason, and contemplates some enterprise of a *general and public nature*. An insurrection, in short, involves an intention to 'levy war against the King,' as it is technically called; or otherwise act in general defiance of the government of the country.[75]

It also gave examples of riot and distinction which illustrated the difference between private and public purposes:

> 7. Examples of insurrection. For example, a mob assembling to pull down or burn a cotton mill, because the proprietor is obnoxious to them, are engaged in a riot. If the object were to attack a barrack or seize a store of arms with a view to arm themselves and make war against government, they would be in a state of insurrection.

The chapter continued with a number of further examples and actual cases and generally supports the distinction made in the definitions, although at times the differences began to blur. The main legal distinction related to punishment as unlawful assembly and riot were punishable at common law by a fine or imprisonment, or both, but participants in an insurrection might be convicted of treason and sentenced to death. The practical consequence of the distinction was that the use of military force against a riot should be the last resort where the civil authorities could not reasonably be expected to cope without military support, which was acknowledged to carry with it the risk of troops firing on the rioters. However, in the case of insurrection, '[t]he existence of an armed insurrection would justify the use of any degree of force necessary effectually to meet and cope with insurrection' and 'force should be repelled by force, care being taken to avoid any unnecessary bloodshed or injury'. In concluding, it recognized the difficulty in ascertaining what is the necessary degree of force and warned that 'the danger of making a mistake in the manner is serious, as any excess in the use of force constitutes a crime'.

The 1884 *Manual of Military Law* was published just prior to Dicey's *The Law of the Constitution* and they share a conception of there being a public duty on officials and citizens to suppress public disorder. In both accounts, soldiers were in the same position as citizens but there is no mention in the manual of acts of indemnity as Dicey suggested would be forthcoming. Perhaps more significantly, there is also no mention of martial law in the chapter on riot and insurrection. The manual

[75] War Office, *Manual of Military Law* (1884) 280–92 (emphasis in original). The definition of insurrection also contains a footnote citing *R v Vincent* 9 Car and Payne, 91 and *Lord Mansfield's charge on the trial of Lord George Gordon in 1781*, State Trials, 644.

uses a typology that adopts the core 'right to repel force with force' but does not use James and Stephen's idea that this may incorrectly be called martial law or Dicey's usage of the right as martial law in the restricted sense. The manual also made an important distinction between municipal law and the 'customs of war'. Municipal law was law in the sense of 'a defined and rigid rule, which must be obeyed in all circumstances, and the infraction of which involves a crime punishable by a legally constituted tribunal' whereas the customs of war were 'principles the enforcement of which must vary considerably according to circumstances, and must, in the case of a military occupation of territory, be subordinate to the safety of the occupying army'.[76] Furthermore, the law as it applied to riot and insurrection was 'law' in the sense defined and, therefore, directly enforceable against soldiers in a way that the customs of war were not. This point is not generally made but does provide a counter-point to the view there was no international law relating to the conduct of hostilities in internal armed conflicts until the Common Article 3 of the 1949 Geneva conventions.

Conclusion

The Jamaica Rebellion began an extensive debate in Britain on the nature and limits of the power of the state in the use of military force in insurrection and rebellion. The debate involved a variety of actors and, in particular, the Jamaica Committee, an interest group formed out of the public abhorrence at the repression of the rebellion, which was instrumental in attempts to hold those responsible accountable under the municipal law. Although the cases that were brought were unsuccessful, the debate before and after them led to the writing of what became foundational texts on the subjects of the limits of the use of military force under martial law and the rule of law. Of these, the most influential was Dicey's *The Law of the Constitution* which introduced the idea of the rule of law. By looking more closely at the foundational texts – the opinion of the Jamaica Committee, the court cases and the writings of Dicey and Finlason – it is possible to draw an important distinction between use of force under martial law and the common law or prerogative right of the Crown to repel force with force. The right to repel force with force is a more limited legal right that is justified by necessity and subject to accountability before the civil courts.

The extension of the municipal law to the use of military force in insurrection and rebellion created the potential for overlap with the laws of war that under *General Order 100* had encompassed insurrection, rebellion and civil war but they were kept separate. Through this separation it became possible for the use of force in the suppression of an insurrection or rebellion to be subject to the scrutiny of the civil courts. However, the potential accountability of state agents under municipal

[76] War Office, *Manual of Military Law* (1884) 2.

law was generally accompanied by an expectation that actions that were necessary would be absolved by an act of indemnity that acted as a bar to proceedings against the civil and military authorities for their actions. It is also possible to see through the writings and court cases a distinction between the offence of treason for 'levying war against the King in his realm' that may be committed in insurrection and insurrection itself. These differing ideas and sources were then developed in the late nineteenth century into government policies that made the deployment of military force a last resort and made a distinction between riot and insurrection by their purpose. In particular, violence in insurrection had a public purpose and it was, therefore, political violence. It is also arguable that this distinction is a legal one in that where the courts looked at violent offences committed in unlawful assemblies, they would distinguish between riot and treason by examining the purpose of the violence. The development of these policies and the underlying distinction between martial law and the right to repel force with military force within the state provides the foundation for understanding the British approach to the development of the paradigms of armed conflict and law-enforcement after the Second World War. It treated everything below a threshold of belligerency as insurrection which could be suppressed through the use of military force subject to municipal law but left open the tension between the actions of the military justified by necessity and their accountability for those actions before the civil courts.

3

Developing the Municipal Law in Internal Armed Conflicts

The British legal theories of martial law and the use of force that were argued over in the publications and court cases that followed the Jamaica Rebellion were seriously challenged by the operations that the British military undertook in the first half of the twentieth century. It has been observed that the British army has a long experience in counter-insurgency stretching back to the nineteenth century but it has tended to look at counter-insurgency piecemeal rather than by developing a military doctrine until it began to look again at the subject whilst engaged in Iraq after 2003.[1] Whilst this critique does have a point, there has been increasing recognition recently of the place of Colonel CE Callwell's (1859–1928) *Small Wars: Their Principles and Practice* that was published in three editions from 1896 to 1906 and General Sir Charles Gwynn's (1860–1963) *Imperial Policing*, published in 1934. Callwell described British and other Western countries' experience in irregular warfare in the late nineteenth century but his book was out of print and largely forgotten until the renewed interest in counter-insurgency after 9/11.[2] Callwell lists a number of categories of 'small wars' that are categorized by their objective from a state perspective including 'quelling an insurrection' by force of arms and the punishment of the insurgents, often through the destruction of property.[3] Gwynn describes the army's 'policing' operations as falling into three categories ranging from small wars; through operations to restore normal civil order that had broken down in which the army was the main agent acting to restore order and might resort to martial law; and operations 'in aid of the civil power' in which the army gave effect to the directions of a civil magistrate.[4]

[1] J Mackinlay, *The Insurgent Archipelago* (London, Hurst, 2009) 11; C Townshend, *Britain's Civil Wars: Counterinsurgency in the Twentieth Century* (London, Faber and Faber, 1986) 19.

[2] CE Callwell, *Small Wars: Their Principles and Practice* (London, HMSO, 1906 – republished by Endeavour Press Ltd, 2016). AWB Simpson refers to it in *Human Rights and the End of Empire: Britain and the Genesis of the European Convention* (Oxford, Oxford University Press, 2001) 63, n14 but says that he was unable to locate a copy. T Mockaitis, *British Counterinsurgency, 1919–60* (Basingstoke, MacMillan, 1990) 17 is a notable exception to this and A Edwards, *Defending the Realm? The Politics of Britain's Small Wars Since 1945* (Manchester, Manchester University Press, 2012) makes Callwell's book a common theme in British counter-insurgency operations after the Second World War.

[3] Callwell, *Small Wars* (1906) (n 2) 23.

[4] Sir C Gwynn, *Imperial Policing* (London, MacMillan, 1934) 3–4.

Townshend and Professor AWB Simpson (1931–2011), who was a leading academic lawyer on legal history and the history of human rights in the British empire, both set out the legal framework for military operations under municipal law and martial law. The legal framework was itself limited, it was based around a small number of statutes, principally the Riot Acts of 1703 and 1714, and what Townshend describes as a minimalist doctrine based on the common law principle of 'necessary force'.[5] It comprised both the right and the duty of the government to 'repel force with force' but required it to use no more and no less force than was absolutely necessary to restore peace. It also held out the possibility that the use of force might subsequently have to be justified before the ordinary courts. The doctrine was based on the principle that the military had the same rights and duties as ordinary citizens and although Townshend says that this had become 'transparently unworkable by the eighteenth century', it nonetheless became enshrined in Dicey's constitutional theory in the late nineteenth century.[6] Simpson goes further and describes Dicey's notion of martial law being unknown to the British constitution as 'grossly and perversely misleading'. In particular, he thought that Dicey's proposition that 'the right and indeed duty of the military to intervene was a mere application of the general right, and indeed duty, of officials *and even private citizens* to take such steps as are necessary to suppress rebellions, riots, or mere breaches of the peace' was 'deeply unreal'.[7] He argues that, having grounded his limited conception of martial law in the common law, Dicey could not then recognize that the common law gave citizens the right to take the sorts of actions that military commanders took in emergencies, such as imposing curfews and shooting those that broke them. As the power to take such actions were clearly not appropriate for or available to private citizens, Dicey reversed the position and identified a single legal principle of necessity, that was to be applied retrospectively, to regulate all circumstances from minor breaches of the peace to major insurrections. This led to a practice of judging the military's use of force by reference to immediate local necessity and overlooking the wider effects that were, in Simpson's view, intended to operate as acts of coercion as part of what he called 'the mechanics of repression'.[8]

In *The Jurisprudence of Emergency*, Nasser Hussain draws on the historiography of the British approach to martial law provided by Townshend.[9] He argues that, in seeking to understand the nature of necessity in determining the difference between lawful and unlawful acts by the authorities, it was in 'those colonies where a social situation of racial difference existed, the legal definition of necessity would prove more varied and vexing'.[10] He identified race as the

[5] Townshend, *Britain's Civil Wars* (1986) (n 1) 19.
[6] ibid.
[7] Simpson, *Human Rights and the End of Empire* (2001) (n 2) 61 (emphasis in original).
[8] ibid 54 and 62.
[9] N Hussain, *The Jurisprudence of Emergency: Colonialism and the Rule of Law* (Ann Arbor, The University of Michigan Press, 2003) 107.
[10] ibid 109.

determining factor and he demonstrated this by examining the 1865 Jamaica Rebellion and the Amritsar massacre in 1919 where 379 people were killed when British troops opened fire on a crowd.[11] Amritsar was an important and brutal incident but it can also be seen in the context being examined here as an example of a military operation which went against British public policy as it was developing at that time: in parliament Winston Churchill, the Secretary of State for War, called it 'an extraordinary event, a monstrous event, an event which stands in singular and sinister isolation'.[12] General Dyer, the commander responsible for the massacre, was heavily criticized by the Army Council and a parliamentary inquiry set up to investigate the massacre and forced to retire. There are different views on whether it was as isolated as Churchill suggested but, from a policy perspective, one of the features Churchill identified which set it apart was that the crowd were not armed and, as it will be seen, this resulted in revised instructions on opening fire that resemble more modern rules of engagement.[13] In this sense, Amritsar is an exception – its significance lies in it being stated to be contrary to the government's policy and General Dyer being censured for it as well as in the dreadful events themselves. The focus of this chapter is instead on the development of government policy in, and as a result of, conflicts in South Africa, Ireland and Palestine. These conflicts provide examples of the use of force in countries or territories which the British recognized as a separate jurisdiction with a system of statutory and common law enforceable through the courts to which military operations short of war were, in theory at least, accountable. The accounts of the British military operations and the use of martial law show clearly, at one level, the justification for the use of force being based in necessity and yet the nature of necessity remains elusive. In particular, the right to repel force with force lacks detail and elaboration. However, by drawing on various papers of the Judge Advocate General's Office held at the National Archives, the *Manuals of Military Law* and other contemporary sources, it is possible to show how the use of force in British military operations in internal armed conflicts occurred within the sphere of municipal law but was also increasingly identified with the laws of war.

This chapter expands on the constitutional theory and practice on the use of force described in the previous chapter. In particular, it argues that by drawing out the separation between martial law and the narrower use of force against force it

[11] The figure of 379 was the official estimate made after the event.

[12] The quotation is given in the record of the parliamentary debate of the report – 'Army Council and General Dyer' *Hansard* HC Deb 8 July 1920, vol 113, cols 1705–819.

[13] See, eg, Mockaitis, *British Counterinsurgency* (1990) (n 2) 24 who sees it as a foundational event in the development of the doctrine of minimum force; H Bennett, *Fighting the Mau Mau: The British Army and Counter-Insurgency in the Kenya Emergency* (Cambridge, Cambridge University Press, 2013) 105–07 who regards it as an example of a practice of the use of 'exemplary force' rather than 'minimum force'; and C Elkins, *Legacy of Violence: A History of the British Empire* (London, Bodley Head, 2022) 140 who sees it as an example of exceptional, but systematic, state-directed violence within the British empire.

can be seen that in the early twentieth century the laws of war provided a recognized standard for the use of lethal force in the conduct of operations and that, in British practice, this standard began to be adopted in the literature on the use of force in internal armed conflicts. It begins by looking in more detail at the sources and commentary on martial law in the period to bring out further the separate right to repel force with force. It then goes on to examine three aspects of the separation: the nature of martial law regulations which generally exclude rules on the use of force in operations; the further development of British constitutional theory and practice on the use of force by different actors within the British government; and the steps towards developing a legal framework for the use of military force in internal armed conflicts. When taken together, these can be seen to cause an overlapping of the spheres of municipal law and the laws of war in the period directly before the creation of the paradigms of armed conflict and law-enforcement in international law. Furthermore, it will be seen that the portrayal of British military operations in Ireland and Palestine given by a contemporary military writer, HJ Simson, in his book *British Rule and Rebellion* showed an unease and uncertainty within the British state over its use of military force in counter-insurgency that resonates with the British military operations in Iraq.[14]

The Colonial Regulations

Although irregular warfare between an organized army and insurgents had become the norm for European powers and the United States in the late nineteenth century, the South African War (Boer War) of 1899–1902 was the exception.[15] It was war as understood as a conflict between states – the Boer republics of the Transvaal and the Orange Free State declared war on the British Cape and Natal colonies in October 1899 and the Boer forces then invaded. However, the British initially treated the conflict as a rebellion on the basis that the Transvaal was a protectorate. The British position changed after an incident in which the British had stopped and searched a French vessel as it revealed a legal disadvantage in treating the conflict as a rebellion since powers of stop and search over other states' shipping arose only in war or a recognized belligerency. The British search was, therefore, illegal and the French government protested.[16] The English courts also recognized the situation as war although they were able to avoid deciding on the actual date that it began.[17] The war is generally described as having three main

[14] HJ Simson, *British Rule and Rebellion* (London, William Blackwood & Sons Ltd, 1937).

[15] JP Cann, 'Low-intensity Conflict, Insurgency, Terrorism and Revolutionary War' in M Hughes and WJ Philpott (eds) *Modern Military History* (London, Palgrave Macmillan, 2006) 108.

[16] SC Neff, *War and the Law of Nations, A General History* (Cambridge, Cambridge University Press, 2005) 263–64.

[17] *Driefontein Consolidated Gold Mines v Janson* [1900] 2 QB 339, CA, [1901] 2 KB 419, HL, [1902] AC 484.

phases: the Boer invasion and early victories over British forces; the British recovery and counter-attack into the Boer republics; and the guerrilla war in which Boer columns operated within the British colonies. However, the legal framework that the British applied was more complex as the invasion by the Boer forces and the support they received from sympathizers within the British colonies created a situation beyond the control of the civil authorities and martial law was declared.

At the start of the Boer War, the British High Commissioner in Cape Colony, Sir Alfred Milner, wrote to the Colonial Office inquiring whether the rules on martial law that were circulated by the Colonial Office in 1867 were still in force as the '[m]ilitary authorities seem imperfectly instructed as to martial law'.[18] Before replying, the Colonial Office contacted the War Office to ask if it regarded the rules as in force and it confirmed that they were.[19] The rules – they are sometimes referred to as the Colonial Regulations – dealt with the division of responsibility between the civil authority and the military for invoking and ending martial law and the trial of civilians to enforce it. They were drawn up by the Colonial Office following the 1865 Jamaica Rebellion and were addressed to the colonial governors in order to provide guidance on the general principles that they were to apply in a civil emergency.[20] They were drafted by a panel of senior military officers, civil representatives of government and a senior legal advisor and approved by the Secretary of State for War and the Field-Marshall Commanding-in-Chief subject to further review.[21] Nevertheless, only one minor change was made to the regulations after their circulation.[22] The letter that was sent out from the Colonial Office with the draft regulations cautioned that 'these regulations have in no respect the force of law, so it is not intended that officers should be under a rigorous obligation to observe them in all cases'.[23] It also explained the scope of the regulations as being that '[t]he first seven regulations relate to the powers and duties of the Governor; the remaining eleven, to the powers and duties of Military Officers and Tribunals'. However, there was one regulation that was very different from the others as it dealt directly with the use of armed force. It provided:

> 12. In subduing the rebels by force of arms, care should be taken as far as possible to avoid injuring non-combatants, women, or children. Men not armed with fire-arms, or offensive weapons, are not to be fired upon, unless actively hostile, without first summoning them to surrender.

[18] TNA, WO 32/8173, 'Martial Law', Telegram from the High Commissioner to Mr Chamberlain, Colonial Office, dated 25 October 1899.

[19] ibid Letter from the War Office to The Under Secretary of State at the Colonial Office (S Wolseley), dated 31 October 1899.

[20] ibid Circular Letter from Downing Street, dated 26 January 1867.

[21] TNA, CO 885/3, folio 8, Letter to the Colonial Office from Edward Lugard (Under-Secretary of State for War), William Paulet (Adjutant-General), Henry K Storks (Lieutenant-General), T Frederick Elliot (Assistant Under-Secretary of State for the Colonies), and Vernon Lushington (Deputy Judge-Advocate-General), dated 14 December 1866.

[22] TNA, WO32/8173, 'Martial Law', Letter from the War Office to The Under Secretary of State at the Colonial Office (S Wolseley), dated 31 October 1899.

[23] ibid Circular Letter from Downing Street, dated 26 January 1867.

> Dwelling-houses, stores, crops, and other property should not be destroyed or injured, except under military necessity.[24]

The status and actual implementation of the rules are difficult to determine given the warning that they did not have the force of law but the War Office's confirmation that it regarded the regulations as in force would suggest that they were regarded as binding on the army as a matter of military law. This can also be seen through notes and correspondence between lawyers in the Judge Advocate General's department after the war as they debated whether military tribunals conducted under the rules of procedure contained in the regulations were illegal as the rules were inconsistent with later regulations made under the Army Acts.[25] There was also legal advice given in July 1901 by the Law Officers (that is the British government's Attorney General and Solicitor General) to the Colonial Secretary that referred to the Secretary of State for War's confirmation that the 1867 colonial regulations 'still held good'.[26] Regulation 12 is, in effect, an early example of a rule of engagement and it is significant in three ways. First, it is a very unusual in recognizing a rule of distinction for internal armed conflicts which excluded non-combatants, this was not recognized in international law until Common Article 3 of the 1949 Geneva conventions regulated the treatment of those 'taking no active part in the hostilities'. However, it also provides that men armed with firearms may be attacked without warning. Second, neither do regulations issued by the British army under martial law in South Africa, Ireland, Palestine or other places nor pro-forma martial law orders prepared by the War Office in 1930 contain a similar rule.[27] Third, it recognizes the application of military necessity as the basis for the destruction of property in internal armed conflicts, an issue that is still unclear as a matter of international law as the rules of targeting that were introduced into international law by the 1977 Additional Protocol I applied to international armed conflicts but were not replicated in relation to non-international conflicts.[28]

Martial Law and the Right to Repel Force with Force

As has been seen, there was great uncertainty and inconsistency in the views taken in the aftermath of the 1865 Jamaica Rebellion on the scope and operation of

[24] ibid Draft Regulations attached to Circular Letter from Downing Street, dated 26 January 1867.

[25] TNA, WO 32/8153, 'Revision of Martial Law Sentences, S Africa'.

[26] TNA, WO 32/8141, 'Detention under Martial Law Sentences after Martial Law has Ceased'. Note of legal advice from the Law Officers (RB Finlay & Edward Carson) to the Colonial Secretary, dated 6 July 1901.

[27] TNA, LCO 53/55 'Martial Law', '1930 Martial Law Chapter on VI for inclusion in Confidential Pamphlet "Notes on Guerilla Warfare" at request of DMO & I War Office. Correspondence. Colonel I/c Mil & Air Force Dept JAG's Office. Martial law in Egypt. Re Preparation of Documents for Declaration of, if necessary. Draft Proclamation under Martial Law. There are also pro-forma documents attached as appendices to the War Office Pamphlet 'Notes on Imperial Policing, 1934'.

[28] I Henderson, *The Contemporary Law of Targeting: Military Objectives, Proportionality and Precautions in Attack under Additional Protocol I* (Leiden, Martinus Nijhoff Publishers, 2009) 12. However, the ICRC *Customary Law Study* applies the same rules to both types of conflict.

martial law but the argument that essentially represented one side of the debate was subsequently adopted as the constitutional position by Dicey in *The Law of the Constitution*. Dicey's theory was challenged by a number of judicial decisions arising out of the Boer War. The first was a decision of the Judicial Committee of the Privy Council, at that time the highest court of appeal for cases brought in the colonies, in *ex p Marais* that '[w]here actual war is raging, acts done by the military authorities are not justiciable by the ordinary tribunals'.[29] The case has been the subject of considerable comment both at the time and since and it is worth noting the words of the actual judgment as they can help to identify the distinction between the legal position that applies under the ordinary law and martial law:

> It may often be a question whether a mere riot, or disturbance neither so serious nor so extensive as really to amount to a war at all, has not been treated with an excessive severity, and whether the intervention of the military force was necessary; but once let the fact of actual war be established, and there is an universal consensus of opinion that the civil Courts have no jurisdiction to call in question the propriety of the action of military authorities.[30]

In reaching the decision, the Privy Council departed from a long-established line of authority that if the civil courts were open, the Crown had no power to try an offender by military tribunal. The judgment was so significant that Dicey revised the treatment of martial law in the next edition of *The Law of the Constitution* to be published after the case. In a new appendix on the subject, he sought to limit the effect of the judgment by taking the view that as a Privy Council decision it did not apply in England and that it should, in any case, be construed narrowly on the basis that, as expressed, its terms were so wide.[31] On a technical level, Dicey may have been correct that Privy Council judgments were not binding as a matter of precedent on the English courts, but to take only a technical view would understate the weight that would have been given to the Privy Council's views as representing the view of the Law Lords, the most senior British judges of the time. In particular, it is notable that the threshold of violence for 'war' in this context is seen as being low, it is not expressed in terms of an invasion or a clash of armies but only more than 'a mere riot, or disturbance neither so serious nor so extensive as really to amount to a war at all'. This formulation continues to resonate in the modern law such as in the exclusion of 'internal disturbances and tensions, such as riots' from the application of the rules applying to non-international armed conflicts.[32]

It was in another case arising from the Boer War that the Privy Council explicitly upheld the right to use force to repel force irrespective of martial law. In *Tilonko v Attorney-General of Natal*, the Privy Council held that

[29] Headnote, *DF Marais v The General Officer Commanding the Lines of Communication and the Attorney-General of the Colony, ex p Marais* [1902] AC 109, PC.

[30] *Ex p Marais* [1902] AC 109, PC at 115.

[31] D Lino, 'The Rule of Law and the Rule of Empire: AV Dicey in Imperial Context' (September 2018) 81 *Modern Law Review* no 5, 739–64 at n 122.

[32] 1977 Additional Protocol II to the 1949 Geneva Conventions, Art 1(2) (in part).

> [t]he right to administer force against force in actual war does not depend upon the proclamation of martial law at all. It depends upon the question whether there is war or not. If there is war, there is the right to repel force by force, but it is found convenient and decorous, from time to time, to authorize what are called 'courts' to administer punishments, and to restrain by acts of repression the violence that is committed in time of war.[33]

Here it is possible to argue that the court was restricting the use of force to war but, as with *ex p Marais*, it is not clear what the court would regard as war. It could be that by 'actual war' the courts are referring to the factual state on which Oppenheim had based his status of belligerency. Alternatively, the English courts at that time took the view that the interpretation of what was 'war' in the context of the treason of levying war against the King was not constrained by a particular definition. However, it was distinguishable from war in the international sense as alien enemies could not be convicted of treason.[34] In the eighteenth century and early nineteenth century there was also an offence of 'a constructive levying of war in peace-time if three or more persons "arose" to alter the established religion or law, or to effect some public purpose'.[35] In *R v Frost* it was said

> that it has been established … that the pomp and circumstances of military array, such as usually attend regular warfare, are by no means necessary to constitute an actual levying of war … [and] [i]nsurrections and risings for the purpose of effecting by force and numbers – however ill-arranged, provided or organized … for redress of supposed public grievances, in which the parties had no special or particular interest or concern, have been deemed instances of the actual levying of war.[36]

The court then held that an armed attack by a mob on a public house in which soldiers were stationed was levying war. There was also an associated notion of going 'armed in a war-like manner' that the courts had used in a sense of a persons armed with weapons of some sort acting as part of a group rather than a narrow sense of war as being fought between armies with firearms and other modern weapons.[37] Lord Haldane (1856–1928), the Secretary of State for War, argued before a parliamentary committee in 1908 that it was a very old expression and 'means "war-like manner" in law, and not according to our military notions of it' so that an attack with 'sticks and stones' would be within it.[38]

The Boer War also called into question Dicey's view that those administering martial law 'may confidently count on the protection of an Act of Indemnity'.[39] As the war progressed there were a number of controversies over the conduct of

[33] *Tilonko v Attorney-General of Natal* [1907] AC 93, PC at 94.
[34] Sir J Baker, *An Introduction to English Legal History* (Oxford, Oxford University Press, 2019) 569.
[35] ibid citing *R v Damaree* (1709) Foster 213, 15 State Tr 521.
[36] *R v Frost and Eleven Others* [1839] 173 ER 771, at 779.
[37] *Beatty and Others v Gillbanks* (1882) 9 QBD 308, QBD at 314.
[38] War Office, *Manual of Military Law*, 6th edn (London, HMSO, 1914) 229.
[39] AV Dicey, *An Introduction to the Study of the Law of the Constitution* (London, MacMillan, 1915) republished by LibertyClassics (1982) 402.

martial law, particularly in relation to what were seen as heavy-handed actions ordered by British military officers and a martial law board was set up in the Cape Colony to oversee the administration of martial law.[40] Then, as the war came to an end, there were calls in the Cape parliament for an inquiry into the conduct of martial law. There was also controversy in Britain over the exercise of martial law and questions were asked in parliament.[41] In response to the controversy, a royal commission was appointed by the imperial government in London to review the sentences of those still detained in South Africa or, in some cases, transported outside South Africa to serve their sentence in another colony.[42] At the same time that the governor and the senior military officers were discussing how to bring martial law to an end and the necessity for an act of indemnity, there was political pressure in the Cape parliament to make the passing of an act of indemnity conditional on the appointment and outcome of a local inquiry into martial law. The correspondence between the governor in the Cape Colony and the Colonial Office displays increasing concern at the speed with which the political situation was moving toward making the conduct of martial law a continuing issue, particularly in relation to compensation. However, after several months of discussion and pressure from the governor and Colonial Office, the Cape government and parliament relented and passed an act of indemnity and, on the same day, martial law was formally withdrawn.[43]

The development of a framework of law prior to the First World War for the use of force in internal armed conflicts based on the common law and applied to South Africa was challenged by the major internal armed conflict that the British army faced in Ireland during and after the First World War. Ireland had been part of the United Kingdom throughout the nineteenth century but had been subject to special emergency powers created under statute to control the periodic disorder there. The statutes contained various restrictions on civic rights such as freedom of assembly and created powers to deal with sedition and disorder. Two insurrections in 1848 and 1867 were dealt with under the legislation in place without resort to martial law.[44] In the First World War, Ireland was subject to the same emergency powers as the rest of the United Kingdom under the Defence of the Realm Act (DORA) passed in 1914 to give the government additional powers for the conduct of the war. There were, however, some differences of application between the British mainland and Ireland, in particular the establishment of courts-martial for the trial of offences created under defence regulations (DORR) made under DORA

[40] C Townshend, 'Martial Law: Legal and Administrative Problems of Civil Emergency in Britain and the Empire, 1800–1940' (1982) 25: 1 *The Historical Journal* 167–195, 178 and 181.

[41] Townshend, *Britain's Civil Wars* (n 1) 184.

[42] TNA, WO 32/8143, 'Revision of Martial law Sentences in Cape Colony', Proposed Royal Commission to enquire into and report on sentences imposed by Military Courts established under Martial Law in S Africa. Telegrams from the Governor of Cape Colony to the Colonial Office dated 4 July and 31 August 1902.

[43] TNA, WO 32/8151, 'Martial Law in Cape Colony', Production of martial law documents.

[44] Townshend, 'Martial Law' (1982) (n 40) 168.

was not applied to Ireland and the right of jury trial for those new offences was preserved in Ireland.[45] Nevertheless, when the Easter Uprising began in Ireland in 1916, the authorities declared martial law throughout Ireland without reference to DORA and did not formally end it, 'it was just said by the Chief Secretary [for Ireland], HE Duke, to have "passed away when the time of insurrection passed".'[46] In 1920 the government passed the Restoration of Order in Ireland Act (ROIA) to supersede the powers available under DORA but the authorities also declared martial law in December 1920 without reference to it. The history of the Easter Uprising in 1916 and the Irish War of Independence (1919–22) has been extensively documented and it is not intended to recount the application of martial law and the conduct of the counter-insurgency by the British forces here. There are, however, two points to make on the law of the use of force in the conflicts: the first is in relation to rules of engagement and the second concerns the development of the legal framework by the courts. In relation to the first point, whether or not troops were serving in a martial law area, the general policy promulgated by General Nevil Macready (1862–1946) – the commander-in-chief in Ireland – was that 'as long as [the security forces] actions to restore order … do not exceed what is reasonably necessary for the purpose, they will meet with his full approval and support' and the emergency powers granted by statute or created by martial law had little further to say on the use of lethal force (other than in punishment following a sentence of the death penalty).[47] The powers deal mainly with the creation of offences and the establishment of military tribunals to hear cases arising from breach of the regulations imposed under the emergency powers. Orders for opening fire, as the rules of engagement were called, were based on the general orders for the whole of Ireland rather than specifically martial law areas but were adapted to local conditions.[48] Apart from an apparent priority to avoid the accidental shooting of other soldiers, the orders are notable for their general restrictiveness for uniformed soldiers, except in relation to persons seen acting suspiciously at night who were to be shot 'at once', and unusual instructions to fire a warning shot if a person failed to stop when challenged and, if firing at a crowd, to aim below the knee. Generally, the policy elsewhere was not to fire warning shots as they risked an accidental shooting of someone else and shots were to be aimed at the person's body. However, the instructions were more cryptic and opaque in their references to orders that could be given for local operations in plain clothes which 'will invariably be under a definite commander and closely controlled'. This seems to hint

[45] Royal Commission on the Rebellion in Ireland, *Report of the Commission* (London, HMSO, 1916) 5.
[46] Townshend, 'Martial Law' (n 40) 184.
[47] TNA, WO 35/173/1, General Routine Orders, C-in-C Ireland, No 145, Friday 17 December 1920.
[48] TNA, WO 35/173/1, General Routine Orders, C-in-C Ireland, No 51, Monday 3 May 1920 and No 27, Friday 8 April 1921; and Major BL Montgomery, 17th Infantry Brigade, 'Summary of Important Instructions (Headquarters' Printing Office, 6th Division, Cork, June 1921), IWM, Strickland Papers, P363. Montgomery was to become a divisional commander in Palestine during the rebellion in 1938–39 and later Field Marshall Montgomery of Alamein.

at an unofficial policy later referred to as 'gunning' which was supported by the Prime Minister, Lloyd George, and the Secretary of State for War, Churchill, and apparently meant selective assassination.[49] However, for the ordinary soldier, the general orders appear to have been interpreted so restrictively that it was necessary to issue a clarification that they did not restrict the firing on anyone armed with firearms or explosives.[50] Overall, these differences reflect the unease and inconsistency about operations in Ireland as part of the United Kingdom.

On the second point, there are a number of important cases from the Irish War of Independence that called into question the important legal developments that arose from the Boer War. Of the two leading cases discussed above in relation to South Africa, it was the judgment in *ex p Marais* that the decisions of military tribunals established under martial law could not be interfered with by the courts that was most attacked. However, although there were a number of conflicting decisions given by the Irish courts in relation to that, the courts in England and Ireland were consistent in their support of the principle upheld by the Privy Council in *Tilonko v Attorney-General of Natal* that there was a right to repel with force. The principle in *Tilonko* was explained in the leading case of *R v Allen* by the Chief Justice of Ireland, Molony CJ, as that in previous armed insurrections the insurgents met the Crown forces in actual battle but that the current insurrection consisted 'exclusively of warfare of a guerrilla character'.[51] Furthermore, during the continuance of the situation as described by the military in evidence, 'the Government is entitled and, indeed, bound to repel force by force, and thereby to put down the insurrection and restore public order'. He also cited from *Tilonko* that 'such acts of justice are justified by necessity by the fact of actual war, and that they are also so justified under the circumstances is a fact that it is no longer necessary to insist upon'. At the highest level, the House of Lords sitting as the supreme court of appeal for cases from Ireland also explicitly upheld the point.[52] There was, however, a contrary decision in *Egan v Macready* which threw the British operations into disarray.[53] In that case, the Master of the Rolls in Ireland, O'Connor PC, found that the detention of a number of persons for offences under martial law regulations was unlawful as the regulations were not made under the ROIA statute and he issued a writ of habeus corpus for their release. He rejected the argument that the regulations could be made under the authority of the Royal prerogative on the basis that the prerogative had been curtailed by statute. This issue led to a major constitutional debate over the Crown's ability to make emergency

[49] C Campbell, *Emergency Laws in Ireland 1918–25* (Oxford, Clarendon Press, 1994) 24.

[50] TNA, WO 35/173/1, General Routine Order No 27, Friday 8 April 1921.

[51] *R v Allen* [1921] 2 IR 268, KBD (Ireland). The decision in *R v Allen* was followed in *The King (Garde and Others) v Major-General EP Strickland and Others* [1921] 2 IR 317, KBD (Ireland) but in *Egan v Macready* [1921] 1 IR 265, CD (Ireland), the judge, O'Connor PC, the Master of the Rolls in Ireland, found that military tribunals lacked jurisdiction to try offences committed under martial law in Ireland even though he recognized that a state of war existed.

[52] *Clifford and O'Sullivan* [1921] 2 AC 581, HL.

[53] *Egan v Macready* [1921] 1 IR 265, CD (Ireland).

regulations under the Royal prerogative.[54] After the establishment of the Irish Free State in 1922, the Irish courts established their own precedent based on the common law that 'there being an armed rebellion, there is but one question – the military necessity of repressing force directed to the overthrow of the lawfully established Government which is entitled to use force to repel force'.[55] It is notable that here the courts are referring to military necessity but it does not appear that there is a specific distinction being drawn between necessity and military necessity. The contrast between them can, however, be seen in the evidence that Lord Haldane gave before the Parliamentary Committee in 1908. The committee was established to investigate the use of military force in civil disturbances as had happened in Belfast in the previous year. Lord Haldane was the Secretary of State for War but he was also a lawyer and his evidence is couched in precise legal language which was seen at the time as setting out the government's policy on the use of troops in aid of the civil power.[56] The committee questioned him on the use of force and he outlined the difficulties of doing so, particularly for officers confronted by civil disorder. He was adamant that the use of force was the officer's responsibility and that 'the judges have laid down, over and over again, that a man is on the verge of two precipices, and has to get along, and he does get along'. When asked if it was possible to draw up specific regulations that would prevent the soldier from falling, Haldane replied, 'If you do you will make the law go over the precipices'.[57]

The Development of Military and Legal Doctrine in Counter-insurgency

The British experience of insurrection and rebellion in parts of its empire and Ireland after the First World War led to two notable attempts to analyze the conflicts and learn lessons for future military operations which can be seen as building on the foundation of a British approach to counter-insurgency set out by Callwell in *Small Wars*. The first was *Imperial Policing*, a book by a former general, Sir Charles Gwynn, published in 1934, and the second, *British Rule and Rebellion*, a book by a former colonel, HJ Simson, published in 1937. In his book, Gwynn offers the traditional disclaimer that the opinions expressed in *Imperial Policing*

[54] See Campbell, *Emergency Laws in Ireland* (1994) (n 49) for a discussion of the prerogative and common law theories of martial law and also critiques of this in C Walker, 'Book Review: *Emergency Law in Ireland 1918–1925* by Colm Campbell, Oxford: Clarendon Press, 1994' (1995) 15(2) *Legal Studies* 311–22 and GR Rubin, 'Book review of *Emergency Law in Ireland, 1918–25* by Colm Campbell' (Oxford: Clarendon Press, 1994)' (1995) *LQR* 111, 520–30. The decision in *Egan* remained a contentious issue for decades but has now been superseded by more recent case law and commentary on the prerogative.

[55] *Rex v General of Provisional Government Forces* [1923] 1 IR 12, HCJ (Irish Free State).

[56] General The Rt Hon Sir N Macready, *Annals of an Active Life*, Vol I (London, Hutchinson & Co, 1924) 136.

[57] War Office, *Manual of Military Law* (1914) 229.

are his own but adds that his 'intention has been to follow the general trend of orthodox doctrine'.[58] By 'orthodox doctrine' I think he means tactical doctrine but nonetheless both books can be seen as putting operational issues within an understanding of the legal framework for the use of force.

Gwynn's book, *Imperial Policing*, was published in the same year that an internal pamphlet on 'Imperial Policing' was produced by the War Office.[59] The title 'Imperial Policing' is rather misleading in a modern context that might not associate policing with the use of military force. Except in small wars which he does not cover in any detail, Gwynn says that in policing operations 'the Army is bound to exercise the minimum force required to attain its object'.[60] However, operations to restore civil order might also involve conditions of 'guerrilla warfare, in which elusive rebel bands must be hunted down'.[61] There is a noticeable resemblance between the pamphlet 'Imperial Policing' and Gwynn's book in the emphasis on the use of minimum force. Although Gwynn states that he will not discuss the legal aspects of the operations, there is a legal distinction in the two categories of policing that he examines in the book. In the case of aid to the civil power, he notes that an officer is not relieved of responsibility by the presence of a civil official and that an officer 'will rarely fail to receive support if he has acted with reasonable moderation and in accordance with what he considered necessary'. However, in the case of armed rebellion, the military may bring its modern weapons to bear and 'the only limitations to their use … are those imposed by the nature of the terrain and the characteristics of the enemy'.[62] He even describes for the benefit of non-military readers the sorts of weapons that may be used, including armoured fighting vehicles, artillery and aircraft.

It has been suggested that Gywnn was the author of both the book and the army pamphlet.[63] However, there is a file of correspondence from the Judge Advocate General's Office held in the National Archives that gives some of the background to the writing of the pamphlet and there is no mention of Gwynn in it. The Judge Advocate General's Office was first asked to become involved in the drafting of a pamphlet entitled 'Notes on Guerilla Warfare' [*sic*] and the drafting was then adapted for the pamphlet published as 'Imperial Policing'.[64] It is perhaps more than coincidental that they were published in the same year with the same title, but they are very different publications. The pamphlet is a small pocket-sized manual of 50 pages which covers a mixture of tactical and legal guidance on operations whilst the book runs to 366 pages and consists of an introduction explaining the principles

[58] Gwynn, *Imperial Policing* (1934) (n 4) v.

[59] War Office, Army Pamphlet, 'Notes on Imperial Policing 1934' (1934).

[60] Gwynn, *Imperial Policing* (n 4) 4.

[61] ibid 5.

[62] ibid 28.

[63] I Becket, *Modern Insurgencies and Counter-Insurgencies: Guerrillas and their Opponents Since 1750* (London, Routledge, 2001) 44.

[64] TNA, LCO 53/55, 'Martial Law', Letter M & AFD4/162/FGC from the Office of the Judge Advocate General to Lt Col HG Martin, dated 19 May 1933.

and doctrine of imperial policing and then illustrates them with ten examples of British operations in different countries from 1919 to 1931. Rather conspicuously, it omitted operations in Ireland from 1920 to 1921 which Gwynn said it was inadvisable to include even though the examples would have been instructive from a military point of view.[65] This was probably because the subject was so controversial but it has been suggested that he may have had personal reasons as his wife's father was a well-known Irish nationalist.[66] There had actually been two pamphlets being drafted, one called 'Notes on Imperial Policing and Irregular Warfare' and the other 'Notes on Guerilla Warfare'. The 'Notes on Guerilla Warfare' had taken some three years to draft and had reached an advanced stage when it was realized that there was some overlap and conflict between the two pamphlets. The 'Notes on Guerilla Warfare' were also thought by the Army Staff to be 'somewhat too complicated and difficult to follow, and more in the nature of a treatise'.[67] The draft pamphlet on 'Imperial Policing' was then adapted and a chapter written on martial law for the 'Notes on Guerilla Warfare' was redrafted for inclusion in it.

Although the idea of creating an institutional approach to martial law within the British army had been raised after the Boer War, it was not taken up and it appears that there was little material available at the time that the 'Notes on Guerilla Warfare' were begun. A note to the Deputy Permanent Secretary of the War Office from the Judge Advocate General's Office dated 18 February 1930, apparently in reply to a request for assistance with the pamphlet, refers to martial law being an 'obscure and difficult subject' on which there was little in ordinary text books and only two references to it in the *Manual of Military Law*.[68] The Judge Advocate General then recommended a Col MacGeagh who, he said, had unique experience of martial law as he had served on the Military Legal Staff in Ireland in 1920–21. He had also prepared a paper on martial law which he had delivered to the Senior Officers' School and the Naval Officers' Course. The Judge Advocate General offered to give it to the Attorney General and said that MacGeagh was willing to write a memorandum on the subject if required. The offer was taken up and a chapter was written for the pamphlet 'Notes on Guerilla Warfare'.[69] It was then reviewed and revised several times before the proposed notes became caught up in the organizational issue over responsibility for drafting and redrafted again.

The correspondence on the draft chapter on martial law for the 'Notes on Guerilla Warfare' and its revision for inclusion in 'Imperial Policing' provide an insight into the development of British legal thinking on martial law and the use

[65] Gwynn, *Imperial Policing* (n 4) 8.

[66] R Johnson, 'Command of the Army, Charles Gwynn and *Imperial Policing*: The British Doctrinal Approach to Internal Security in Palestine 1919–29' (2015) 43: 4 *Journal of Imperial and Commonwealth History* 574. The reference is to 574.

[67] TNA, LCO 53/55, 'Martial Law', Note BM SD4/4650/11 to AG 3 from SD4 dated 31 October 1933.

[68] ibid Note to the Deputy Permanent Secretary of the War Office from the Judge Advocate General's Office, dated 18 February 1930.

[69] ibid '1930 Martial Law Chapter on VI for inclusion in Confidential Pamphlet "Notes on Guerilla Warfare"'.

of force as they comment on and explain various provisions. Much of the description of martial law contained in the original draft written by MacGeagh in 1930 remained unchanged in the pamphlet 'Imperial Policing' as published. It defined martial law as

> in reality not 'law' at all in the accepted sense of the term. It denotes the suspension of ordinary law and its supersession by Military rule during war or rebellion and amounts merely to the exercise of the will of the Military Commander upon whom has fallen the task of ensuring the safety of the State and the restoration of law and order.[70]

This is a description of martial law that combines two formulations pre-dating the Jamaica Rebellion. One is attributed to Lord Hale (1609–76), a leading jurist from the period of the English Civil War, who had described martial law as 'no Law, but something indulged rather than allowed as a Law'.[71] The other was by the Duke of Wellington from a debate in the House of Lords on rebellion in Ceylon in 1849: 'Martial law is neither more nor less than the will of the general who commands the army; in fact, martial law is no law at all'.[72] However, it is less frequently noted that Wellington then added that it was the duty of the commander to promulgate 'the rules and regulations and limits according to which his will has to be carried out'.[73] The notes then distinguished martial law from duties in aid of the civil power where assistance is given to quell a riot – 'The essential distinction is that under Martial Law the Military Authorities are supreme for the time being'. It also had a section on acts of indemnity that was virtually unchanged through the drafts. It explained that it was usually expedient to pass an act of indemnity after a war or rebellion was over to protect officers and soldiers from claims in damage from those who thought they were wrongly imprisoned or punished under martial law. However, it would only protect those 'whose acts were done *bona fide* and in the honest belief that they were doing their duty'.[74]

The descriptions of martial law in the pamphlets are not consistent with the treatment of it in the then current edition of the *Manual of Military Law*. The Judge Advocate General's remark that there were only two references to martial law in the 1929 *Manual of Military Law* is not correct and, whilst brief, there was

[70] ibid Draft (2B) Chapter II – Martial Law, dated 1 April 1930. The version in the War Office Pamphlet, 'Notes on Imperial Policing' is the same other than some changes of capitalisation.

[71] Cited in W Forsyth, *Cases and Opinions on Constitutional Law, And Various Points of English Jurisprudence, Collected and Digested from Official Documents and Other Sources; with Notes* (London, Stevens and Haynes, 1869), 'Joint Opinion of the Attorney and Solicitor General, Sir John Campbell and Sir RM Rolfe, 1838', 198 and C Clode, *The Administration of Justice Under Military and Martial Law* (London, John Murray, 1872) 158. The reference is from Sir M Hale, *The History of the Common Law of England* (London, E and R Nutt and R Gosling, 1739) – see C Moore, *Crown and Sword: Executive Power and the Use of Force by the Australian Defence Force* (Canberra, ANU Press, 2017) 130 n 3.

[72] Forsyth, *Cases and Opinions* ibid, cited in Author's notes, 211: *Hansard*, 'Affairs of Ceylon' HL Deb vol 115, cols 843–82 at 880–81 (1 April 1851).

[73] RW Kostal, *A Jurisprudence of Power: Victorian Empire and the Rule of Law* (Oxford, Oxford University Press, 2005) 203.

[74] War Office, 'Notes on Imperial Policing' (1934) (n 59) 35.

a discussion of the nature of martial law in the introduction.[75] It began by noting that use of the term 'martial law' frequently led to confusion as it was used in different senses. It then explained that although the English constitution made no permanent provision for situations of riot or war in the way that some other countries did through the state of siege, that

> [i]n time of invasion or rebellion, or in expectation thereof, exceptional powers are often assumed by the Crown … for the suppression of hostilities or the maintenance of good order within its territories (whether the United Kingdom or British possessions); and the expression 'martial law' is sometimes employed as a name for this common-law right of the Crown and its servants to repel force by force in the case of invasion, insurrection or riot, and to take such exceptional measures as may be necessary for the purpose of restoring peace and order.

However, the proclamation of martial law

> of itself in no degree suspends the ordinary law, or substitutes any other kind of law in its stead, but operates only by way of warning that the Government is about to resort, in a given district, to such forcible measures as may be necessary to repel invasion or suppress insurrection.

It tried to explain the conflict arising from the co-existence of the common law right to take action and the ordinary law by reference to an act of indemnity but it does so in such a way that it is not clear to what extent an act is necessary. It stated:

> To obviate any question as to the legality of the measures taken for this purpose (whether or not they had been preceded by a proclamation of martial law) it has been usual subsequently to pass an Imperial or local Act of Indemnity for the protection of those engaged, so far as the steps taken by them have been reasonably necessary for the purpose and carried out in good faith, and for the confirmation of the sentences passed by military courts.

It footnotes one of the Indemnity Acts for the Boer War and then the Indemnity Act 1920 that had dealt primarily with sentences passed by military tribunals in the First World War and notes that '[i]f no Indemnity Act was passed in a such a case, the ordinary courts could, at the suit of an aggrieved person, enquire and decide whether the circumstances justified the servants of the Crown in their actions'. It is noticeable that the test applied in the *Manual of Military Law* is both objective – 'steps that were reasonably necessary' and subjective – 'carried out in good faith' whilst the War Office pamphlet has only a subjective test of good faith.

It is possible that the discrepancies between the descriptions of martial law are due to editorial oversight. The introduction on martial law in the *Manual of Military Law* was originally written for the first edition in 1884 by Parliamentary Counsel. The manual had been updated a number of times and the 1929 version was the seventh edition. Each edition began with an introductory section that set

[75] War Office, *Manual of Military Law*, 7th edn (London, HMSO, 1929) 4–5.

out the scope of the manual and its basis in English law. The section was revised for each edition and the changing conceptions and concerns around martial law are reflected in them, including the Boer War, but it still kept much of its original conception. As already noted, the Judge Advocate General seemed mistaken about its treatment in the *Manual of Military Law*, perhaps because of its being confined to a short section in the introductory pages. Nonetheless, the significant differences illustrate the confusion and contestation in the understanding of martial law. It may also be that the common law conception is attributable to Parliamentary Counsel's own views in 1884 and the view taken by the Judge Advocate General's department in the 1930s reflected military views based on military operations abroad from the Boer War onwards. Apart from revision to the introduction, the main chapters of the *Manual of Military Law* on riot and insurrection and on the laws of war changed very little as the result of actual military operations in the Boer War, the First World War, or in Ireland or elsewhere in the 1920s. The chapter on the laws of war in the 5th edition published in 1907, the first revision to be published after the Boer War, was deleted pending the outcome of the 1907 Hague Conference and replaced by appendices containing the text of international conventions on the laws of war to which the UK was party. However, the chapter on riot and insurrection, was unchanged except for references to the Boer War in the introduction and the addition of an appendix containing extracts of a report into the 1893 Featherstone Riots.[76] The appendix on the Featherstone Riots includes an extract from the report that sets out two conditions for the use of military force in a riot; that what was done was 'necessary, and no more than necessary, to put a stop to or preventing felonious crime' and that the military 'exercise all ordinary skill and caution, so as to do no more harm than could be reasonably avoided'. If those conditions were met, it said that a guilty ringleader who was shot dead was justifiable homicide and an innocent person killed was an accidental death so long as there was no negligence.[77] In 1914 the chapter on the laws of war was completely rewritten to take account of the 1907 Hague conventions but without any change to the chapter on riot and insurrection other than the addition of another appendix containing the report of the Secretary of State for War to parliament in 1908 on the use of the military in internal disorder.[78] A further update in 1929 had included some changes to the introduction on martial law and to the chapter on riot and insurrection to take account of the emergency powers legislation put in place for industrial disputes and other civic disputes after the First World War but the substantive advice on riot and insurrection was not changed.[79]

[76] War Office, *Manual of Military Law*, 5th edn (London, HMSO, 1907).
[77] War Office, *Manual of Military Law* (1914) 233.
[78] ibid 225–32.
[79] War Office, *Manual of Military Law* (1929).

Developing Rules of Engagement for Colonial Conflicts

The comments provided by Colonel MacGeagh on the draft 'Notes on Guerilla War' pick up the distinction on the use of force in a riot and in a rebellion without mention of the description in the *Manual of Military Law* and treats it in its own way. In his comments on the draft chapter, he says that there is no 'rule of thumb which will relieve an officer from the use of his judgment in distinguishing between "enemy (rebel) forces" however loose their formation, whom it is his duty to destroy, and a "crowd" whom it is his duty to disperse'. However, he was concerned that officers might have a mistaken idea that the amount of force that could be used against civilian crowds under martial law was different from operations in support of the civil power. He drafted a section on orders for opening fire on crowds that was intended to instil some caution on officers which was hardly changed in the pamphlet as published. It provided:

> The principle which has consistently governed the policy of His Majesty's Government in directing the methods to be employed when military action in support of civil authority is required may be broadly stated as the use of the minimum force necessary. Consequently, should it become necessary to fire on a crowd, the firing should not be continued a moment longer than is necessary to effect the immediate object of dispersing the crowd. To prolong the firing beyond this point with the ultimate object of impressing the population generally and discouraging rebellion in other localities should not be countenanced. The principle enunciated above will not, however, apply in time of guerrilla warfare or rebellion to bodies of the enemy or rebels in engaged in hostilities.[80]

Other than the last sentence, this paragraph was a verbatim extract of a letter from the Secretary of State for India to the Viceroy written in May 1920 to set out government policy in the light of the Amritsar shooting.[81] MacGeagh's draft had included an additional sentence on selecting ring-leaders among the crowd to be shot by marksmen which was omitted but it was the addition of the last sentence that provoked most comment. There was a handwritten note on one of the drafts saying that the Judge Advocate General was concerned about it and a note from another department in the War Office, MO1 [Military Operations]:

> Suggest that this paragraph requires re-drafting. The word 'crowd' in this sense is somewhat ambiguous. It presumably means an unarmed or partially armed mob. But in the case of a collection of fully armed rebels (which might be also called a crowd) it is presumed that the maximum of casualties should be inflicted.[82]

[80] War Office, 'Notes on Imperial Policing' (n 59) 41.
[81] TNA, LCO 53/55, BM SD4/4650/11 to AG 3 from SD4, dated 31 October 1933.
[82] ibid Letter to Col CT Tomes (Assistant Adjutant-General) from The Office of the Judge Advocate General, dated 8 March 1933 with 'Revision of notes on "Irregular Warfare"'; and Copy/FGC 'Proposed Amendments to Chapter II. "Notes on Guerilla Warfare"' [undated – c March 1933].

Taking the remarks in the context of the other notes, the point that the Judge Advocate General was concerned about implied a distinction between the two situations: in a riot firing was to be strictly limited but the laws of war would apply in the case of attacks on rebels. The phrase 'bodies of enemy or rebels engaged in hostilities' evokes ideas of the enemy that is familiar in the context of laws of war, in particular the principle of military necessity which referred to 'the complete submission of the enemy'.[83] It also echoes the italicized wording in the original copies of *General Order 100* that referred to military necessity as permitting the destruction of '*armed* enemies' that it has been suggested was a modified rule created by the US Army Board for the American Civil War. Furthermore, it implies that there are persons who take no active part, or no direct part, in hostilities (as it would now be phrased) to whom the restricted rule of engagement would apply. This is consistent with Churchill's remarks in parliament in the debate on Amritsar in which he said that the questions 'is the crowd attacking?' and 'is the crowd armed with lethal weapons?' were the fundamental questions for the decision to open fire without warning but that '[m]en who take up arms against the State must expect at any moment to be fired upon. Men who take up arms unlawfully cannot expect that the troops will wait until they are quite ready to begin the conflict'.[84] In *Imperial Policing* Gwynn illustrates the point on firing in riots with several examples and particularly incidents that arose in riots during an insurrection in Cyprus in 1931 where he noted 'how immediately effective was the result of the very few rounds that were fired to disperse dangerous rioters' and on one particular occasion the firing of a single shot dispersed a dangerous crowd.[85] However, he also revealed that the military were prepared to use considerably more force if the insurrection had developed into the use of armed force as a flight of aircraft had been sent to Cyprus 'equipped for machine-gun action … but they were never required to fire'. He also records that in effect a rule of distinction applied in that in the stone-throwing riots, some of which would have involved firing on the crowd, '[n]on-combatants, who included a number of women and children, were not interfered with'.[86]

Gwynn had been a senior staff officer and his book was, he said, intended to educate the public but it was also an expression of a War Office view. An alternative view was given by another recently-retired senior staff officer, HJ Simson. Simson had served as Chief of Staff in Palestine and wrote a book *British Rule and Rebellion* based on his experience in Ireland and Palestine in the 1920s and 30s. In it, he described the tension in maintaining public order in modern conditions of rebellion. It was, he wrote

> subversive, stealthy, and secret, and depends for success on intimidation … Intimidation, in turn, depends for success on deliberate murder, carefully planned, after a long watch on the movements of the target, so that it can be done without risk to the perpetrators. Rebellion is too good a name for the thing. It is proposed to call it sub-war.[87]

[83] War Office, *Manual of Military Law* (1929) 271.
[84] *Hansard*, HC vol 113, col 1726 (8 July 1920).
[85] Gwynn, *Imperial Policing* (n 4) 359 and 363.
[86] ibid 357.
[87] Simson, *British Rule and Rebellion* (1937) (n 14) 34.

He observed that '[o]pposing it requires the good co-ordination of the four means of rule – civil, police, legal, and military, and a good understanding of the other side'.[88] However, in performing their roles

> [t]he civil power is particularly puzzling. The history of sub-war leaves it uncertain whether the civil power regards itself as a body which really takes part in the struggle to restore complete order, or whether it regards itself as a kind of referee between its own forces which it can control, and those of the other side which it cannot control.[89]

Furthermore, '[a]s well as the civil power taking it upon itself to act as referee, the law also acts as a referee and the two referees are generally at logger-heads'.[90] Simson's observation on the need for good co-ordination became a central theme of British counter-insurgency writing in the 1960s but his critique which identified a conflict within government went deeper than that and will be seen again in British military operations in the subsequent chapters.

It seems from these various sources from the 1930s that there was a common understanding of a framework for applying the laws of war to the use of force in internal armed conflicts but that the conceptions on martial law were remarkably different. It is difficult to be precise on the details of the framework as some principles and rules are explicitly mentioned whilst others may be implied. It appears to be taken for granted that an officer would know the main tenants of the English common law, particularly in relation to the protection of persons and property. The regime that is being applied to internal armed conflicts is then creating exceptions to the common law by reference to the laws of war and, in particular, a rule of distinction. There are clear references to a category of non-combatants which amount to a recognition of the principle of distinction and treats armed rebels as legitimate targets whilst distinguishing between them and non-combatants, including women and children. The rule of distinction was supported by the *Manual of Military Law* that contained, in the introduction to successive editions, a reference to soldiers being, for the purposes of the Army Act, on active service in a riot and the armed rioters were the 'enemy'.[91] The reference was provided to give context to provisions of the Army Act regulating the conduct and terms of service of the military but it made the point that 'rioters are an enemy only while actually resisting, and when force ceases to be used, whether prisoners or otherwise, must be tried or dealt with according to civil law'.[92] The Army Act defined the 'enemy' for the purposes of the Act as including 'all armed mutineers, armed rebels, armed rioters, and pirates' and soldiers were on 'active service' when, among other things, they were 'engaged in operations against the enemy'.[93] As such, the reference supported the emphasis in the pamphlet 'Imperial Policing' on the necessity

[88] ibid 35.
[89] ibid 68.
[90] ibid 83.
[91] See, eg, War Office, *Manual of Military Law* (1914) 2.
[92] ibid.
[93] War Office, *Manual of Military Law* (1929) 602 and 599 respectively.

of offensive action against armed rebels.[94] Simson, illustrates the effect of this framework and the consequences of being on active service in military operations against insurgents in Ireland and Palestine in the 1920s which he had labelled 'sub-war':

> Officially, of course, sub-war is a form of peace; for example, armed rebels do not have to comply with the laws and usages of war on land by carrying their arms openly, wearing distinctive uniforms to prevent confusion with non-combatant inhabitants, or by treating prisoners in the recognized manner. Military sub-war is a mixture. Soldiers are only on active service for death, wounds, and discipline … if a man is killed his dependents may receive a pension … if a soldier commits a military offence when engaged in sub-war he can be punished as severely as in international war, that is, more severely than in peace.[95]

When it came to applying the laws of war, the writers were not arguing that the armed rebels should be subject to the laws of war but rather that, as per the *Manual of Military Law*, the rebels would be answerable under the ordinary law. In addition to the rule of distinction that is also the beginnings of a rule of proportionality. In the pamphlet 'Imperial Policing', there is a chapter on the use of aircraft in support of military operations. It precludes the use of armed aircraft in operations in aid of the civil power except

> (i) To prevent, or terminate, the unlawful use of aircraft.
> (ii) To support or extricate small parties of troops which are being attacked or have been ambushed, or to prevent the destruction of property. In these circumstances consideration should be given to the risk of damage to friendly or innocent persons.[96]

However, it then provides that '[w]hen the hostile forces are in open opposition and are armed, offensive air action should be taken whenever opportunity offers.'[97] There is also perhaps a sense of proportionality in reference by Gwynn in *Imperial Policing* to terrain limiting the use of weapons such as artillery:[98] for example, in an urban environment.

Beyond a rule of distinction and the consideration of proportionality, it is possible that other rules may be implicit but here the position becomes more speculative. For example, under the laws of war there were clear prohibitions against killing an enemy who had surrendered and giving no quarter and it would seem implicit that the substance of the rules would apply either as a rule under the laws of war or as an expression of the common law rules on murder and manslaughter which would preclude killing except where justified by necessity.[99] Conversely, the common law rule against murder would conflict with a rule permitting reprisals and in the pamphlet

[94] War Office, 'Notes on Imperial Policing' (n 59) 7.
[95] Simson, *British Rule and Rebellion* (n 14) 84.
[96] War Office, 'Notes on Imperial Policing' (n 59) 21.
[97] ibid.
[98] Gwynn, *Imperial Policing* (n 4) 28.
[99] The Hague Regulations (1907), Art 23 (c) and (d).

'Imperial Policing' it was deliberately placed in the chapter on martial law on the basis that they could not be taken at other times.[100] At that time, the *Manual of Military Law* stated that, although reprisals were not mentioned under the Hague Regulations, they were permitted by the customary laws of war in retaliation for illegitimate acts of war by the enemy and for hostile acts committed by individual inhabitants during an occupation, but only in serious and urgent cases.[101] The form of the reprisals was at the discretion of the commander but they were to be applied coercively as a last resort to enforce compliance rather than as punishment.[102] The rules also extended to the methods of warfare as both the British army and the IRA accused the other of using 'dum-dum' bullets in the Irish War of Independence, 'dum-dum' bullets are a type of expanding bullet that flattens on impact to cause more severe wounds and were prohibited under the 1899 Hague Declaration. Rather oddly, the British army also treated ambulances as being subject to the Geneva convention-based rules against their use for moving arms or ammunition in the Irish War of Independence.[103] To go beyond these examples of implied rules would perhaps involve some interesting speculation and, yet, on a practical level, it does seem possible to suggest that given the limited number of rules for the conduct of hostilities under the laws of war as they then stood, an officer or soldier would have had a sense of what it meant to apply the laws of war in an internal armed conflict.

Although the British army had taken some steps towards formulating a doctrine of martial law and the use of force in internal conflicts, the issue of martial law was raised afresh in May 1940 at a meeting attended by the Attorney General and the Judge Advocate General on the possibility of the application of martial law in the event of an invasion.[104] The Judge Advocate General, who was then Sir Henry MacGeagh who had earlier written the 'Notes on Guerilla Warfare', followed-up the meeting with advice to the Attorney General including noting that there were forms of proclamations and orders for martial law contained in the 1934 pamphlet *Imperial Policing*.[105] The meeting led to a major debate in government on the Crown's ability to declare martial law with the Judge Advocate General and the Adjutant General taking a position based on the Royal prerogative and colonial practice and the Attorney General and the Home Office taking a different view based on Dicey's constitutional doctrine that martial law powers were grounded in the common law and the need to authorize any other emergency powers by statute.[106] After several months of debate, the Home Office's views prevailed and official policy fell in behind a notice printed by

[100] TNA, LCO 53/55, 'Martial Law', Letter M & AFD4/162/FGC from the Office of the Judge Advocate General to Lt Col HG Martin, dated 19 May 1933.

[101] War Office, *Manual of Military Law* (1929) 331 and 343.

[102] ibid 343.

[103] TNA, WO 35/173/1, General Routine Order No 109, dated 20 September 1920, 973.

[104] TNA, LCO 53/55, 'Martial Law', Letter from Office of the Judge Advocate General to the Attorney General, dated 20 May 1940.

[105] ibid.

[106] TNA, WO/32/9485, 'Martial Law 1940', various file notes dated 6 June 1940 headed 'PUS' (Sir Alexander Maxwell, Permanent Under Secretary at the Home Office), Notes of S of S (through CM), dated 9 June 1940; Notes from MacGeagh to Gordon-Finlayson, dated 20 May 1940 and Gordon-Finlayson to MacGeagh, dated 22 May 1940.

the War Office entitled 'Notes on the Powers of His Majesty's Armed Forces engaged in active operations in the United Kingdom, with regard to the civil population and property' dated May 1940 which contains a classic exposition of the common law power 'of the repelling of attacks, whether by land or air, or in dealing with an armed insurrection'.[107] In the course of the discussion on the powers available under martial law, the Law Officers also advised the government of the powers available to it in the event of an invasion.[108] Part of the discussion concerned requests for assistance from members of the civilian population and it was thought that if they refuse 'they cannot be coerced by the use of force or the infliction of punishment by the military authorities, unless there has been some further specific Instruction dealing with this point'. There is a manuscript note at the side with 'Martial Law Order' presumably indicating that the requirement to give assistance should be made enforceable through martial law orders backed-up by the jurisdiction of military tribunals to try breaches of them. There appears to have been no thought given to the contradiction between the Diceyian notion that the common law power to use force is founded on citizens and soldiers having the same duty to repel attacks and uphold public order that underlay the notions of martial law and the advice that, whilst soldiers had military obligations to act, the duty could not be enforced against civilians.

Conclusion

The period from the Boer War to the Second World War is usually portrayed as involving the increasing use of statutory martial law – the use of powers granted by legislation, such as DORA and ROIA, rather than based in the common law. However, statutory martial law can be better seen as granting wider powers to try and punish offences in addition to the separate common law power to use lethal force. It was made subject to a framework provided by the municipal law and the laws of war whether or not martial law was applied and contained some basic rules of engagement. It was also adapted so that war included guerrilla warfare. These developments appear to have institutional and geographical elements to them. The chapters on riot and insurrection were written by Parliamentary Counsel by reference to the law as it was in Great Britain and not by the War Office whose experience lay outside it. The War Office's notion is more draconian both perhaps for the racial reason explained by Hussain but also because, as Finlason had identified, the state had to exercise power more coercively if it was to maintain control where its forces were scattered more widely and thinly. The exposition of it also reflected the varying threats to the State as can be seen in the more expansive notion in the face of a real threat of invasion in 1940 becoming more limited as the threat receded. Underlying these differing

[107] TNA, LCO 53/55, 'Martial Law', 'Notes on the Powers of His Majesty's Armed Forces Engaged in Active Operations in the United Kingdom, With Regard to the Civil Population and Property', dated May 1940.

[108] ibid Letter from Donald Somerville to Sir Thomas Barnes, dated 23 May 1940.

notions there are recurring references or allusions to Dicey and the use of the concept of the rule of law to constrain the use of force in internal circumstances which is reflected in the increasing use of 'statutory martial law'. However, the adoption of rules on the conduct of hostilities within a municipal law-enforcement framework had the effect of applying the laws of war to situations which were not formally within the definition of war and creates an area of overlap. In the overlap, the justification for the use of force is always necessity whatever the level of violence that is encountered. Nonetheless, there was perhaps an implicit sliding-scale that applied a stricter form of necessity to justify the use of force in riots but which moved nearer to military necessity to permit the attacking of armed rebels and echoes the qualification added by the italicized wording in the original copies of *General Order 100* that referred to the destruction of '*armed* enemies' in the American Civil War.

The redefining and limiting of the interpretation of the common law powers to justify the use of force in 1939–40 as the fear of invasion receded revealed a tension between the differing offices of the State in how they viewed the use of force. The tension is also perhaps behind the different interpretations of martial law given in the *Manual of Military Law* and the pamphlet 'Imperial Policing' and it was most obvious in the decision by O'Connor MR in *Egan v Macready* that reinstated habeus corpus in Ireland in conditions recognized as war. It can also be seen in the differing views of senior military officers, Gwynn and Simson. Gwynn essentially explained the War Office view of its policy and operations that combined military, legal and political elements in a supportive construct. Simson was much more critical and provided an important insight into the tension between the civil authority, the police, the military and the judiciary in the maintenance of public order in conditions which he described as 'sub-war'. In particular, he drew attention to the dual roles taken on by the public authority and the judiciary in upholding public order whilst also acting as referees of the amount of force that could be used by the police and military against rebels. It is easy to see in this the frustrations of a soldier who saw the government using the military as 'a dog in a dog fight',[109] but his identification of the conflicted position of government and the competition between government and the judiciary within a common cause of the maintenance of public order in the face of armed rebellion is a feature that resonates with the martial law discussions in 1940 and the experience of the British army in Iraq. Simson's critique might be seen as an example of the separation of powers between government and the judiciary operating as it should or of effective civil control over the military but it also a reflection of the inherent tension that arises from the political choices that governments make when ordering troops to deploy to restore public order, choosing the legal paradigm and powers that will apply, and then acting as prosecutor in a criminal trial if it determines that the amount of force used was unnecessary. These tensions will be seen again in the development and operations of the paradigms of armed conflict and law-enforcement in the second half of the twentieth century which will considered in next two chapters.

[109] Simson, *British Rule and Rebellion* (n 14) 82.

4

The Laws of War in Internal Armed Conflicts: Hague and Geneva Law and the Creation of the Paradigm of 'Armed Conflict'

Up to the Second World War there was a clear distinction that the laws of war applied only between states and not within a state unless, in theory at least, an armed conflict within a state had reached the status of belligerency. The publication of *General Order 100* in 1863 and its promotion abroad by Lieber more or less coincided with the first steps in a movement that led to the creation of the International Red Cross and the first Geneva convention in 1864. The two initiatives became part of different strands of the laws of war that came to be known as Hague law and Geneva law, each being named after the location of their major treaties. Hague law meant the laws regulating the conduct of hostilities, whilst Geneva law referred to the law protecting those who did not or no longer participated in hostilities, such as the wounded and prisoners of war.

Although *General Order 100* was said to be based on existing customs and usages of war, there was little consensus at that time on the status of the customs and usages of war as law. The expression 'custom and usages of war' is now taken to be part of customary international law but in the late nineteenth century the term could be used in that sense or in the sense of a military practice that was argued to carry with it only a moral obligation. This chapter examines the development of the laws of war that led to their expansion to non-international armed conflicts under the 1949 Geneva conventions. It begins with a review of the development of the laws of war under international treaties from the Hague conventions in 1899 and 1907 through to the Geneva conventions in 1949. It distinguishes between the laws of war as applied to states in war and the regime introduced by the 1949 Geneva conventions which created the paradigm of armed conflict and included under Common Article 3 of the four conventions 'armed conflicts not of an international character'. It looks at what the parties at the time understood Common Article 3 to provide and in what circumstances it was to apply in order to separate those views from current views of Common Article 3. It also looks at some of the differences of opinion on some seemingly small but important points of law which shaped some states' positions during negotiations and continue to have importance today, for example, on the effect of recognising rebel combatant status during and after the conflict. It shows that views of Common Article 3 among states and within the ICRC have changed significantly since it was created in 1949. Based on the drafting history of Common Article 3 and its express terms, it argues that Common Article 3 should be seen as a limited provision which introduced measures protecting those who did not or no longer participated in hostilities in non-international armed conflicts as a humanitarian measure but it did not necessarily carry with it Hague law – the laws of war that govern the conduct of hostilities. Furthermore, its origins suggest that it was thought of as giving basic civil rights under municipal law the force of international law. The implications of this will be explored in subsequent chapters, particularly with regard to the effect that this may have in the area where the paradigms of armed conflict and law-enforcement overlap. Within this overlap, the differing views on the scope and application of Common Article 3 created and continue to create legal uncertainty and gave states, the ICRC and others the opportunity to apply their own interpretation of it. It is also within the area of overlap that the problems of calibrating the use of lethal force and justifying the killing of insurgents become acute as the laws of war and international human rights law may both apply but have different parameters.

Regulating the Conduct of Hostilities – Hague Law (1899 and 1907)

The initiative that was to lead to the Hague Conventions of 1899, the first international treaties containing rules of the laws of war regulating the conduct of hostilities, is generally traced to the Brussels Conference of 1874.[1] The Russian Government proposed a text that was based on *General Order 100* and the book, *The International Law of War*, by Bluntschli that also drew heavily from it.[2] The Brussels Conference was not able to reach agreement on a text of the laws of war and made only a non-binding declaration containing the draft rules that had been proposed with some alterations.[3] The conference was followed by an initiative led by Bluntschli through the newly-formed Institute of International Law to draft a manual of the laws of war. It was published in 1880 and became known as the 'Oxford Manual' but it was not adopted by European governments. The only country to adopt it was Argentina and it was heavily criticized by the German

[1] The first modern international convention on the laws of war on land was the 1868 St Petersburg Declaration Renouncing the Use, in Time of War, of Explosive Projectiles Under 400 Grammes Weight. It dealt with weapons, often referred to as the 'means' of warfare.

[2] K Nabulsi, *Traditions of War, Occupation, Resistance and the Law* (Oxford, Oxford University Press, 1999) 5 and 7.

[3] ICRC, 'Project of an International Declaration concerning the Laws and Customs of War. Brussels, 27 August 1874' (in the Introduction).

authorities in particular for lacking any means of enforcement.[4] Nonetheless, the issue was taken up again at an international peace conference at The Hague in 1899. The conference was convened by the Russian Tsar, Nicholas II, and a set of regulations on the conduct of hostilities based on the Brussels Declaration was adopted and ratified under Hague Convention II. The Hague Conference then met again in 1906 and a very similar set of regulations was adopted under Hague Convention IV in 1907.[5] The convention also contained a general participation clause that provided, as had 1899 Hague Convention II, that the regulations applied only to the states that were party to it, and then only if all the belligerents were parties to the convention.[6] When war came in 1914, one of the belligerents, Serbia, was not a party to the convention and so, on one view, the Hague conventions did not apply to the First World War according to their terms.[7]

The Hague Regulations consisted of a simplified set of rules governing the conduct of hostilities based on the rules in *General Order 100* and only applied to war between states.[8] For example, rules limiting reprisals were proposed as part of the discussion at the Brussels conference in 1874 but they were so controversial in the light of allegations of unjustly severe reprisals carried out by the Prussian Army in the Franco–Prussian War of 1870–71 that the proposals were dropped and not raised again for 50 years.[9] However, there is also a deeper omission that is fundamental to understanding the laws of war on the conduct of hostilities contained in the Hague Regulations in that they, unlike *General Order 100*, do not contain reference to the principle of military necessity but assume its application in war. They are, to that extent, one sided in that they contain restrictions on the conduct of hostilities but are silent on the permissiveness of the use of force in doing so. As Oppenheim expressed it at the time: 'Apart from such means as are expressly prohibited by treaties or custom, all means of killing and wounding that exist or may be invented are lawful'.[10] This becomes important later in relation to the special regime created for internal armed conflicts under Common Article 3 of the 1949 Geneva Conventions as, in general, treaties restrict means and methods of war – they say what cannot be done – as opposed to setting out what can be done so long as it is justified by the principle of military necessity.

Once the Hague conventions had been ratified, a number of states, including France, the United Kingdom and the United States, duly produced their own

[4] C Andler, *'Frightfulness' in Theory and Practice as compared with Franco-British Usages* (London, T Fisher Unwin, 1916) 94; Nabulsi, *Traditions of War* (1999) (n 2) 8.

[5] ICRC, 'Convention (II) with Respect to the Laws and Customs of War on Land and its annex: Regulations concerning the Laws and Customs of War on Land. The Hague, 29 July 1899' (in the Introduction).

[6] JM Spaight, *War Rights on Land* (London, Macmillan and Co Limited, 1911) 6–7.

[7] W Schabas, *The Trial of the Kaiser* (Oxford, Oxford University Press, 2018) 131.

[8] G Best, *War and Law Since 1945* (Oxford, Clarendon Press, 1997) 41.

[9] G Best, *Humanity in Warfare, The Modern History of the International Law of Armed Conflict* (London, Weidenfeld and Nicholson, 1980) 171.

[10] L Oppenheim, *International Law, A Treatise, Vol II War and Neutrality* (London, Longmans, Green, and Co 1912) §116.

forms of instructions in accordance with the obligation in article 1 of the Hague Regulations to issue instructions to their armed forces conforming with the regulations.[11] The British produced a handbook for each of the 1899 and 1907 regulations and the later one was then adopted wholesale as a completely revised chapter on the laws of war in the 1914 edition of the *Manual of Military Law*.[12] The United States produced its own *Rules of Land War* based on the 1907 regulations, the first set of rules since *General Order 100* was adopted in 1863 and reprinted in 1898 for the conflict in the Philippines.[13] Germany, however, did not produce a new set of instructions and what was regarded as a semi-official German military handbook of 1901, the *Kriegbraunch im Landkrieg* [*The Usages of Land Warfare*], produced after the 1899 regulations was not up-dated. It treated the laws of war as only usages and not binding.[14] The revised British and US Manuals for their part went a great deal further than the Hague Regulations. The *British Manual* made the now customary disclaimer that it had been prepared by the War Office but could not be regarded as official and then stated that as none of the existing 'conventions and declarations deal exhaustively with their subject matter … it has been found necessary to supplement the rules of the conventions and declarations by the rules of warfare sanctioned by custom and usage'.[15] The *US Manual* similarly contained an extensive set of rules mostly drawn from *General Order 100* to supplement the Hague Regulations. For example, it included rules restricting reprisals taken from *General Order 100* that had been so controversial at the Brussels conference and were omitted from the Hague Regulations.[16] The status of the Hague Regulations continued to be disputed after the First World War but they were treated as having become customary international law by 1939 by the Nuremberg Military Tribunal in 1946, although without any proof being cited in the case report.[17]

The Limited Development of the Laws of War (1907–1949)

It is possible to portray the period up to 1949 as one of the progressive advancement of the laws of war with similar rules being developed and agreed in different

[11] For France, see Andler, *'Frightfulness' in Theory and Practice* (1916) (n 4) 138; For Germany, see Best, *Humanity in Warfare* (1980) (n 9) 178.

[12] TE Holland, *The Laws and Customs of War on Land, as defined by the Hague Convention of 1899* (London, Harrison and Sons, 1904); and Col JE Edmonds and L Oppenheim, *Land Warfare. An Exposition of the Laws and Usages of War on Land for the Guidance of Officers of His Majesty's Army* (London, HMSO, 1912).

[13] US War Department, *Rules of Land Warfare* (Washington, GPO, 1914).

[14] Best, *Humanity in Warfare* (n 9) 146 and 178.

[15] Edmonds and Oppenheim, *Land Warfare* (1912) (n 12) 'Preface'.

[16] US War Department, *Rules of Land Warfare* (1914) 132–34.

[17] International Military Tribunal, Nuremberg, 'Trial of the Major War Criminals before the International Military Tribunal' (IMT, Nuremberg, 1947) 253; ME O'Connell, 'Historical Development and Legal Basis' in Fleck (ed), *The Handbook of International Humanitarian Law* 15.

instruments over the period or as one of a lack of consensus among states as seen in the conferences that did not reach a binding agreement, such as the 1874 Brussels Conference, the Hague Rules on Aerial Warfare of 1923 and even the limited nature of Common Article 3.[18] However, beneath these differing views, it is difficult to determine what status the laws of war were given as 'law' in the enforceable sense. There is evidence that some states, including France, the United Kingdom and the United States, treated them as applying to their own forces through their military manuals but there is no clear view on whether they were enforced. For example, the laws and customs of war that had been codified in the Hague Regulations were used publicly to identify violations of those laws and customs in the Balkan Wars in 1913.[19] They were used again to denounce German war crimes at the beginning of the First World War but the references to the laws and customs of war as the basis for German war crimes were deleted from the final report of the Allied commission set up to inquire into German war crimes after the First World War, partly due to uncertainty about their legitimacy.[20] In the case of enforcement against 'the enemy' at that time, the 1914 *British Manual* provided that soldiers who carried out orders that breached the rules of war could not be prosecuted but that the official or commander who gave the order, if captured, could be – although by implication this was unlikely to happen.[21] If the commander were to be captured, there was then a fear that prosecutions for war crimes would result in reprisals by the enemy.[22] In the case of enforcement against the country's own soldiers, Britain and the United States treated breaches of the laws of war as breaches of their military law. So, for example, shooting a prisoner might be charged as murder rather than a war crime as such and, by implication, it is very difficult to find evidence of cases that had an underlying basis in the laws of war.[23] Nonetheless, by the Second World War, the British government and the UN War Crimes Commission referred to the right to try war crimes as customary international law but without producing any examples.[24] It is, however, at least possible to say that the military authorities were capable of taking their obligations seriously. In Britain, as early as 1903, a report of a Royal Commission at the ending of the South African War noted that no new instructions had been produced to comply with the UK's obligation under the 1899 Hague conventions.[25] Notes in

[18] O'Connell, 'Historical Development and Legal Basis' ibid 15.

[19] Schabas, *The Trial of the Kaiser* (2018) (n 7) 140.

[20] ibid 148.

[21] M Garrod, 'The British Influence on the Development of the Laws of War and the Punishment of War Criminals: From the Grotius Society to the United Nations War Crimes Commission' in R McCorquodale and JP Gauci, *British Influences on International Law* (Leiden, Brill Nijhoff, 2016) 322.

[22] ibid 346.

[23] R McLaughlin, 'The Use of Lethal Force by Military Forces on Law Enforcement Operations – Is There a "Lawful Authority"?' (2009) 37: 3 *Federal Law Review* 444. McLaughlin cites two cases of shooting a prisoner of war whilst trying to escape that were tried as murder: *HM Advocate v Sheppard* [1941] JC 67; and *Hajdamovitz v Attorney General* (1944) 11 *Palestine Law Reports* 140.

[24] Garrod, 'The British Influence on the Development of the Laws of War' (2016) (n 21) 357.

[25] TNA, WO 32/8153, 'Revision of Martial Law sentences, S Africa', Memorandum by the Commissioners for the Revision of Martial Law Sentences, received 3 January 1903.

the War Office files in response to that report remark that the chapter on the laws of war in the *Manual of Military Law* was being revised by Professor Holland to include the Hague conventions and that no action was required.[26] As it turned out, Holland's work was published separately and the changes to the main chapter on the laws of war in the *Manual of Military Law* were postponed to allow for the further conference at the Hague in 1906.[27] In 1914 the chapter in the *British Manual* on the laws of war was completely rewritten to take account of the 1907 Hague conventions in the expanded commentary written for the War Office by Professor Oppenheim and Col Edmonds in 1912. A further update to the *British Manual* in 1929, however, surprisingly made no changes to the chapter on the laws of war. An editor's note explained that, although there had been considerable advances in weaponry in the First World War, there had not been any changes in international law to reflect them and, with minor exceptions, 'the chapter has been left in its previous form, not necessarily as a code universally accepted, but as the best guide at present available upon the subject of which it treats' – this was the 'code' written in 1912 by Oppenheim and Edmunds.[28] Professor Arnold McNair (1885–1975), one of the leading international lawyers of the period, explained the apparent lack of attention to the laws of war as being due to a switch to efforts to condemn war as an instrument of policy as seen in the League of Nations and the condemnation by 50 states of the war between Italy and Abyssinia (the predecessor state of modern Ethiopia) in 1935. He said that 'the changes were due to the destructiveness of the weapons used in the Great War and the suffering of combatants and non-combatants alike'.[29] As well as states, this change of emphasis was also the work of concerned individuals, 'Internationalists', who 'maintained that war was a barbaric way to resolve disputes and the best way to resolve controversies was through international institutions'.[30] After the experience of the Second World War, this change was made and the use of force by states was restricted under the Charter of the United Nations but, unlike the experience after the First World War, there was also a large extension of the laws of war under the 1949 Geneva conventions.

There was also only limited development of Geneva law before 1949. The first Geneva convention covering the treatment of the wounded was updated and extended in 1906 and a further convention on the treatment of prisoners of war was entered into in 1929. Whilst these conventions applied only to war between states, there were the beginnings of attempts to extend Geneva law to civil wars. Some writers date the initiative to extend the application of the convention on the treatment of the wounded beyond war between states to 1882 whilst others

[26] ibid file note to GGMI.

[27] Holland, *The Laws of War on Land* (1904) (n 12); and War Office, *Manual of Military* Law, 5th edn (London, HMSO, 1907).

[28] War Office, *Manual of Military Law*, 7th edn (London, HMSO, 1929) 270.

[29] AD McNair, *Collective Security, An Inaugural Lecture* (Cambridge, Cambridge University Press, 1936) 11. McNair later became the first judge to be appointed by the UK to the ICJ and then the first president of the ECtHR.

[30] OA Hathaway and SJ Shapiro, *The Internationalists: How a Radical Plan to Outlaw War Remade the World* (New York, Simon & Schuster, 2017) xxi.

prefer 1912.[31] The ICRC explained that when a draft convention on the role of the Red Cross in civil wars and insurrections was submitted to the International Red Cross Conference in 1912, the proposals were not 'opened to detailed discussion and vote'.[32] Best gave another explanation, he said that the attempt at extension was blocked by the chief Russian delegate who said that 'insurgent bands or revolutionaries … can only appear in the eye of the law as criminals.'[33] The ICRC was itself split between sceptics and advocates of extending the coverage of the laws of war to internal armed conflicts. It developed a practice of humanitarian relief being provided by national Red Cross societies in such circumstances, for example, by the Russian Red Cross during the civil wars following the Russian Revolution.[34] Although the extension of the convention beyond the formal legal conception of war had been generally resisted by states, the ICRC did have some success in extending the scope in practice, for example: it had persuaded the parties to the civil war in Upper Silesia in 1921 and to the Spanish Civil War (1936–39) to comply with the Geneva conventions on the treatment of the wounded and prisoners of war.[35] The involvement of national Red Cross societies in the post-First World War civil wars also led to a non-binding resolution being passed at the Tenth International Conference of the Red Cross held in Geneva in 1921 calling for the humane treatment of political detainees captured in civil wars.[36] However, a further attempt made at the 1938 conference to extend humanitarian protection during civil wars failed to gain sufficient support even among national societies.[37] Overall, then, until the end of the Second World War, it was generally recognized that the Geneva conventions applied only in war and states resisted attempts by the ICRC to become involved in internal armed conflicts.[38] This makes what happened afterwards all the more remarkable, and contested.

Extending the Laws of War after the Second World War

In the aftermath of the Second World War there was renewed effort to uphold and extend the laws of war. The International Military Tribunals at Nuremberg and

[31] T Rodenhäuser, *Organizing Rebellion: Non-State Armed Groups under International Law* (Oxford, Oxford University Press, 2018) 33; and E Castrén, *Civil War* (Helsinki, Suómalainen Tiedeakatemia, 1966) 84; respectively.

[32] ICRC, *Commentary on the First Geneva Convention: Convention (I) for the Amelioration of the Condition of the Wounded and Sick in Armed Forces in the Field* (Cambridge, Cambridge University Press, 2016) 'Commentary of 2016. Article 3: Conflicts not of an international character' §362.

[33] Best, *Humanity in Warfare* (n 9) 299.

[34] G Mantilla, *Lawmaking Under Pressure: International Humanitarian Law and Internal Armed Conflict* (New York, Cornell University Press, 2020) 54.

[35] ICRC, *Commentary on the First Geneva Convention: Convention (I) for the Amelioration of the Condition of the Wounded and Sick in Armed Forces in the Field* (ICRC, 1952), 'Commentary of 1952. Article 3: Conflicts not of an international character' 40.

[36] Mantilla, *Lawmaking Under Pressure* (2020) (n 34) 55–56.

[37] ibid 63.

[38] H Wilson, *International Law and the Use of Force by National Liberation Movements* (Oxford, Clarendon Press, 1988) 21 citing GI Draper, *The Red Cross Conventions* (London, Stevens, 1958) 10.

Tokyo tried individuals for war crimes and in their judgments declared that the rules set out in the Hague Regulations had by 1939 become regarded as customary international law.[39] This meant that the rules applied to all states regardless of whether they were parties to the Hague conventions and, more specifically, Germany was subject to them and liable for breaches made by its armed forces in the Second World War. The Conference of National Red Cross Societies held in 1946 also proposed applying the principles of the 1929 Geneva Convention on the treatment of prisoners of war to both sides in a civil war, unless one of them announced its intention not to do so.[40] At the same time, however, an insurrection in Greece from 1946–49 was suppressed by the government as a war even though a special commission appointed by the United Nations' Security Council concluded that the conflict did not amount to a civil war and the ICRC were unable to convince the parties to observe the Geneva conventions.[41]

As the ICRC conference proposals for new Geneva conventions were developed into drafts updating the existing conventions and proposing a new civilian convention, the ICRC extended the proposed scope of application of the conventions. The draft Convention for the Protection of War Victims submitted to the XVIIth International Red Cross Conference held at Stockholm in 1948 contained a common article setting out their application. The article provided that it applied to all cases of declared war or any other armed conflict between two states party to the conventions. This introduced the conceptual change of the application of the laws of war to armed conflicts rather than war and it then went on to provide that

> [i]n all cases of armed conflict which are not of an international character, especially cases of civil war, colonial conflicts, or wars of religion, which may occur in the territory of one or more of the High Contracting Parties, the implementing of the principles of the present Convention shall be obligatory on each of the adversaries.

This extension to 'cases of armed conflict not of an international character' in effect created a paradigm of armed conflict covering both international and non-international armed conflicts. After discussion at the conference the draft was adopted with the omission of the specific reference to 'cases of civil war, colonial conflicts, or wars of religion'. There are a number of different accounts for this. The 1952 ICRC Commentary refers simply to the omission and comments that this enlarged the scope of application of the conventions whereas the 2016 updated *Commentary on the First Geneva Convention* states that it was omitted as 'the view prevailed that too much detail risked weakening the provision, as it was impossible to foresee all future circumstances and as the character of a situation is independent of its motives'.[42] The broader reference to 'armed conflict not of an

[39] G Solis, *The Law of Armed Conflict: International Humanitarian Law in War* (Cambridge, Cambridge University Press, 2016) 61.

[40] ICRC, 'Commentary of 1952. Article 3' (n 35) 41.

[41] Castrén, *Civil War* (1966) (n 31) 66.

[42] ICRC, 'Commentary of 2016. Article 3' (n 32) §373.

international character' can be seen as a specific attempt to broaden the scope of coverage. Prior to the Second World War, the ICRC had tended to use the term 'civil war' loosely to apply to its attempts to intervene in internal armed conflicts but this was often resisted by states arguing that there was no civil war.[43] However, as will be seen, the phrase was open to different interpretations and the British delegation to the 1949 conference approached it from a traditional perspective based on the application of the laws of war in belligerency. This still followed the views of Oppenheim expressed in his *Treatise on International Law* since its first publication in 1906, and by 1949 in its sixth edition, that war was a contention between states but there was also a de facto state of war that could exist within a state. A further issue flowed from this, how this de facto state would be recognized and the British generally followed two lines of negotiation: to reserve the determination to the state concerned and to avoid any prescriptive definitions.

The drafts approved by the Stockholm Conference consisted of four conventions: three draft conventions updating and expanding existing conventions on the treatment of the sick and wounded, the ship-wrecked and prisoners of war; and a new draft convention – the Convention for the Protection of Civilian Persons in Time of War – commonly known as the Civilian Convention.[44] It is generally noted that these drafts were to apply to armed conflicts 'not of an international character' but there was a subtle distinction between them as the obligation of the state parties under the updated Prisoners of War Convention and the new Civilian Convention were to be 'subject to the adverse party likewise acting in obedience thereto'.[45]

The British government had opposed the application of the conventions to internal armed conflicts on an objective test and 'sought to apply the draft conventions to civil wars only where the Sovereign Power had recognised the existence of a state of war'.[46] They had explained this on the basis that to do otherwise would mean that rules intended for war, as defined by international law, would be applied to circumstances that were not war and create great confusion as well as appearing to give the status of belligerents to insurgents.[47] At the beginning of the 1949 conference, however, a large majority of states supported a general application of the conventions to civil wars. This was partly a reflection of their pre-Second World War experience, particularly of the Spanish Civil War, but, at the same time, many states were also concerned that the conventions should not be applied to situations that did not amount to organized armed conflict.[48] There was also an

[43] Mantilla, *Lawmaking Under Pressure* (n 34) 62.

[44] TNA, LO2/673, Law Officers' Department: Geneva Conventions 1949 Publications.

[45] ibid.

[46] TNA, LO2/674, 'Law Officers' Department: Geneva Conventions 1949, Drafting & Signing of Conventions', Extracts from Sir Robert Craigie's Report relating to questions previously considered by the Cabinet.

[47] ICRC, *Final Record of the Diplomatic Conference of Geneva of 1949* (Berne, 1949) Vol IIB, 10.

[48] N Zamir, *Classification of Conflicts in International Humanitarian Law: The Legal Impact of Foreign Intervention in Civil Wars* (Cheltenham, Edward Elgar, 2017) 29.

overlap between states which were occupied during the Second World War and colonial powers which complicated matters both as a matter of law and policy. The overlap derived in part from the draft provisions determining when a war and an occupation of a state, or part of it, terminated. Once it did, any further conflict was, in law, no longer subject to the laws of war unless it could be classified as a non-international armed conflict. States that had experienced occupation in Europe and suffered from Nazi operations that fell outside of the protection of the laws of war were sensitive to this and, in general, more inclined to be in favour of provisions providing protection in those circumstances, particularly as they concerned the protection of both civilians and those engaged in continuing armed opposition, such as the French Resistance. However, the same provisions would also apply to other types of internal armed conflict in relation to which the imperial powers and newly-recognized states had particular concerns over their ability to take repressive measures against insurgents. The overlap sometimes led to differences of view between and within state delegations on issues of protection but, as the conference progressed, the discussion of the detail of the drafts began to reveal substantial difficulties with a general application to non-international armed conflicts. For example, in relation to the draft Prisoner of War Convention, it was doubted that non-state parties would be able to implement the detailed provisions of that convention. The real difficulties, however, began to emerge in relation to the draft Civilian Convention and, in particular, it was unclear how the protections accorded to civilians who were 'protected persons' in a conflict or an occupation would have applied to civilians in territory recaptured by the state forces.[49] Furthermore, there was a provision that restricted the right of the occupier to try protected persons for offences committed prior to the occupation and it was unclear how the provision would apply or which party was to be treated as an 'Occupying Power' in a non-international armed conflict.[50]

The opposition of the British delegation hardened further as the scrutiny of the drafts widened within the UK government although it was not consistent between departments and varied between the doctrinaire and the pragmatic. In the initial stages, the Home Office produced a draft note on the application of the Civilian Convention that included a typology of internal conflicts.[51] It made reference to the classic formulation of war as a contention between states but its typology of internal conflicts was unusual as it referred to insurgency but made

[49] The term 'protected persons' is one of the key concepts providing protection to civilians under the convention. Under Art 4, they are defined as 'those who, at a given moment and in any manner whatsoever, find themselves, in case of a conflict or occupation, in the hands of a Party to the conflict or Occupying Power of which they are not nationals'.

[50] Under Art 70 of the Civilian Convention, protected persons 'shall not be arrested, prosecuted or convicted by the Occupying Power for acts committed or for opinions expressed before the occupation … with the exception of breaches of the laws and customs of war'.

[51] TNA, LO2/674, 'Law Officers' Department: Geneva Conventions 1949, Drafting & Signing of Conventions', Letter to ME Reed from the Home Office, dated 24 March 1949 enclosing a note from the Home Office on draft Article 2 of the Civilian Convention.

no reference to insurrection or rebellion. It then took the view that circumstances that equated to the recognition of belligerency might give rise to the application of the Civilian Convention but not lower levels of disorder and that the UK's view was that it would apply only when the success of the rebels meant that a de facto state had to be recognized. However, at a meeting held by the Attorney General at the Lord Chancellor's Office and attended by representatives of the government departments involved, the Attorney General gave instructions for the negotiations that 'in no circumstances should the Delegation accept the application of the Civilian Convention in Civil War'. Nonetheless, the other conventions might apply if the sovereign power declared that a state of civil war existed.[52] The UK's main objection was explained again as that the application of the convention could 'encourage revolt by facilitating premature recognition of belligerency' but there were also thought to be practical difficulties in applying the conventions to a civil war 'without hampering the Sovereign Power in applying legitimate measures for the suppression of subversive movements'.[53] The British delegation was, therefore, to try to separate any terms that were to apply from the recognition of belligerency and avoid any references to 'civil war'. It was also to avoid conditions analogous to belligerency and focus on the readiness and ability of the parties to the conflict to apply carefully selected provisions. The provisions themselves would be limited to those having a strictly humanitarian effect.[54]

Common Article 3

As the conference progressed, the range of views seemed to be widening on the potential outcomes. They ranged from acceptance of the Stockholm drafts to complete rejection of the application of the conventions to civil war. There was, nonetheless, a 'willingness of the vast majority of states to extend humanitarian protection to all types of armed conflicts … without hampering their right to quell rebellions'.[55] Within this, the French position had become more opposed as the negotiations proceeded and turned from detailed objections to the draft to rejection of the general application of the Civilian Convention. The United States, Canada, Australia and Burma were also opposed to the application of the conventions to civil war but only short of belligerency whilst the Soviet Union was in favour.[56] The British were aware that they were in a minority position in thinking

[52] ibid Letter to ME Reed at the Law Officers' Department from [Johnston] at the Cabinet Office, dated 26 May 1949. The writer's name is unclear.

[53] ibid Letter from R Craigie at the UK Delegation at Geneva to HA Caccia at the Foreign Office, dated 9 May 1949.

[54] ibid.

[55] Zamir, *Classification of Conflicts* (2017) (n 48) 217.

[56] TNA, FO369/4150, (General – 1949), Note of 7th Meeting of the United Kingdom Delegation, dated 28 April 1949.

that the conventions should not apply at all but at that time they thought that, if the conventions were to apply, they should continue to apply after termination of the civil war to protect the rebels from subsequent trial. Most states found this position difficult to understand and the United States and the Soviet Union, by contrast, took the opposite view.[57] This is a significant difference of opinion on the law and helps to explain why the British government were so resistant to accepting a lower threshold of armed conflict for the conventions as it links to their insistence that they should retain the power to try rebels as criminals during and after the conflict. To do so, the conflict had to remain subject to municipal law and not become a non-international armed conflict subject to the Geneva conventions. In an attempt to reach a compromise, the issue was referred to a committee under French chairmanship and it produced a draft that was, with minor changes, the form adopted as Common Article 3. The draft was based on a preamble to the draft Civilian Convention that was subsequently deleted but which provided an interesting link between the laws of war and human rights. It had provided:

> The High Contracting Parties, conscious of their obligation to come to an agreement in order to protect civilian populations from the horrors of war, undertake to respect the principles of human rights which constitute the safeguard of civilisation and, in particular, to apply, at any time and in all places, the rules given hereunder:
>
> (1) Individuals shall be protected against any violence to their life and limb.
> (2) The taking of hostages is prohibited.
> (3) Executions may be carried out only if prior judgment has been passed by a regularly constituted court, furnished with the judicial safeguards that civilised peoples recognise to be indispensable.
> (4) Torture of any kind is strictly prohibited.
>
> These rules, which constitute the basis of universal human law, shall be respected without prejudice to the special stipulations provided for in the present Convention in favour of protected persons.[58]

The preamble was deleted mainly because states and the ICRC could not agree its purpose or what it should contain.[59] Nonetheless, although deleted and largely forgotten until recent research revived an interest in it, the preamble can be seen to express a different spirit and approach to the application of the provisions that were to become Common Article 3. It has been suggested recently that the preamble in effect identifies the Civilian Convention as the first human rights instrument.[60] A closer reading of the text, however, shows that it should be seen as more limited

[57] ibid and Cabinet Paper GEN 281/1, Application to Civil War of Geneva Conventions on War Victims, Report of Official Working Party, dated 21 May 1949.

[58] TNA, LO2/673, 'Law Officers' Department: Geneva Conventions 1949 Publications. Draft Convention for the Protection of Civilian Persons in Time of War'.

[59] B van Dijk, *Preparing for War: The Making of the Geneva Conventions* (Oxford, Oxford University Press, 2022) 92.

[60] B van Dijk, 'Human Rights in War: On the Entangled Foundations of the 1949 Geneva Conventions' (2018) 112: 4 *American Journal of International Law* 553–82.

than that as the preamble was self-contained. It referred only to the rules in the preamble itself and the nature of the rights in the convention is quite different from the individual rights created by human rights instruments. For example, it is fundamental that the laws of war purport to bind both parties to a conflict whereas under human rights law only the state is bound.[61] Furthermore, under the convention itself, the rights are not given to all individuals who may be affected by an armed conflict as the citizens of neutral states and co-belligerents are not within the main class of 'protected persons'.[62] However, the link between the preamble and Common Article 3 suggests the idea that the extension of humanitarian protection to internal armed conflicts did not necessarily carry with it other elements of the laws of war, in particular the rules on the conduct of hostilities. The current view on Common Article 3 as expressed by the ICRC in its updated commentary to the First Convention is that 'when common Article 3 is applicable, it is understood that other rules of humanitarian law of non-international armed conflict, including those regarding the conduct of hostilities, also apply'.[63] This is a common modern position but it is not quite clear-cut as the rather reserved language – 'it is understood' – suggests. It has also been thought to be the product of the ICRC's 2005 *Customary Law Study* which sought to identify and document the customary laws of war.[64] More widely, it can be seen in the existence of separate categories of war crimes in the 1998 Rome Statute. There are different sections for serious violations of Common Article 3 and for '[o]ther serious violations of the laws and customs of war applicable in armed conflicts not of an international character' and it is the latter section that includes breaches of rules on the conduct of hostilities.[65] The preamble also raises a question about the British government's attitude at the Geneva conference to the negotiations on the laws of war and the negotiations on human rights at the United Nations in New York that were proceeding at the same time. There was an awareness at departmental level that the British government should seek to keep these apart and to keep colonial issues out of the human rights discussions.[66] On the other hand, it was the Legal Advisor at the Foreign Office – the most senior lawyer in the department and the leading adviser within government on international law – who was best placed to see the potential for an overlap between them as he saw papers from both sets of negotiations but there is no indication that he considered there was one. Perhaps the issue resolved itself with the deletion of the preamble but it may also be seen as an unsurprising separation in

[61] Y Dinstein, *The Conduct of Hostilities under the Law of International Armed Conflict* (Cambridge, Cambridge University Press, 2016) 28 citing *Prosecutor v Kunarac et al*, ICTY, Trial Chamber (2001), §470.

[62] 1949 Fourth Geneva Convention, Art 4 and 6. The nationals of neutral states are, however, protected persons within occupied territory.

[63] ICRC, 'Commentary of 2016. Article 3' (n 32) §389.

[64] J Pejic, 'The Protective Scope of Common Article 3: More than Meets the Eye' (2011) 93 *International Review of the Red Cross* no 881, 219.

[65] 1998 Rome Stature of the International Criminal Court, Art 8.2(c) and (e) respectively.

[66] van Dijk, *Preparing for War* (2022) (n 59) 115.

the context of the time as, from a British perspective, the laws of war applied to international armed conflicts abroad and human rights would apply to the United Kingdom at home in peacetime. If it could, it would keep the position with regard to the colonies separate. Nevertheless, the preamble to the Civilian Convention might have given the government pause for thought on this division.[67]

By July 1949, the conference was in something of a deadlock as the discussions had reached a point of offering the possibility of no provision on civil wars, the Stockholm text, or various working party texts. The British ruled out any support for the Stockholm text and discussed the other options around versions of the draft article produced by the French-led committee based on the preamble.[68] Faced with the quite different positions and the possibility of nothing being agreed at the conference, a consensus then appeared within a short time on the new draft article and it was adopted as Common Article 3 of the four conventions. There were, however, some residual concerns and at the British cabinet meeting to approve the ratification of the conventions, the cabinet's attention was drawn generally to the provisions on civil war and war crimes as well as a few detailed matters. It was noted on Common Article 3 that

> the present provision would make it more difficult to deal promptly and effectively with rebellion, and that some of the provisions could not be carried out in practice. It was to be hoped, for example, that no endeavour would be made to argue that the Convention should apply to the operations now in progress in Malaya.

However, it was agreed that it was impolitic to raise any further objection to Common Article 3 given the unfavourable position that the UK had been in during the earlier negotiations.[69] The quotation is also interesting in its reference to Malaya and this will be examined further in chapter six.

The application of Common Article 3 was considered at length in the ICRC's commentaries on the 1949 conventions, the first of which appeared in 1952. It noted that 'the burning question' which arose again and again at the conference was what was meant by a 'conflict'. Some governments

[67] For example: TNA, LO2/674, 'Law Officers' Department: Geneva Conventions 1949, Drafting & Signing of Conventions', Letter to CG Kemball at the Foreign Office from ME Reed [Legal Officer] dated 16 May 1949 – in the letter Reed states his strong objection to any provision that would prevent the government treating insurgents as traitors and notes that the issue concerns colonial governments more than others; TNA, IOC (HR)(48)4, 'Cabinet Steering Committee on International Organisations Working Party on Human Rights', Note by the Joint Secretaries dated 24 January 1948 – the notes recognize the potential for the International Covenant to 'cause some of our Colonial territories serious difficulties and embarrassment in the conduct of their affairs'.

[68] TNA, LO2/674, 'Law Officers' Department: Geneva Conventions 1949, Drafting & Signing of Conventions', Letter to HA Caccia at the Foreign Office from the United Kingdom Delegation to the Diplomatic Conference for the Protection of War Victims, dated 19 July 1949, entitled 'Civil War Articles'.

[69] TNA, CAB 130/46, 'Cabinet Gens 281–91', Minutes of a Meeting of Ministers held on 2 December 1949 entitled 'Revision of Geneva Conventions'.

> feared that it might be taken to cover any act committed by force of arms – any form of anarchy, rebellion, or even plain banditry. For example, if a handful of individuals were to rise in rebellion against the State and attack a police station.[70]

The ICRC commented that the difficulty in resolving the issue of the meaning of armed conflict led to the attempt being abandoned and replaced by the adoption of a limited number of provisions that would apply. It did, however, think it useful to include a list of the conditions that had been discussed as applying to the determination as to whether a non-international armed conflict existed for the purposes of the conventions. The list is detailed and includes that the insurgent party possessed an organized military force with control over territory and the means of respecting and ensuring respect for the convention, and that it became necessary for the lawful government to use regular military forces against the insurgents. It also listed the requirement for recognition of the insurgents as belligerents by the lawful government that had so concerned the British delegation and that the dispute had been admitted to the agenda of the Security Council or the General Assembly of the United Nations as being a threat to international peace, a breach of the peace, or an act of aggression. It was noted that the list was a list of the criteria that had been discussed, it was not describing a cumulative test, and the ICRC stressed that the criteria were not determinative. An alternative way of viewing it is that the list contained the points on which the states could not agree and the article itself represented all that could be agreed.[71] However, the ICRC then said that in its view

> the Article should be applied as widely as possible. There can be no reason against this. For, contrary to what may have been thought, the Article in its reduced form does not in any way limit the right of a State to put down rebellion. Nor does it increase in the slightest the authority of the rebel party. It merely demands respect for certain rules, which were already recognized as essential in all civilized countries, and enacted in the municipal law of the States in question, long before the Convention was signed.[72]

Looked at in the light of the wider context, this is a revealing opinion as it identifies the origin of the rules – or, to use a more common term, rights – within the municipal law of certain states, 'civilised countries' in its phrase. The rules were, in effect, incorporated into international law which gave them force against all states that are parties to the conventions and limited a state party's ability to disapply the rules under emergency legislation. Following the logic of the argument further then, for those states that already had such rules in their municipal law, the rules were reinforced by, rather than introduced through, international law. This connection seems to have been recognized within the ICRC as, in internal discussions, they noted that the provisions should not apply until the conflict had reached the stage

[70] ICRC, 'Commentary of 1952. Article 3' (n 35) 49.
[71] Mantilla, *Lawmaking Under Pressure* (n 34) 86.
[72] ICRC, 'Commentary of 1952. Article 3' (n 35) 49–50.

where it could not be regulated by municipal law.[73] The US delegation similarly thought that the provisions should not apply until an insurrection had stabilized into a rebellion or civil war.[74] However, there was no such distinction made in the provisions themselves, which allowed states and the ICRC to take very different positions of its application to a particular conflict. The Inter-American Court of Human Rights has also recognized the connection with municipal rights in a number of cases, for example, in the leading *La Tablada (Abella)* case. In it, the court stated that '[Common] Article 3 basically requires the State to do, in large measure, what it is already legally obliged to do under the American Convention [on Human Rights].'[75] These opinions are notably silent on any implied powers under Common Article 3 to conduct operations under the laws of war. It suggests that the context of Common Article 3 at the time that it was adopted did not include the full range of the laws of war permitting the use of force not, as the modern commentary implies, by omission even though it was within the scope of applicable international law, but as a consequence of its design. The content of Common Article 3 was drawn from municipal rules which did not contain permissive rules for the conduct of hostilities based on a balance of military necessity and humanity as the Hague Regulations and customary international law do. For example, English law uses a different test and standard of necessity for the use of force. Common Article 3 does not on its face cover the use of lethal force in military operations against insurgents in the field until they had been injured or detained as it applied only to persons 'taking no active part in the hostilities'. The deleted preamble also shows that it has a closer connection to a human rights-based approach than is generally recognized, certainly before a connection was made between the subject matter of Common Article 3 and human rights when human rights became prominent in the 1960s.[76] It is possible to find some contemporary references to its connection to human rights but they are rare. For example, RR Baxter, a legal adviser to the US State Department in the 1950s, recognized the human rights nature of provisions in the Civilian Convention but thought that human rights was a 'dirty word' at the time and that he should not characterize the provisions as a human rights convention.[77] However, the human rights it recognized are limited by comparison with those set out in contemporary human

[73] van Dijk, *Preparing for War* (n 59) 126.

[74] ibid.

[75] M Odello, 'Fundamental Standards of Humanity: A Common Language of International Humanitarian Law and Human Rights Law' in R Arnold and N Quénivet (eds), *International Humanitarian Law and Human Rights Law: Towards a New Merger in International Law* (Leiden, Martinus Nijhoff Publishers, 2008) 36.

[76] van Dijk, 'Human Rights in War' (2018) (n 60) 578.

[77] ibid 554 citing DF Vagts, T Meron, S Schwebel & C Keever (eds), *Humanizing the Laws of War: Selected Writings of Richard Baxter* (Oxford, Oxford University Press, 2014). D Schindler, 'International Humanitarian Law: Its Remarkable Development and its Persistent Violation' (2003) 5 *Journal of the History of International Law* 170–71 also made the argument on Common Article 3 being more in the nature of a human rights provision but it is doubted that this was the majority view at the time – Arnold and Quénivet, *International Humanitarian Law and Human Rights Law* (2008) (n 75) 3.

rights instruments, in particular the European Convention on Human Rights, the International Covenant and the American Convention on Human Rights, as it was looking at those rights that were considered as continuing to exist in conditions of war. In a sense it is the counterpart of the rights as they would exist under the human rights conventions after permitted derogation.

Recent research into the negotiations of the Geneva conventions has sought to explain the outcome of the conference as the product of the national negotiating objectives of the principal actors, primarily the major state actors Britain, France, the Soviet Union and the United States, but also others such as Burma which acted as something of a representative of post-colonial states and the ICRC as the main non-state actor. This produces contrasting views of the motives and performance of the various actors but the authors generally agree that there is a disparity in views between what was understood to be the scope of Common Article 3 at the conference and its subsequent implementation. This is usually portrayed as a difference in view on its application to colonial conflicts between Britain and France, on the one hand, and the ICRC supported by former colonial states and the Soviet Union on the other. They tend to take what is at best a sceptical view of the sincerity of the UK's negotiating position but the British records also show a wide range of views within the British government at the time. This is not to suggest that such scepticism cannot be justified but that the position is quite nuanced. The records give less of an impression that Common Article 3 was fully understood as applying to internal armed conflicts which had not reached the scale where belligerency applied and, together with other records, suggest that the modern understanding of Common Article 3 is open to reinterpretation to the extent that it applies to a conflict that falls short of a belligerency-standard of civil war. The British thinking seems to have included two strands that sometimes appeared to overlap but were not looked at in an integrated way. On the one hand, there was a focus on the provisions that would apply under the Civilian Convention from the perspective of occupation, that is after a state had gained control over hostile territory. The War Office in particular were concerned about the provisions related to grave breaches – the term used in the conventions for war crimes – and wanted to ensure that 'nothing must be included in the Convention which would restrict freedom to carry out operations, particularly bombing' in military operations in war or in any subsequent occupation.[78] On the other hand, their approach to internal armed conflict was to examine the new provisions and question how they would apply in both government and rebel-held territory. So, for example, they objected strongly to provisions that would have the effect of restricting the occupying power's ability to try captured fighters for treason or other municipal criminal offences such as the provision limiting prosecution of offences prior to occupation. It is tempting then to see a systematic analogy being applied between the provisions that

[78] TNA, LO2/674, 'Law Officers' Department: Geneva Conventions 1949, Drafting & Signing of Conventions', Letter to WH Gardner [UK Delegation in Geneva] from GD Roseway [War Office], dated 9 June 1949.

would apply in occupation and those that would apply in rebel-held territory in an internal armed conflict, however, this would be mistaken as the government's position was more complex. In particular, it contained within it different points of view which were not always consistent and could be institutionally focused. It was the Colonial Office which was more concerned about restrictions on conducting operations against insurgents and prosecuting them when captured whilst the War Office were more concerned about the potential war crimes arising from military operations, particularly aerial bombing, and a failure to achieve more protection for soldiers captured by rebels if the Prisoner of War Convention did not apply to non-international armed conflicts.[79] The Home Office was aware of the War Office and Colonial Office concerns but did not see these as overriding its general concern on the Civilian Convention having application within the United Kingdom and the Lord Chancellor emphatically rejected it.[80] The Foreign Office, on the other hand, which led the negotiations in Geneva, focused on the diplomatic relationships at the conference and its perception of their effects on the UK's reputation rather than the concerns of other departments. The Legal Advisor at the Foreign Office dismissed the War Office's concerns over grave breaches in the Civilian Convention on the basis that it 'is only applicable in territory which is occupied by the belligerent in question, and no belligerent bombs territory in its own occupation', which is an indication of how some officials thought of the application of the convention to occupation and colonial conflicts separately but, at the same time, is an extraordinary view for someone so senior to express given, for example, the extent of bombing carried out by the Royal Air Force in Palestine in the 1930s.[81]

Conclusion

The laws of war were developed in important ways in the first half of the twentieth century but were concerned with war between states until the advent of Common Article 3. There was significant movement by states in agreeing the Hague Regulations in 1899 and 1907 to regulate the conduct of hostilities but the actual effect of their adoption was disputed, particularly by Germany from the

[79] ibid Letter to CG Kemball at the Foreign Office from ME Reed [Legal Officer], dated 16 May 1949; Letter to WH Gardner [UK Delegation in Geneva] from GD Roseway [War Office], dated 9 June 1949; and Letter to ME Reed at the Law Courts from the Cabinet Office, dated 9 April 1949 enclosing a draft note to brief the Prime Minister on the issue of the application of the Conventions to Civil War. TNA, CAB 130/46-281-291, 'Cabinet, Ministerial Committee for the Revision of the Geneva Conventions on War Victims', Memorandum by the Secretary of State for Foreign Affairs, dated 25 November 1949.

[80] ibid Letter to ME Reed at the Law Courts from the Cabinet Office, dated 9 April 1949 enclosing a draft note to brief the Prime Minister on the issue of the application of the Conventions to Civil War; and Letter to ME Reed from The Lord Chancellor's Office, dated 11 April 1949 containing a note of conclusions reached in a meeting held by the Attorney General.

[81] ibid Letter to CG Kemball from WE Beckett, dated 17 June 1949.

time of the conventions but also by the allied states and their lawyers during and after the First World War. Some states, such as France, the United Kingdom and the United States, followed their obligations to include the Hague Regulations in their own internal instructions and, in the case of the British and Americans, their military manuals went considerably further in describing a 'code' that applied a wider range of rules. The British and Americans then considered these binding upon their soldiers under military law, if not international law. There was some expansion of Geneva law as it applied to the wounded and prisoners of war, but other attempts to expand the laws of war were largely subordinated to the attempt to avoid war itself. The experience of the Second World War and the wars preceding it changed that, particularly the Spanish Civil War. The Nuremberg Tribunal confirmed that the Hague Regulations were customary international law and the Geneva conventions introduced an extensive expansion of the laws of war both in the detail of the rules that were to apply in armed conflicts between states and in the 'remarkable achievement' of Common Article 3 that was to apply to non-international armed conflicts.[82] Remarkable as it undoubtedly was, the process of negotiation and compromise left it open to a number of interpretations both at the time and subsequently such that states, particularly Britain and France, could argue that it did not apply to a large number of colonial conflicts but at the same time it gave the ICRC an opening through which to raise its concerns. However, the modern interpretation of Common Article 3 given in the commentaries on the 1949 Geneva conventions produced by the ICRC can be seen as different from how the article was conceived and came to be understood. The contemporary debate was deliberately imprecise on the type of internal armed conflict to which Common Article 3 would apply and silent on the modern understanding that the extension of the rules to non-international armed conflicts carried with them, as a matter of international law, rules on the conduct of hostilities based on the balance of military necessity and humanity. Both can be seen to be contingent outcomes. As will be seen, the ICRC's view on the type of conflicts to which Common Article 3 applied gradually came to be widely accepted but the British never fully accepted it. The records of the 1949 conferences also suggest that Common Article 3 had a quite limited scope. It is better understood as a humanitarian provision extending to international law, and so to all states that were parties to the conventions, basic municipal rules of protection recognized by 'civilised countries'. The persisting disagreements on the scope of the conflicts to which Common Article 3 applied and the omission of the connection to the laws of war regulating the conduct of hostilities in relation to non-international armed conflicts forms part of the argument for reinterpreting the area of overlap between the paradigms of armed conflict and law-enforcement. It calls into question the level of hostilities at which an armed conflict within the meaning of Common Article 3 should be seen to arise, particularly as the definition was deliberately imprecise, and whether this

[82] Best, *Humanity in Warfare* (n 9) 300.

should include insurrection and rebellion. Pushing the threshold higher reduces the weight of the permissive nature of the laws of war provided though the principle of military necessity which is one of the most apparent consequences of crossing the threshold into armed conflict. As will be seen in the next chapter, another feature of the overlap is that the law-enforcement paradigm was conceived as permitting a more extensive use of lethal force in the area of overlap through the exception to the right to life for quelling an insurrection.

5

The Law-enforcement Paradigm under International Law and the Right to Life in International Human Rights Law

At the same time that the international community was extending protection under the laws of war to persons who did not or no longer actively participated in non-international armed conflicts, it also took up the issue of the protection of individuals' human rights through international law. The initiatives to expand the scope of international law to these areas that had traditionally be regarded as sovereign rights were pursued separately: negotiations on the laws of war were arranged by the International Red Cross and held at Stockholm and then Geneva whilst the first steps towards international protection of human rights centred on the United Nations in New York. Although the subject matter would overlap, the laws of war and human rights were mostly kept in what had been the separate spheres of war and peace. Even the occasional glimpses of overlap, such as in the draft Preamble to the Civilian Convention, were lost by its deletion and the apparent separation of the paradigms of armed conflict and law-enforcement was reflected in the provision for derogation from human rights law in times of war. This chapter considers the development of the law-enforcement paradigm after 1945 through the creation of international human rights law. It includes the history of the drafting of the right to life in the International Covenant and the European Convention on Human Rights (ECHR)[1] and the application of it by the European Court of Human Rights (ECtHR) in law-enforcement. The history of the drafting of the main human rights instruments shows in explicit and implicit ways how much the use of lethal force by the State against rebels was accepted as an exception to the right to life: explicit in that it was part of the discussion on the drafting of the first instrument to be drafted, which became the International Covenant; and implicit in that there is no record of its discussion when the provision for insurrection was included in the draft exceptions to the ECHR. This implies that it was uncontroversial but it also results in an absence of background material that would assist in understanding whether 'insurrection' was thought to be autonomous or to have a particular meaning and what circumstances it was

[1] Convention for the Protection of Human Rights and Fundamental Freedoms (Rome, 4 November 1950).

thought to cover. This acceptance will be seen later to be in marked contrast to the absence of its use by states in cases brought before the ECtHR and illustrates the degree to which its non-use is a choice made by states. The first cases brought before the court in relation to the use of lethal force in military operations were cases in which the British army was acting in support of the police and the leading case, *McCann v United Kingdom*,[2] included consideration of rules of engagement and the elements of the justification of self-defence to an allegation of unlawful killing by state agents in law-enforcement. As will be seen in chapter seven, the judgment in the case then became the basis of future judgments on military operations in very different circumstances of internal armed conflict.

The main sources for the history of the drafting of the International Covenant and the ECHR are their *travaux préparatoires* – the official records of the negotiation of treaties – but there are also records of the negotiation of them by the British delegation and government departments. The *travaux préparatoires* of the ECHR were prepared by the Council of Europe. They were originally published in 1961–64 and kept confidential to the member states, the European Commission on Human Rights and the ECtHR but were approved for general publication in 1972 and republished in 1975.[3] They contain the full text of the registry of the Council of Europe's internal working documents and, in addition to them, the registry has produced summary notes on individual articles. There are summaries of all of the main rights and some other articles, except for article 2, the right to life, for which there is inexplicably no summary.[4] The *travaux préparatoires* of the ECHR show a close connection between the drafting of the ECHR and the early discussions on the drafting of an International Covenant, which was being prepared at the same time by the United Nations, to implement the Universal Declaration of Human Rights in a binding instrument. The UN had been working on the two documents in parallel but a decision was taken in 1948 to complete the non-binding Universal Declaration and to continue work on the International Covenant. Work that eventually led to the signing of the International Covenant of Civil and Political Rights in 1966. The *travaux préparatoires* for the International Covenant bring out a number of points about it and the ECHR. In particular, they show the extent of the discussions on the right to life or its exceptions and the number of different forums and constituencies which were involved. There is actually no record of any discussion in the *travaux préparatoires* of the ECHR to the right to life itself or its exceptions although they record that what became article 2.2(c) was modified during the drafting process to remove an additional exception for the defence of national security sites. The records of the drafting of the International Covenant do provide evidence of discussion of the right to life and a greater diversity of

[2] *McCann v United Kingdom* App no 18984/91 (1995) ECHR 31.

[3] Council of Europe, *Collected Edition of the 'Travaux Préparatoires'* (The Hague, Martinus Nijhoff, 1975).

[4] Explanatory note on the website of the registry of the Council of Europe. The notes provided include for example: Articles 1 (Obligation to respect Human Rights), 3 (Prohibition of torture) and 15 (Derogation in time of emergency).

proposed exceptions but also consistent objection to setting out a list of exceptions, particularly from the United States. In both cases there were significant divergences in approach between those who favoured a broad approach to the enumeration of the rights in the individual treaty on the basis that there would be detailed national implementation of the rights and those that insisted that, if the treaty was to be binding, it had to be definitive of the rights. Eventually, there were compromises in both cases but the different approaches were enshrined in the treaties themselves with the ECHR having a detailed set of exceptions and the International Covenant narrowing only slightly its broad wording.

Drafting the International Covenant and the ECHR

The United Nations had initially conceived of creating a bill of human rights and referred the drafting of it to the Economic and Social Council and the Commission on Human Rights. After the decision was made to press ahead with a non-binding declaration of rights – the Universal Declaration of Human Rights – and follow it with a second, binding instrument – the International Covenant – the early work continued in parallel. The Commission on Human Rights' work on the binding International Covenant began its initial phase in June 1947 and lasted until 21 May 1948, whilst the discussions on the Universal Declaration were still continuing.[5] There were a number of proposals made formally and informally for the initial draft and at the 1st Session of the Drafting Committee of the Human Rights Commission in June 1947 the UK delegation put forward a draft proposal for the right to life that simply provided that

> [i]t shall be unlawful to deprive any person of his life save in the execution of the sentence of a court following on his conviction of a crime for which this penalty is provided by law.[6]

The Second World War and its aftermath had led to a number of different groups and forums being set up to promote peace and unity in Europe. In May 1948, whilst work was continuing on the draft covenant at the United Nations, the first initiative for a European convention was taken by the European Movement, a non-governmental organisation created in 1947 to promote greater unity in Europe. At the same time that it was working on the idea, a Congress of Europe was held in The Hague attended by delegations from 18 nations and prominently supported by leading politicians. Among the discussions about the need for a new political order to ensure peace in Europe 'there also emerged the need to define a specifically European concept of human rights and of the relationship between citizens and the state in order to differentiate from the Universal Declaration of Human Rights

[5] MJ Bossuyt, *Guide to the "Travaux Préparatoires" of the International Covenant of Civil and Political Rights* (Dordrecht, Martinus Nijhoff, 1987) 113–25.
[6] ibid 113.

that was being drawn up at the same time'.[7] There was also a call for the creation of a European Court of Human Rights. These various initiatives led to the formation of the Council of Europe by ten European governments in consultation with the European Movement. Although a draft outline of a convention on human rights was prepared by the European Movement, the committee of ministers which was formed from the foreign ministers of each of the states in the council was reluctant to put human rights on the agenda for the first meeting of the assembly as it thought this would prejudice the position of the International Court of Justice and the United Nations.[8] However, the issue was taken up at the First Session of the Parliamentary Assembly of the Council of Europe and a list of fundamental freedoms was proposed based on the Universal Declaration and a collective guarantee given by member states. The Universal Declaration was adopted by a resolution of the General Assembly of the United Nations on 10 December 1948 and article 3 provides: 'Everyone has the right to life, liberty and the security of person'. On 30 August 1949, the legal committee of the assembly considered the draft and, after extensive deliberation, made amendments to some articles but none to the article on security of the person and it recommended that the committee of ministers draw up a draft convention. In November 1949 the committee of ministers accepted the proposal for a convention but appointed a committee of legal experts to prepare a draft convention directing that '[d]ue attention should be paid to the progress which has been achieved in this matter by the competent organs of the United Nations'.[9] It was expected at that time that the final text of a draft UN agreement would be prepared and put before the Economic and Social Council in March to May 1950 and then submitted to the General Assembly for approval in the Autumn 1950.[10]

At the United Nations, the Second Session of the Drafting Committee was held at about the same time that the European Movement raised the issue of a European Covenant and the wording of the draft International Covenant was amended slightly by the UN Secretariat for submission to the Commission of Human Rights. The draft was accompanied by a list of possible exceptions drawn up from suggestions made by states. The exceptions (and their proposers) were:

1. Suppression of rebellion or riot (Union of South Africa);
   Deprivation of life by the military or state officers in a national emergency (USA);
2. Self-defence and defence of another (Union of South Africa and USA);
3. Killing in attempting to effect arrests for certain offences (Union of South Africa);

[7] The Congress of Europe in The Hague (7–10 May 1948), 'The European Court of Human Rights'.

[8] *Council of Europe, Travaux Préparatoires*, Vol I – Preparatory Commission of the Council of Europe, Committee of Ministers, Consultative Assembly: 11 May–8 September 1949, 4.

[9] ibid Vol. II – Consultative Assembly, Second Session of the Committee of Ministers, Standing Committee of the Assembly: 10 August–18 November 1949, 290.

[10] UN Commission on Human Rights, 'Report of the Fifth Session of the Commission of Human Rights to the Economic and Social Council', dated 23 June 1949, 12.

4. Killing by accident (USA);
5. Killing for violation of honour (USA);
6. Killing of persons caught in the commission of a felony (USA);
7. Killing to prevent an escape (USA);
8. Killing by medical operation in absence of gross negligence or malpractice (USA);
9. Killing through a voluntary medical operation (USA);
10. Killing by officers of the law to prevent the commission of a crime (USA);
11. Killing by officers of the law in a local emergency (USA);
12. Killing by a member of the military in time of war (USA).[11]

Following circulation of the draft, the British cabinet committee responsible for overseeing the negotiations within government coordinated a review of the draft covenant in order to produce a briefing note for the British delegation at the United Nations. In its note, the Home Office commented on which of the exceptions to the article on the right to life were necessary as a matter of English law to cover killings that were considered to be justifiable or excusable homicide. It listed killings: in defence of the person or property from unlawful violence; in attempting to effect an arrest or prevent an escape; in prevention of the commission of a felony by open force – felonies were the English law category of serious offences; and in order to quell a riot. It said that these would cover the limitations numbered 1, 2, 3, 6, 7, 10 and 11 in the Secretariat's list. In relation to exception 1, it suggested that the US proposal was not sufficient as, under English law, the duty to suppress a riot extended to ordinary citizens as well as state officers. It would appear that the Home Office thought that the suppression of a rebellion fell within the exception for the prevention of a felony by open force rather than requiring an explicit reference to insurrection, rebellion or levying war against the King.[12] The department also questioned whether the exception for killings in time of war was relevant as the covenant would not extend to the military in time of war. It added that, if the proposed exception were to be included, the proposed wording was too wide as not all killings in war were lawful and that it should be limited to 'circumstances where military operations are in progress'.[13] The references to killings in the prevention of a felony by open force and military operations would implicitly support the notion that killings carried out in repelling force with force would be justifiable. However, when the internal Foreign Office briefing note for the delegation was produced, this was made explicit as insurrection was added to the list of exceptions.[14] This was probably for the benefit of, or at the suggestion of,

[11] Bossuyt, *Travaux Préparatoires of the ICCPR* (1987) (n 5) 114 – the anomolous numbering is in the original.

[12] TNA, CAB 134/424, IOC (HR) (49)9, 'Cabinet Steering Committee on International Organizations, Working Party on Human Rights', Draft Covenant on Human Rights, Observations by the Home Office, dated 14 April 1949.

[13] ibid addendum, dated 20 April 1949.

[14] TNA, CAB 134/424, IOC (HR)(49)13, 'Cabinet Steering Committee on International Organizations, Working Party on Human Rights', Fourth Session of the Human Rights Commission, dated 26 April 1949.

the Colonial Office as there is no record in the various minutes of the War Office having been consulted.

The Commission on Human Rights discussed the draft and the UN *travaux préparatoires* recorded that '[t]here was general agreement regarding the importance of safeguarding the right of everyone to life through the covenant although various opinions were held as to how the right should be formulated'. It also noted that there were differing views on whether a list of exceptions should be included setting out when the taking of life was justified.[15] The United Kingdom, Lebanon, Australia and India were among those that thought that the scope of the right should be defined as closely as possible. Others, including the Soviet Union, the United States, France, Chile and the Soviet Republic of Ukraine, thought that a list of exceptions would always be incomplete and convey the idea that the exceptions were more important than the right. Some, including the United States and the Soviet Union, were also concerned that a provision with exceptions might be seen as authorising killing rather than safeguarding the right to life. The notes of the British delegation are rather more candid about the discussion. The British regarded the draft article as unsatisfactory and had formally reserved its position. The main British delegate, Miss Marguerite Bowie, sent a report to the Foreign Office noting several points that she thought needed to be understood for future discussions, in particular that 'the rather brutal drafting using the word "killings" roused considerable opposition' and 'the suggestion that "killings" might be justified in defence of property was rejected by everyone else'. The exception for killings in time of war was also opposed but appeared to be accepted as part of the derogations clause.[16]

The Commission of Human Rights met again for its Fifth Session from 9 May to 20 June 1949 to discuss the draft covenant and during the course of the session the United Kingdom made four drafting proposals to specify the exceptions but none of them was voted upon. The four clauses were essentially variants of one form and even at this stage very similar to what would become article 2 of the ECHR but with an additional exception for the protection of national security sites. Following the discussions, the Secretary General forwarded a report of the session and a draft International Covenant to member states for comments to be received by 1 January 1950. The right to life appeared in article 5 of it simply as 'No one shall be deprived of his life'. There was provision made in article 5 for capital punishment but, otherwise, there were no exceptions. Derogations under the covenant were permitted '[i]n time of war or other public emergency threatening the interests of the people' but the provision for exclusions to derogation was left blank.[17] Extracts of the report were also sent to the Council of Europe. In internal discussion, the British noted that 'the present text is meaningless'

[15] Bossuyt, *Travaux Préparatoires of the ICCPR* (n 5) 115.

[16] TNA, FO 371/72810, IOC (49) 163, 'Report on the Fifth Session of the Commission on Human Rights' by Marguerite Bowie, 5.

[17] UN Commission on Human Rights, 'Report of the Fifth Session of the Commission of Human Rights', 12 and 29.

and said it was recognized as such in the commission.[18] The UK supported by Australia, Denmark, France and Lebanon then submitted comments on the draft International Covenant once again including the previous proposals for exceptions and a derogation for killings in time of war.[19]

Linking the Drafting of the International Covenant to the ECHR

When the committee of experts appointed to draft the European convention met in February 1950, the UK expert, Sir Oscar Dowson – a former Legal Adviser to the Home Office – proposed amendments to the right to life, among other rights. The Legal Adviser is the most senior legal official in the Home Office and generally regarded as one of the most senior legal advisors to the British government. According to the *travaux préparatoires*, these were the same as those in the then latest draft of the International Covenant, presumably this is how the British officials described them.[20] However, this is somewhat misleading – a number of similar forms of exception clause had indeed been proposed by the United Kingdom at the United Nations but none were voted upon and there were no exceptions to the right to life in the draft.[21] There is then no record of discussion of the right to life in the committee of experts on the ECHR on 15 February 1950 but after these meetings the revised draft of the convention provided simply 'Everyone has the right to life, liberty and security of person'.[22]

The meetings of the committee of experts revealed similar differences of approach to the drafting of the convention as had been seen at the United Nations. France was the main supporter of a form that provided the principle of each right and required that the rights were to be enacted in the domestic law of the member states. Others, particularly the UK and the Netherlands, argued for more detailed definitions of rights to be included in the convention itself.[23] In order to reflect the differences of opinion, the committee of experts drew up alternative 'Preliminary Draft Conventions', one with the wording on the right to life as proposed by the UK and the other contained the older wording derived from the Universal Declaration. The Report of the Committee of Experts contained an extensive commentary on the version based on the Universal Declaration but said that the articles on the right to life and the prohibition on torture in the detailed

[18] TNA, CAB 134/424, IOC (HR)(49)16, 'Cabinet Steering Committee on International Organizations, Working Party on Human Rights', Foreign Office memo, dated 16 July 1949.

[19] *Council of Europe, Travaux Préparatoires*, Vol III – Committee of Experts 2 February–10 March 1950, 158.

[20] ibid 186.

[21] Bossuyt, *Travaux Préparatoires of the ICCPR* (n 5) 116.

[22] *Council of Europe, Travaux Préparatoires*, Vol III, (n 19) 236.

[23] ibid 288.

form 'require no comment'.[24] The Third Session of the Committee of Ministers was then held on 1 April 1950 and the committee decided to refer the issue on form of the convention to a conference of high officials 'to prepare the ground for the political decisions to be taken by the Committee of Ministers', adding that 'it would be helpful if the Committee had a single text to consider'.[25]

At the time that the committee of ministers was meeting and convening a conference of senior officials, the Commission of Human Rights, Sixth Session was also meeting in New York, a session that lasted from 27 March to 19 May 1950. During the session, several versions of the more detailed form were proposed by the British and others and eventually a form of it was voted on but not adopted by five votes to five with four abstentions. Following the meetings and votes, the Report on the Sixth Session of the Commission of Human Rights, dated 29 May 1950 contained a revised form of draft covenant and included records of national comments including the UK's and other countries' comment that the article required a list of exceptions along the lines proposed by the UK and that article 2 should include a derogation for lawful acts of war. However, the right to life included in the draft covenant attached to the report was limited to the simple statement that 'Everyone's right to life shall be protected by law' and it contained three exceptions for 'the execution of a sentence of a court, or in self-defence, or in the case of enforcement measures authorized by the Charter' and a provision on capital punishment.[26] An internal briefing note for the British delegation explained how unsatisfactory this was from a British point of view as it did not reflect the English legal systems approach to justified killing. In addition, the meaning of the reference to 'self-defence' was quite different in the French text. It used the term 'défense légitime' which was thought to cover lawful acts of war but 'it is extremely doubtful whether "self-defence" in the context of [the article] is sufficient to cover lawful acts of war'.[27]

Just after the report of the proceedings at the UN was published, the Committee of Senior Officials of the Council of Europe met for the first time. At a meeting on 8 June 1950 the UK representative, Mr S Hoare, a Deputy Under-Secretary at the Home Office, explained that the draft text of the detailed form of the convention was based on the work done at the UN on the International Covenant. The initial view taken at the committee of senior officials was that it was impossible to combine the two versions of the rights and freedoms as they were based on 'entirely different systems' but the officials were aware of the request to produce a

[24] ibid Vol IV – Third and Fourth Sessions of the Committee of Ministers, Conference of Senior Officials, 30 March–17 June 1950, 32.

[25] ibid 84.

[26] UN Commission on Human Rights, 'Report of the Sixth Session, 27 March–19 May 1950', dated 29 May 1950.

[27] TNA, CAB 134/424, IOC (HR)(49)16, 'Cabinet Steering Committee on International Organizations, Working Party on Human Rights', Draft Brief on Amendments to the First Eighteen Articles of the Draft Covenant on Human Rights, dated 10 July 1951.

single text.[28] There was extensive discussion of the approach to various questions and particular articles, including whether to include a court and access to it and articles that were controversial such as the right to vote, but there is no mention of the right to life. After much discussion the officials voted on the form and a majority were for the detailed draft following the British approach. A new single draft text was then prepared for the conference of senior officials and a draft report. It recorded that the draft covenant was based on the decisions of the majority of senior officials although the states representing the majority varied between different clauses. It also contained a minor amendment to the exception to the right to life omitting the exception for the protection of national security sites. Further drafts were prepared and discussed by the committee of senior officials, the foreign ministers, the legal committee and sub-committee of the committee of ministers but there were only minor changes made to the right to life and the provision for derogation in time of war or national emergency.[29] The sub-committee of the committee of ministers could not, however, agree on the inclusion of a 'colonial clause' that would extend the rights contained in the convention to the colonies of the member states.

Having been provided with a single draft as they had requested, the committee of ministers met and discussed points that had not been agreed by the advisors. In particular they discussed five open points, including the 'colonial clause' which extended the application of the convention to the colonies of member states, but there was no discussion of the right to life or derogation. The form of draft convention adopted by the committee of ministers on 7 August 1950 included some minor drafting changes from the previous draft and was sent to the Consultative Assembly. On the right to life, it provided:

> Art. 2 1) Everyone's right to life shall be protected by law. No one shall be deprived of his life intentionally, save in the execution of a sentence of the court following his conviction of a crime for which this penalty is provided by law.
>
> 2) Deprivation of life shall not be regarded as inflicted in contravention of this Article when it results from the use of force which is not more than is absolutely necessary:
>
> (a) in defence of any person from unlawful violence;
> (b) in order to effect lawful arrest or to prevent an escape from lawful custody;
> (c) in action lawfully taken for the purpose of quelling a riot or insurrection.
>
> Art 15 1) In time of war or other public emergency threatening the life of the nation a State may take measures derogating from its obligations under this Convention to the extent strictly required by the exigencies of the situation, provided that such measures are not inconsistent with its other obligations under international law.
>
> 2) No derogation from article 2, except in respect of deaths resulting from lawful acts of war, or from Articles 3, 4 (para 1) and 7 can be made under this provision.[30]

[28] *Council of Europe, Travaux Préparatoires*, Vol IV, (n 24) 100–102.

[29] ibid Vol V – Legal Committee, Ad Hoc Joint Committee, Committee of Ministers, Consultative Assembly, 23 June–28 August 1950, 40.

[30] ibid 120.

This is very close to the final form although there were to be some minor drafting changes made before the convention was signed. Within the record of the proceedings, a glimpse of the atmosphere is given by the excerpts of speeches and remarks that were made in the various stages of discussion. The initial focus seems to have been on the prevention of states slipping into totalitarianism through the progressive removal of democratic rights as had happened in Nazi Germany and the potential for newly liberated states to slide back into totalitarianism – 'a warning bell against another Dachau' was one phrase that was used.[31] Over the short time of the drafting, there was also a growing awareness of the Cold War and a determination to be seen to entrench human rights as part of the internal and external political battle against communism. At the assembly meetings in August 1950, a French delegate drew attention to the danger of 'cold' wars turning into 'hot' wars and the provisions of international law allowing exceptional rules in wartime against nationals of enemy countries, including 'arrest, internment … and special penalties for espionage, sabotage etc' and put his remarks in the context of the conflicts in Greece and Korea. He suggested that greater powers to suspend the liberties of foreign nationals might be called for but made no mention of the adequacy, or otherwise, of the exceptions to the right to life in such circumstances.[32] Prior to signing, the UK also noted the possibility of conflict with the UN agreement under discussion and in the discussions it was suggested that the European convention might be stricter than was possible within the wider community of the United Nations.[33] The convention was signed on 4 November 1950.

Progress on the UN's International Covenant slowed considerably after 1950 as tensions increased in the Cold War and an ideological and political battle was fought over decolonization and the scope of individual and collective rights. The draft International Covenant was discussed by the Third Committee of the General Assembly, 5th Fifth in December 1950 and the record includes a revised list of exceptions to the right to life including those in the European convention and several others, together with a list of proposers.[34] The Commission of Human Rights met for its Eighth Session in 1952 and the UK proposed once again a similar form of exceptions clause to those presented previously. Notably, the wording about the 'absolute necessity' of the use of force that was in the previous drafts and in the final form of the ECHR (and has since been expressed as the particular basis for decisions by the ECtHR) had been moderated to that which was 'necessary' but the proposal was not voted upon. The United States and India also made drafting proposals around the wording for self-defence and India proposed again

[31] ibid Vol II, (n 9) 16 and 240.

[32] ibid Vol VI – Consultative Assembly, 14.

[33] ibid Vol VII – Standing Committee of the Consultative Assembly, Confirmed Consultative Assembly, Committee of Experts, Committee of Ministers, Legal Committee 3 November 1950–15 May 1951, 30.

[34] Bossuyt, *Travaux Préparatoires of the ICCPR* (n 5) 116.

an exception for 'circumstances of grave civil commotion'. None were adopted. The drafting process went on until 16 April 1954 when the Commission on Human Rights sent two draft covenants to the Economic and Social Council and then onto the Third Committee of the General Assembly. The Third Committee, Twelfth Session met in 1957 to discuss the drafts and, in relation to the right to life, the main provision that was discussed again was in relation to the form of the right and whether an affirmation of the inherent right to life was being included as a specific protection or just a declaratory statement.

Throughout the discussions at the Fifth Session (1949), the Sixth Session (1950) and the Eighth Session (1952) there was a persistent view among some states that it would be preferable not to list exceptions but to affirm that 'no one shall be arbitrarily deprived of his life'. However, a United States' proposal on this was rejected in 1949. The final form of the right in the International Covenant emerged gradually through the sessions. A formulation that 'No one may deprive another person of his life' was adopted in 1949 and subsequent attempts in 1950 to reinsert the word 'arbitrarily', made by the United States, or 'intentionally', made by the United Kingdom, were rejected in 1950. The limitation of the clause to 'intentional' killings had been a recurrent theme of British comments as it was thought that the clause should not extend to accidental deaths and the word was included in article 2 of the ECHR.[35] In 1952 a further proposal by the United States and Chile for the wording 'no one shall be arbitrarily deprived of his life' was adopted but the objection made to this wording continued at the Ninth Session (1954) and the Twelfth Session (1957). When the formulation was discussed again, the United Kingdom and Australia argued once again that the right was vague as the meaning of 'arbitrarily' was not clear. Discussion of it revealed that different states had different interpretations of it thinking it meant 'illegally' or 'unjustly', or both, and the United Kingdom again pointed out that it included accidental death. The United States and some other states saw no objection. The wording was re-adopted in 1957 by 46 votes to 12 with 14 abstentions. A proposal by the Netherlands at the Twelfth Session in 1957 to use the ECHR wording was rejected by 50 votes to 9 with 11 abstentions. Following the 1957 votes, the final form was settled and became article 6 of the International Covenant on Civil and Political Rights (ICCPR), it provides:

> 1. Every human being has the inherent right to life. This right shall be protected by law. No one shall be arbitrarily deprived of his life.

The International Covenant itself was eventually signed in 1966 and entered into force in 1976.

[35] TNA, CAB 134/424, IOC (HR)(49)9, 'Cabinet Steering Committee on International Organizations, Working Party on Human Rights', Draft Covenant on Human Rights, Observations by the Home Office, dated 14 April 1949.

The Right to Life in the International Covenant and the ECHR

The history of the drafting of the right to life in the ECHR and the International Covenant reveals a number of interesting points relating to it and its interpretation:

First, as a matter of interpretation, there is no guidance available from the *travaux préparatoires* of the ECHR to confirm the meaning of the exceptions but the British records show how they conceived of the exceptions as covering the exceptions to homicide contained in English criminal law. However, the reference to 'légitime défense' in the French text was thought to incorporate a much wider scope than 'self-defence' that included *jus ad bellum*, for example, it is used in the French text of article 51 of the UN Charter as the exception for the prohibition on the use of force by states in international relations.[36] There were reservations about whether it was broad enough to include lawful acts of war but the wider meaning will be seen later to have some resonance in the later case law of the court although it does not seem to have been based on this difference in language.

Second, there is no evidence that the exceptions to the right to life that were agreed in the ECHR were seen as controversial other than the proposed exception for the protection of national security sites which was removed from the draft. It does, however, provide an interesting link to the emergency laws that were used in British colonial conflicts which will explored in the next chapter. The exception for the defence of property had been removed prior to submission of the exceptions after receiving no support in the discussions at the United Nations. In relation to the exceptions for riot and insurrection, the *travaux préparatoires* of the International Covenant show that there was general support from members, including the United States, the Soviet Union, the United Kingdom and France, for an exception in circumstances that might generically be called violent internal conflict and that this was separate from the right of self-defence. There is no particular evidence available to explain why the exception in the ECHR does not include rebellion. It had been raised in the list of potential exceptions produced as part of the initial drafting of the International Covenant and, as has been seen, would have been part of the traditional legal hierarchy of internal armed conflict as understood at the time. However, it is possible to see that, as a matter of common law that formed the basis of the British and Commonwealth governments' approach to the drafts, insurrection was a more particular legal term and it could be said that every rebellion included insurrection. It may also be because the word 'insurrection' is the same in the French text.

Third, in relation to the right to life in time of war and other public emergencies, it was originally proposed in the initial drafting sessions of the International Covenant that the right to life should not apply in relation to killing by lawful

[36] UN Commission on Human Rights, 'Report of the Sixth Session, 27 March–19 May 1950, Supplement No 5' (Lake Success, New York) 25.

acts of war. However, following objections to this, the approach moved to one of derogation. This led to some important distinctions between the ECHR and the International Covenant. First, it raises a question of interpretation as to the meaning of 'in time of war' in the ECHR and brings in the issue of territorial application of the convention. The ECHR requires a derogation from the right in time of war whereas lawful acts of war are taken to fall outside of the right to life in the International Covenant by virtue of their not being 'arbitrary', at least to the extent that they are not in violation of international humanitarian law.[37] Similarly, in order to be lawful, killings by state agents would have not to be 'arbitrary' under the International Covenant but, under the ECHR, they have to fall under one of the exceptions in article 2.2. The judicial interpretation of these provisions will be considered further below but, despite the differences in the provisions and their negotiating histories, in general it is thought that the exceptions to the right to life in the ECHR will also apply to the International Covenant.[38] There was one potential difference in that it was thought that the UN Human Rights Committee might deem killings in the course of a war fought contrary to the prohibition on the use of force under the UN Charter to be a violation of the individual right to life.[39] This has now been confirmed by the committee in their recent guidance that 'States parties engaged in acts of aggression as defined in international law, resulting in deprivation of life, violate *ipso facto* article 6 of the Covenant'.[40] In addition, in relation to killing by state agents, 'arbitrary' may cover more than 'intentional killing'.[41] The committee of experts who looked at the issue of consistency between the treaties for the committee of ministers of the Council of Europe 'concurred … that arbitrary deprivation of life contained elements of *unlawfulness* and *injustice*, as well as those of *capriciousness* and *unreasonableness*'.[42] However, the general view taken in the literature is still that the cases of permissible deprivation of life by state organs listed in article 2(2) of ECHR cannot be viewed as arbitrary within the meaning of article 6(1) of the International Covenant.[43]

Fourth, given the commonality of some of the main state actors, it is reasonable to assume that the rights were intended to be the same in substance. There was a self-view that the Europeans were able to adopt a more rigorous form of rights than the UN but there is no indication that this was a particular issue for the right to life. The forms of the articles then came down to different views and negotiation, and resulted in very different forms. This may suggest that the widely-held view

[37] M Nowak, *UN Covenant on Civil and Political Rights, CCPR Commentary* (Kekl, Germany, NP Engel, 2005) 126; UN HRC, 'General comment No 36: Article 6, Right to Life (2018)' §64.

[38] ibid 128.

[39] ibid 125–26.

[40] UN HRC, 'General comment No 36: Article 6, Right to Life (2018)' §70.

[41] S Joseph and M Castan, *The International Covenant on Civil and Political Rights: Cases, Materials and Commentary* (Oxford, Oxford University Press, 2013) 170.

[42] Nowak, *CCPR Commentary*, (2005) (n 37) 128.

[43] W Schabas, 'The Right to Life' in A Clapham and P Gaeta (eds), *The Oxford Handbook of International Law in Armed Conflict* (Oxford, Oxford University Press, 2014) 368.

that they are still in substance the same is the product of an ideological stand-point that human rights are universal rather than relying on conventional legal interpretation. This requires the courts and commentators to stretch or even ignore the normal meaning of words to maintain consistency and, as will be seen in the next section, in some cases to develop the rights.

Applying the ECHR

Although the ECHR was signed in 1950, it was slow to develop. The European Commission was formed in 1954 and it received its first complaint in 1958. It was made against the UK by Greece over the detention of suspects in the insurgency in Cyprus. The ECtHR was created in 1959 and Britain submitted to it in 1966. There were some early cases brought against Britain in relation to the Troubles in Northern Ireland in the 1970s and 80s including cases on the treatment of detainees in internment and one case on riot. However, the starting point for any consideration of the Court's jurisprudence on the use of lethal force is *McCann v United Kingdom* as it was the first case in which the Court fully considered the issue and it has repeatedly returned to the judgment as a source for its interpretation of article 2.

McCann concerned the killing of three members of the Irish Republican Army (IRA) in Gibraltar by members of British special forces in 1988 during what the authorities thought was an attempt to detonate a car bomb. It established five points of law explicitly and arguably one more. In its explanation of the applicable law, the court decided, first, that the provisions of article 2 should be strictly construed and that they should be interpreted and applied so as to make its safeguards practical and effective. Second, that the standard of 'absolute necessity' 'indicates that a stricter and more compelling test of necessity' than applied to the rights in articles 8 to 11 of the ECHR and '[i]n particular the force used must be strictly proportionate to the achievement of the aims set out in sub-paragraphs 2 (a), (b) and (c) of Article 2'. Third, that in considering an operation of the type mounted in Gibraltar, the court must consider whether 'the anti-terrorist operation was planned and controlled by the authorities so as to minimise, to the greatest extent possible, recourse to lethal force'. Fourth, that the protection of the right to life includes the lives of the security forces. Fifth, that the self-defence rules of engagement issued to the soldiers reflected the substance of English law and the ECHR convention. More arguably, there may also be a principle that a killing in self-defence cannot be premeditated. Although this was not within the court's description of the applicable law, it considered at some length the applicants' contention that the killings had been premeditated but found that they were not. In rejecting the applicants' case, the court referred to an earlier judgment of the commission that found that

> this provision (art 2-2) extends to, but is not concerned exclusively with, intentional killing. As the Commission has pointed out, the text of Article 2 (art 2), read as a whole, demonstrates that paragraph 2 (art 2-2) does not primarily define instances where it

> is permitted intentionally to kill an individual, but describes the situations where it is permitted to 'use force' which *may result*, as an *unintended outcome*, in the deprivation of life[44] [emphasis added]

This is a confusing passage as its interpretation of article 2 runs directly against the text of the article but it has been used repeatedly in subsequent judgments. The prohibition in the second sentence of article 2.1 refers only to intentional killing and logically article 2.2 would set out exceptions which would be required only if a killing would otherwise have fallen within the prohibition, that is it was intentional. The reference to 'intentional' deprivations of life was originally included to address a concern that without it the positive statement of the right to life would result in the state being responsible for accidental deaths.[45] However, by referring to 'unintended outcomes' the court is saying that a death may be the unintended result of lethal force used for one of the purposes set out in article 2.2. It is not clear which exceptions 'may' result in an unintended outcome but if it were correct, the particular exception would be unnecessary as the person never 'intended' to kill, only to act in self-defence, make an arrest, etc.

To understand this particular point it is necessary to look further back as the passage quoted above had been used by the European Commission on Human Rights in relation to a case of riot in Northern Ireland. During the riot, a soldier fired a baton round at an adult rioter but, as the soldier fired, he was hit by stones thrown by the rioters, missed his target and killed a boy of 13, Brian Stewart.[46] Baton rounds are made of plastic and were designed to be used in riot control as a non-lethal alternative to live ammunition. The commission were grappling with a concern that the exceptions should not be seen as setting out circumstances where killing was permitted and the issue that if the prohibition in article 2 was construed as only meaning intentional killing, it did not cover the incident at all as, in the ordinary meaning of the word, the soldier did not intend to kill the boy.[47] The problem in this situation arose from the addition of the word 'intentionally' in article 2.1 and how a court interprets it. 'Intention' is an element of the crime of murder in English law and there were different approaches that an English or Northern Irish court could have taken in the circumstances. One approach would be to apply a doctrine known as 'transferred fault' which addresses the situation where a person intended to injure one person and for whatever reason injured or killed another. It allows the law to avoid the consequence that the striker did not 'intend' to injure the second person in the ordinary sense of the word and operates by transferring both the fault and any defence to it.[48] It is not clear how it was dealt

[44] *McCann v United Kingdom* (n 2) §§146–47, 149, 194, 192, 156 and 148 respectively.

[45] TNA, CAB 134/424, 'Cabinet Steering Committee on International Organisations', Addendum to IOC(HR)(49) 9 (Home Office Observations on the Draft Covenant of Human Rights), dated 20 April 1949.

[46] *Stewart v United Kingdom* App no 10044/82 (1984) EHRR 453.

[47] The *Concise Oxford English Dictionary* defines 'intentional' as 'done on purpose; deliberate'.

[48] J Horder, *Ashworth's Principles of Criminal Law* (Oxford, Oxford University Press, 2016) 212.

with in the proceedings in Northern Ireland, the proceedings took the form of an inquest and the jury gave an open verdict – one that is chosen where there is insufficient evidence for any other verdict. In Northern Ireland at that time, a coroner could only give an open verdict if he or she believed that there was no-one who could be held responsible for the death as otherwise they had to make findings of fact and leave the matter of a prosecution to the Director of Public Prosecutions in Northern Ireland.[49] Nonetheless, despite not being held responsible, the government paid compensation to the boy's mother. When the case came before the Commission, in order to avoid the problem of 'intent', they interpreted article 2.1 as containing a positive obligation on the state that was not limited to intentional killing and based it on reasoning that went against the construction of article 2.1 and 2.2.[50] This passage then became a justification for a wider reading of the right to life and was simply repeated in subsequent cases. This is a potentially important extension in the context of the use of lethal force to quell an insurrection as it could bring persons other than the person targeted within the scope of the exception under article 2.2(c) of the ECHR where they would otherwise have been excluded by the word 'intentionally'. By doing so, it creates a link to the concept of collateral damage which is one of the features of proportionality under the laws of war, as will be discussed further in the final chapter.

The *McCann* case also established that the English law standard of self-defence was consistent with the terms of article 2 even though it uses different terminology by referring to 'reasonably justifiable', 'reasonable necessity' or a similar phrase rather than being 'absolutely necessary'.[51] The argument has been made on a number of occasions that English law and the ECHR have to be consistent and are not.[52] The debate usually focuses on the extent to which the test of necessity is objective or subjective – does the act have to be reasonable in the circumstances as they actually were or only as the defendant believed them to be? However, the debate on consistency raises an issue of what is called a category mistake in that it applies the meaning from one body of law to another.[53] Here the potential category mistake is that the courts are seeking to establish the rights of a victim under international human rights law by reference to the rights of the defendant under municipal criminal law. Not only are these different regimes of law with different internal rules, the rights also relate to different persons. Theoretically, as these rights are in separate categories, it should be possible for a state to be in violation of the right to life even though no-one is guilty of a criminal offence. This is

[49] M Urban, *Big Boys' Rules: The SAS and the Secret Struggle Against the IRA* (London: Faber & Faber, 1992) 79.

[50] This was a change from the Commission's previous position that an unintentional killing could not be grounds for a claim under Art 2 – *Stewart v United Kingdom* (n 46) 167.

[51] The phrase 'reasonably justifiable' was the standard in Gibraltar under its constitution but the same principle has been applied in other cases – eg *R (Bennett) v HM Coroner for Inner South London* [2006] EWHC Admin 196, QBD, §25–27.

[52] D Ormerod and K Laird, *Smith and Hogan's Criminal Law* (Oxford, Oxford University Press, 2015) 437–38.

[53] JD Ohlin and L May, *Necessity in International Law* (Oxford, Oxford University Pres, 2016) 137.

the position in English law where, for example, a person may not be guilty of the criminal offence of murder but may be liable in tort for the killing.[54] However, by combining the categories, the ECtHR may be left in the position that, as no state agent is criminally liable, the state is not liable. To address this potential outcome the court has implied additional rights under article 2 – in particular the requirement for an operation to be planned and controlled by the authorities 'so as to minimise, to the greatest extent possible, recourse to lethal force'.[55] Whilst I think that there is a form of category mistake in the court's practice, it is also one that is embedded in the drafting of the ECHR. The exceptions to the right to life proposed by the British delegation which were to become article 2.2 were originally based on what the law considered to be justified or excusable homicide.[56] It is an example of where municipal law has itself had to deal with the problem of conflicting rights.[57] In that case they were rights between individuals but human rights law is about the relationship between the individual and the state. What then happened is that international human rights law developed separately from municipal criminal law. This can be seen both from the original negotiations at the United Nations in which the English law exception for the defence of property was excluded, and also from the judicial development of the exception for self-defence by the ECtHR.

Conclusion

The period after the Second World War saw the development of a new paradigm of law-enforcement that combined municipal law and international law. Prior to that law-enforcement was a matter of sovereign rights that was based in municipal criminal law but it also protected, among other things, the lives of individuals. These two elements were combined in the negotiation of what became the ECHR and the International Covenant. The drafting of the treaties began with a simple expression of a right to life and a list of 12 exceptions proposed by various countries at the discussions at the United Nations on the International Covenant but gradually became a more limited set covering capital punishment and the use of force in self-defence, arrest or the prevention of escape from custody, and the quelling of a riot or insurrection that is contained in article 2 of the ECHR. The draft of the International Covenant developed more slowly but eventually took a different form which prohibited the arbitrary deprivation of life. Although the form of the right can be seen to develop through the *travaux préparatoires* for the International Covenant and the ECHR, they give no detailed guidance on what

[54] Ormerod and Laird, *Smith and Hogan's Criminal Law* (2015) (n 52) 439.

[55] *McCann v United Kingdom* (n 2) §194.

[56] TNA, CAB 134/424, Addendum to IOC(HR) (49) 9 (Home Office Observations on the Draft Covenant of Human Rights), dated 20 April 1949.

[57] Horder, *Ashworth's Principles of Criminal Law* (2016) (n 48) 132.

was understood by the exceptions. The British records show, however, how they conceived of these exceptions as covering killings that were treated as justified or excusable homicide under English criminal law. Once additional exceptions that might also have been covered by English law had been removed, in particular an exception for the defence of property, there is no evidence in the records that the exceptions to the right to life that remained were seen as controversial. Furthermore, in relation to the exceptions for riot and insurrection, the *travaux préparatoires* of the International Covenant show that there was general support from members, including the United States, the Soviet Union, the United Kingdom and France, for an exception in circumstances of internal disturbances and that this was separate from the right of self-defence. The commonality of the main states involved in the negotiation of the two treaties in their early stages as well as the subject matter have resulted in the different formulations of the right to life being seen as consistent. A killing that falls within the exceptions in the ECHR is generally seen as not 'arbitrary' within the meaning of the right to life under the International Covenant but, in order for the reverse to be true, it must either fall within one of the exceptions under the ECHR or into the derogation for lawful acts of war.

The ECtHR has developed the interpretation of the exceptions to the right to life in cases involving the use of lethal force by state agents through a framework it first set out in *McCann*. It has three main elements: any use of force must be no more than absolutely necessary for one or more of the purposes set out in paragraphs (a) to (c) of article 2.2; 'absolute necessity' is a stricter and more compelling test of necessity; and that the force used must also be 'strictly proportionate' to the achievement of the aims set out in subparagraphs (a), (b) and (c). Although the case concerned a killing carried out by soldiers and included consideration of their rules on engagement, the operation in which they were involved was conducted within a law-enforcement environment and the court's approach to more war-like military operations will be considered in chapter seven. The meaning of the exception for insurrection in the ECHR, however, remains unexplored, in particular whether it has an autonomous meaning. The evidence presented here makes it clearer what the British understood by it and how it fitted into municipal law in the United Kingdom but there is little more through which to understand it in the context of international law. It is clear though how much the British government shaped the drafting of the exceptions and how it was satisfied that homicides that were lawfully justified under English law would not be in breach of the ECHR, except for killings in defence of property which remains an exception to crimes of violence under English law. None of this is to say, of course, that the court is bound by this understanding but it helps to support an argument about how the various exceptions were intended to operate individually and together. The exclusion of property appears to have been a common view amongst the states on the UN Commission on Human Rights that were drafting the International Covenant and was seen again in the British and US rules of engagement in relation to looting in Iraq which excluded opening fire in defence of property. The extent of British involvement and the level of confidence that they seemed to have in the drafting of the exceptions is then part of the overall picture in which it will be seen Britain, and other states, have chosen to avoid using the exception for insurrection that they created. Before that, however, the practical application and development of the paradigm of armed conflict will be further explained and brought up-to-date in the next chapter.

6

Choosing Paradigms: The Selectivity of the Protection of Civilians and Insurgents in Internal Armed Conflicts

The initiatives to develop international law in the aftermath of the Second World War in the fields of armed conflict and human rights were conceived as a response to the internal and international conditions leading up to and during the war. They involved lengthy negotiations between states but also influential non-state actors, primarily the ICRC. The treaties they produced, which formed the basis of the paradigms of armed conflict and law-enforcement, involved compromises by states that left some of the provisions ambiguous, sometimes deliberately so in order that states could agree to them. This, in turn, allowed and continues to allow the continuation of the contestation – or selectivity – of the application of the laws of war to internal armed conflicts both in practice and in historical works.

This chapter considers how the paradigm of armed conflict continued to develop after the signing of the Geneva conventions as a matter of law and in military theory and practice. Military theory and practice can be seen through the development of the strategy of counter-insurgency in response to the increase in internal armed conflicts and the changing character of war. At the same time, many argued that Common Article 3 should be implemented in those conflicts, but different understandings of Common Article 3 can be seen in the views and practice of states, the ICRC and other interested groups. Through practice, or more accurately, through a perception that there was a lack of practice, from the 1960s the scope of the law relating to non-international armed conflicts was increasingly seen as inadequate. This led to further initiatives to update and expand the application of the laws of war, now beginning to be referred to as 'international humanitarian law', principally through what became the 1977 additional protocols to the 1949 Geneva conventions. The chapter shows how significant differences have arisen between modern views that have come to be accepted on the application of the Common Article 3 and the 1977 additional protocols and state views and practice in relation to internal armed conflicts, particularly British practice in Malaya, Kenya, Cyprus and Northern Ireland. The chapter begins to put in the final pieces of the jigsaw and to bring together some of the earlier pieces. In particular, it includes the emergence of the modern interpretation of the application of Common Article 3 with a lower threshold of armed conflict and the coupling of it with military necessity which realized a concept that was formulated in the Lieber Code. As so interpreted, and for the first time as a matter of international law, it applied the laws of war that were developed for inter-state conflicts to circumstances of insurrection and rebellion. This in turn permitted modern rules of engagement based on the laws of war to be set and applied by states in insurrection and rebellion which have a higher degree of permissibility of the use of force than had existed in municipal law in comparable circumstances. However, this development also introduced a dilemma in that politically, if not legally, the use of such rules carried with it the spectre of recognition of the insurgents.

Differing Approaches to the Use of Lethal Force in Colonial Conflicts

British colonial experience in the 1940s, 50s and 60s and armed violence in Northern Ireland and elsewhere in the 1970s led to a number of works which tried to put a more theoretical framework around past operational practices. For example, in *Low Intensity Operations*, one of the most influential British authors of the time, General Sir Frank Kitson (1926–2024), mainly used his experience in Malaya, Kenya and Cyprus to give practical advice on supposedly hypothetical examples. He began, though, by looking at the subject more broadly and commented on the multiplicity of terms, including 'insurgency' and 'insurrection', and how they may be used by different authors in different ways. He thought the best term to describe the armed violence of the period was 'revolutionary warfare' but that it was too politically charged and he used 'insurgency' instead.[1] At that time, the terminology of revolutionary war and guerrilla fighters was particularly associated with Mao Tse-Tung (1893–1976), and other communist leaders, who emphasized the political character of wars. Kitson then distinguished between peaceful and violent opposition to a government and referred to the former as 'subversion'. Like Gwynn, Kitson did not attempt to define the legal sphere that applied to his theories of counter-insurgency except within a general framework of the rule of law.

The meaning of the rule of law is somewhat difficult to encapsulate and has vexed legal commentators but, broadly, it may mean either acting accordance with the rules of the law, or satisfying a broader notion of justice. Sir Robert Thompson (1916–92) who was a counter-insurgency advisor to the British, Malayan and South Vietnamese governments, wrote in his famous 'Basic Principles of Counter-Insurgency' that it was important for the government in an insurgency to function in accordance with the law and not treat insurgents as outlaws, that is as criminals who were summarily killed when they could have been detained.[2]

[1] F Kitson, *Low Intensity Operations: Subversion, Insurgency, Peacekeeping* (London, Faber and Faber, 1971) 2.

[2] Sir R Thompson, *Defeating Communist Insurgency: Experiences from Malaya and Vietnam* (London, Chatto & Windus, 1966) 52.

This policy became known as a 'hearts and minds' approach to counter-insurgency which emphasized the importance of using 'minimum force'.[3] As part of a post-2001 renewal of interest in counter-insurgency and more recent histories of British colonial conflicts, the view of British strategy being based in practice on the minimum use of force has come under considerable attack by revisionist historians and the existence of a 'hearts and minds' approach has even been denied.[4] Rather than there being no such approach, it has become much clearer that the amount of force used within the policy of 'minimum force' could be, and was, considerable as local commanders were left to decide what was the minimum amount necessary to restore order. Furthermore, when public order breaks down, whether measures to restore it are legal or illegal is, as a domestic matter, determined in accordance with the rules made by the government and governments have increasingly resorted to emergency laws rather than martial law to legitimize the use of force.[5] Within the limits of international law and its emergency powers under municipal law, it is then the government that can set the parameters of 'the rule of law'. This aspect of colonial conflicts has received considerable attention in recent historical writing but it has left gaps in the analysis of what was the law and how it applied in circumstances of insurrection which will be explored in this chapter.

The ICRC's original view of Common Article 3 was that the article should be applied as widely as possible.[6] In his book, *Organizing Rebellion*, Tilman Rodenhäuser looked at the application of Common Article 3 in practice and concluded that there was little state practice on it in the 1950s but by the early 1960s the ICRC had taken the view that 'Common Article 3 conflicts exist "if the hostile action, directed against a legal government, is of a collective character and consists of a minimum amount of organization"'.[7] This is considerably wider than the indicative criteria that the ICRC had noted in its commentary and supports a view held among some academics and practitioners that the ICRC and some courts have sought to lower the threshold at which Common Article 3 applied.[8] There is, however, now a general recognition that British state practice did not support the ICRC's position and the counter-insurgency operations in the 1950s suggest a different interpretation of the application of Common Article 3. It has already been noted that, at the meeting held to consider ratification of the 1949 Geneva conventions, the cabinet expressed the view that '[i]t was to be

[3] P Dixon, 'Hearts and Minds? British Counter-Insurgency from Malaya to Iraq' (2009) 32: 3 *Journal of Strategic Studies* 353.

[4] M Hughes, 'Introduction: British Ways of Counter-insurgency', (2012) 23: 4–5 *Small Wars & Insurgencies* 580–90.

[5] D French, *The British Way in Counter-insurgency, 1945–1967* (Oxford, Oxford University Press, 2011) 74–76 and 137.

[6] ICRC, *Commentary on the First Geneva Convention: Convention (I) for the Amelioration of the Condition of the Wounded and Sick in Armed Forces in the Field* (ICRC, 1952) 'Commentary of 1952. Article 3: Conflicts not of an international character' 49–50.

[7] T Rodenhäuser, *Organizing Rebellion: Non-State Armed Groups under International Law* (Oxford, Oxford University Press, 2018) 44 – citing the ICRC Report, *Humanitarian Aid to the Victims of Internal Conflicts, Meeting of a Commission of Experts in Geneva* (ICRC, 1962) 82.

[8] See, eg, S Sivakumaran, *The Law of Non-International Armed Conflict* (Oxford, Oxford University Press, 2012) 162 and G Mantilla, *Lawmaking under Pressure: International Humanitarian Law and Internal Armed Conflict* (New York, Cornell University Press, 2020) 114.

hoped … that no endeavour would be made to argue that the Convention should apply to the operations now in progress in Malaya'.[9] The cabinet were, then, regarding Malaya as a sovereign matter and, at about the same time, the Army pamphlet 'Imperial Policing' which set out its policy on counter-insurgency was up-dated and changed from stressing the principle of the necessity of offensive action to the principle of 'the minimum use of force'.[10] Nonetheless, this could include, if necessary, 'the use of all force at the commander's disposal'.[11] In practice in Malaya and subsequent colonial conflicts, the army continued to emphasize the need to take the offensive within the principle of minimum force which included ambushes of armed rebels and aerial bombing of rural or jungle targets. The effects of the bombing in Malaya were said to be 'meagre' and having more of a psychological effect than a military one but it could be effective when combined with ground operations.[12] Nevertheless, despite the scale of the military operations, a magistrate had to determine whether the killing of each guerrilla had been justifiable.[13] Simpson, a leading authority on British human rights practice, thought that the British forces had applied the laws of war as well as emergency powers in Malaya which might indicate that Common Article 3 should have been applied but he said that, in legal terms, it was an insurrection subject to municipal law.[14] His view is, therefore, consistent with the proposition made in chapter three that the British approach to insurrection combined municipal law with certain laws of war on the conduct of hostilities. After the Second World War, however, it is possible to see a more structured approach to the separation of the paradigms of armed conflict and law-enforcement beginning in Malaya. The legal frameworks that supported the colonial operations had a common foundation in the 1939 Emergency Powers (Colonial Defence) Order-in-Council and the measures taken first in Malaya in the late 1940s and early 1950s included a mixture of emergency laws and common law rules that together provided the municipal law basis for mounting a counter-insurgency campaign to quell the insurrections. The measures that were taken provide an insight into the link between emergency regulations and the development of international human rights law for, as noted in the last chapter, one of the

[9] TNA, CAB 130/46, 'Cabinet Gens 281–291', Minutes of a Meeting of Ministers held on 2 December 1949 entitled 'Revision of Geneva Conventions'.

[10] War Office, Army Pamphlet, 'Notes on Imperial Policing 1934' (1934) and War Office, WO Code No 8439 'Imperial Policing and Duties in Aid of the Civil Power' (1949) 5.

[11] A Edwards, 'Misapplying Lessons Learned? Analysing the Utility of British Counterinsurgency Strategy in Northern Ireland, 1971–76', (2010) 21: 2 *Small Wars & Insurgencies* 303–30 citing WO 7 January 1963. Keeping the Peace: Part 1 – Doctrine (London, The War Office, WO Code No 9800).

[12] R Stubbs, 'From Search and Destroy to Hearts and Minds: The Evolution of British Strategy in Malaya 1948–60' in D Marston and C Malkasian (eds), *Counterinsurgency in Modern Warfare* (Oxford, Osprey Publishing, 2008) 125. The quote is cited in A Edwards, *Defending the Realm? The Politics of Britain's Small Wars Since 1945* (Manchester, Manchester University Press, 2012) 66.

[13] R Thornton, 'The British Army and the Origins of the Minimum Force Philosophy', (2004) 15: 1 *Small Wars & Insurgencies* 99 citing TR Mockaitis, *British Counter-Insurgency 1919–60* (Basingstoke, MacMillan, 1990) 54.

[14] AWB Simpson, *Human Rights and the End of Empire: Britain and the Genesis of the European Convention* (Oxford, Oxford University Press, 2001) 833.

proposed exceptions to the right to life in the European Convention on Human Rights (ECHR)[15] was an exception for national security sites. Following the introduction of emergency laws in Malaya, the governor could designate as 'protected places' properties or areas where anyone who failed to stop after being challenged three times by a police officer could 'be arrested by force which force may, if necessary to effect the arrest, extend to the voluntary causing of death'. Among the places designated as 'protected places' were military barracks and a military airfield as well as government buildings, schools and factories.[16] As the emergency in Malaya worsened, the emergency regulations were then extended to permit the designation of 'special areas' in order 'to prevent malicious injury to persons or property' in them and among the places designated as 'special areas' were parts of districts in which insurgents were operating. The new regulation provided that:

> (2) It shall be the duty of any person in a special area to stop and submit to search by an officer when called upon so to do, and if any person fails to stop when challenged or called upon to stop by an officer, he may be arrested and searched by force if necessary, and such force may, if such officer considers such action necessary to effect the arrest, extend to the use of lethal weapons.[17]

As can be seen, the new regulation retained the requirement to challenge a person to stop but reduced it from three times and made the threat of the use of lethal force in attempting to make an arrest more explicit. These emergency regulations then became the model for the emergencies in Kenya, Cyprus and elsewhere.

The conflict in Kenya is one of the most controversial of the colonial conflicts in terms of the severe and extensive coercion applied by British and local government forces in the suppression of a rebellion by the Mau-Mau movement, particularly in the maltreatment of detainees. Following the declaration of the emergency in Kenya in October 1952, a new military commander, General Sir George Erskine (1899–1965), was sent to lead the security forces there 'charged with the conduct of all military measures to restore law and order in the Colony'.[18] In his post-tour report, he noted that he had the option to declare martial law but thought that it was too extreme a measure unless the civil government lost control. Instead, he based the operations against the Mau-Mau on a mixture of emergency laws and the common law. In addition to 'control' measures such as detention without trial, the measures included the use by the Kenyan government of a power based

[15] Convention for the Protection of Human Rights and Fundamental Freedoms (Rome, 4 November 1950).

[16] TNA, CO 717/167/3, 'Law and Order, Emergency Legislation Various. (Malaya – 1949)', Copy of Regulations made under The Emergency Regulations Ordinance, 1948 (amendments made up to 22 Marc 1949 – complied by B Lee Tian Huat, Attorney-General's Chambers), Regulation 10 and various orders made under the regulations.

[17] ibid Regulation 10A.

[18] General Sir George Erskine KCB, KBE, DSO, 'Report: The Kenya Emergency, June 1953–May 1955', dated 25 April 1955, IWM, Documents. 7570d, *Private papers of General Sir George Erskine GCB KBE*, IWM 75/134/4, 1.

on the emergency regulations in Malaya to designate certain areas as 'special' or 'prohibited' areas. In special areas, government forces had the right to challenge persons and, if they failed to stop, they could be fired upon. In prohibited areas to which entry was not permitted, however, no challenge was required and the government mounted offensive operations in which 'troops were able to operate on a straight forward war basis knowing that anybody they met must be enemy'.[19] This approach was applied to what was called 'the forest' or jungle from where the Mau-Mau operated and, as well as offensive ground operations with close air support, the security forces developed direct bombing attacks which, unlike Malaya, it was thought caused large numbers of Mau-Mau casualties. When the regulations were introduced at the start of the emergency in 1952, the regulation that permitted the creation of 'prohibited areas' provided that anyone who failed to stop when challenged could be 'arrested by force, which force may, if necessary to effect the arrest, extend to a voluntary causing of death'.[20] Orders were then made designating certain jungle areas where the Mau-Mau were located as 'prohibited areas' but the regulation was amended in April 1953 by the addition of a new subsection that stated:

> (7) Any authorized officer may within a prohibited area take such measures, including means dangerous or fatal to human life, as he considers necessary to ensure that no person prohibited from entering into or remaining or being in a prohibited area shall enter into or remain or be in such area.[21]

An authorized officer meant any member of the police, the British armed forces or any administrative officer. As can be seen, it is still based on necessity and somewhat opaque but its terms made necessity a subjective decision and changed the purpose of opening fire from making an arrest to maintaining the prohibition on entry and remaining in the area. When put into the context of the military operations being planned and conducted at that time, it seems to have been introduced to facilitate air operations that were intended to harass the Mau-Mau – hence the dispensing with the requirement for challenge – but it also formed the basis of offensive ground operations and particularly ambushes where it had been found that issuing challenges had allowed the Mau-Mau the opportunity to use their superior jungle knowledge and skills to escape. By contrast, in the 'special areas' anyone could be called upon to halt for the purposes of identification or search and, if they failed to stop, the regulations permitted the use of 'such force as, in the circumstances of the case, may be reasonably necessary, which force may extend to the use of lethal weapons, to effect an arrest or to prevent escape from arrest'.[22] In practice, this was interpreted as meaning that they could be shot. Outside of the

[19] ibid 5.

[20] TNA, CO 822/728, 'Emergency Powers Legislation, Kenya', The Emergency Regulations 1952, dated 30 October 1952.

[21] ibid Amendment Slips arising out of Emergency Regulations made during the period 6 March 1953 to 22 April 1953.

[22] ibid Telegrams between the Secretary of State for the Colonies and Kenya (Sir E Baring), dated 9 and 10 January 1953.

'prohibited areas' and 'special areas', the legal basis of the security forces' actions was 'the obligation under the common law to protect the inhabitants against a felony and in doing so to use the minimum force as judged by the Officer in Command to achieve his purpose' and the operations were said to be 'simply those of troops employed in aid of the Civil Power to quell civil disturbance'.[23] In similar vein to General Macready's orders in Ireland in 1920, troops were required to do what was necessary to restore order and instructed that '[i]f, in the course of those operations, troops are unfortunate enough to cause the death of an innocent person, or damage to property, the Law will regard this as an unavoidable accident'.[24] This general understanding of operations being based in the common law is consistent with the views of the Home Office during the drafting of the International Covenant and the ECHR but with the addition of powers created under emergency regulations. It represented a shift away from reliance on the common law right to repel force with force in that it was no longer expressly focused on armed rebels and it shows a further development of the legal–military framework that reflected both the increasing protection of civilians under international and municipal law and, conversely, the increasing use of emergency legislation to create exceptions in municipal law. The reference at the time to the idea that the common law excluded liability for accidents is also significant for later operations for, as was seen in the last chapter, the European Court of Human Rights (ECtHR) has since developed the interpretation of the right to life so that it includes accidental death.

The mode of operations based on segregated areas and differentiated rules of engagement used in Malaya and Kenya was then followed in Cyprus and Aden.[25] In the conflict in Cyprus (1956–59) emergency legislation was introduced to permit the creation of 'danger areas' which were the equivalent of the 'prohibited areas' in Kenya with the same rule on opening fire on persons found in the area.[26] The 'danger areas' that were created were mountainous areas where the insurgents would hide and train and troops mounted offensive operations, particularly counter-ambushes, against them. As these were increasingly successful, the insurgents moved to greater use of road-side ambushes and the danger areas were extended to strips of land alongside roads where troops were liable to be ambushed to cover places which the insurgents might use as firing points for gunmen or the detonation of road-side bombs.[27] However, it appears that the regulation was not

[23] Erskine, 'The Kenya Emergency' (1955) (n 18) 4–5 and 16.

[24] Edwards, *Defending the Realm* (2012) (n 12) 102 citing Major-General Heyman, 'Confidential: Operations in Special Areas and in the Reserve', dated 7 January 1954, IWM, *Erskine Papers*, 75/134/4.

[25] See B Drohan, *Brutality in an Age of Human Rights: Activism and Counterinsurgency at the End of the British Empire* (Ithaca, Cornell University Press, 2017) 88. The rules of engagement in Aden were among the harshest of the measures adopted as they permitted the engagement of animals as well as individuals and deprived the local population of the ability to keep livestock.

[26] TNA, CO 926/1083, 'Emergency Regulations Legislation in Cyprus', Copy of No 781 The Emergency Powers Orders in Council, 1939 and 1956, Regulation made by the Governor under Section 6, Regulation 38A(4).

[27] ibid Telegram to the Secretary of State for the Colonies from Cyprus (Sir H Foot) sent 17 October 1958 at 18.10 hrs (No 1767).

used to its full extent in practice as the army said that troops continued to issue challenges before opening fire as it perceived there was too great a risk of shooting civilians.[28] This self-limitation may have reflected a number of differences between the operations in Kenya and Cyprus, including an awareness of the potential liability created through the extensive use of proceedings in the local courts on behalf of insurgents and affected civilians in Cyprus. The potential liability had already led to the exclusion of claims for injuries caused in the 'danger areas' as well as emergency legislation which restricted cases against the security forces by providing that proceedings against them required the consent of the Attorney General. This was later extended beyond the ending of the emergency, partly in what was seen as a quid pro quo for an amnesty for former insurgents.[29] In Cyprus, the rules of engagement were summarized in a 'Red Card' issued by the army (the rules were actually printed on a small red card), although it also expressly stated that they were not covered by the emergency regulations.[30] The instructions stated that opening fire must be a last resort but also that, in addition to the right of self-defence, the soldier had a duty to open fire if it was the only way to protect other troops, police, 'peaceful inhabitants' or government property against serious attack; to disperse a riotous mob which posed a serious risk to life or property; or to arrest persons who were committing acts of violence, or whom the soldier honestly believed had done or were about to do so, and to prevent their escape. These instructions would seem to be based on the traditional common law view that soldiers had a duty to suppress a riot or an insurrection but they are significantly more assertive in stating that duty than the Yellow Card later used in Northern Ireland in the Troubles. In legal terms, though, the difference was more of style than substance.

There is a recurring question in the historical literature on the conflicts that were fought as Britain withdrew from its colonies as to whether it had breached its obligations to apply Common Article 3 to the conflicts. This is not only an historical question as a review carried out by a British government lawyer in the 1970s in connection with the Troubles in Northern Ireland concluded that the British had indeed 'denied' the application of Common Article 3 to situations in Malaya, Kenya and Cyprus but the word 'denied' is ambiguous as it is not clear whether the denial was thought to be incorrect.[31] Research carried out by Heather Wilson supports the view that it was incorrect as she thought that the denial reflected an unwillingness to admit that the level of internal disturbance amounted to an armed conflict.[32]

[28] TNA, WO 106/6020, 'Report on Cyprus Emergency', Report by KT Darling, Director of Operations, dated 31 July 1959, 52.

[29] TNA, CO 926/1083, 'Emergency regulations legislation in Cyprus', Memorandum Concerning Proposed Termination of Emergency, dated 14 April 1959.

[30] 'Instructions to Individuals for Opening Fire in Cyprus', CS/1060/A/Dec 55, IWM, Documents. 5442, British Forces Cyprus documents, 1955–1958, Misc 93 (1391).

[31] TNA, DEFE 24/1770, 'Human Rights – Guerrilla Warfare and Humanitarian Law', Letter from JD Gutteridge (DS 11) to DS 10 Legal Secretariat, 'Humanitarian Law – Applicability of Protocols I and II to the Northern Ireland Situation', dated 17 October 1977 attaching a draft FCO report.

[32] H Wilson, *International Law and the Use of Force by National Liberation Movements* (Oxford, Clarendon Press, 1988) 47.

Others see a more wilful denial of its application.[33] Nevertheless, within this extensive historical discussion, there are three points that can be made. First, as a legal matter, Britain was not obliged to comply with Common Article 3 until it ratified the 1949 Geneva conventions, which did not occur until 23 September 1957 – that is after the conflict in Malaya and during the later parts of the emergencies in Kenya and Cyprus.[34] It has also been argued that the delay in ratification was made to avoid the recognition of rebels,[35] and this concern can certainly be seen in the records but, again as a legal matter, Common Article 3 explicitly excludes recognition. Alternatively, it might be argued that Common Article 3 applied as a matter of customary international law but the evidence presented here and the opinions of others such as Rodenhäuser suggest that there was a lack of practice rather than the sort of a widespread and uniform practice or the defence of claims of breach that would be necessary to establish its customary status in this period. This would also be consistent with the views of a number of writers who assess that Common Article 3 did not become customary law until the 1970s or 80s.[36] Second, as critics such as Mantilla acknowledge, what constituted a non-international armed conflict was far from clear and was disputed by and between states and the ICRC.[37] This remains more of an issue than many of the critics allow. Third, as argued in chapter four, Common Article 3 was not understood to incorporate rules on the conduct of hostilities at that time and the standards that were required by Common Article 3 were the same as those of rights-based municipal systems. The real issue is then non-compliance, particularly in relation to the treatment of detainees. Taken together, the arguments on legal uncertainty and non-compliance in practice form part of the argument made here that the regulation of the use of force in internal armed conflicts below the level of civil war may be more effectively pursued through a modern human rights-based framework that recognizes the right of the State to quell insurrection but also the restrictions and accountability that accompany it.

Moves Toward Further Extending the Laws of War

The uncertainty over the application of Common Article 3 led to a call for further regulation of internal armed conflicts in what was to become the 1977 Additional

[33] See, eg, Drohan, *Brutality in an Age of Human Rights* (2017) (n 25) 49; Mantilla, *Lawmaking under Pressure* (2020) (n 8) 102; C Elkins, *Legacy of Violence: A History of the British Empire* (New York, Alfred A Knopf, 2022) 488; and H Lovat, *Negotiating Civil War* (Cambridge, Cambridge University Press, 2020) 43.

[34] Bennett has also argued that between signature and ratification there is an obligation under international law 'to refrain from acts which would defeat the object and purpose of a treaty'. His argument is based on the Vienna Convention on the Law of Treaties (1969), article 18 but this is a more modern treaty and he does not claim that it was a customary law obligation at that time –H Bennett, *Fighting the Mau Mau: The British Army and Counter-Insurgency in the Kenya Emergency* (Cambridge, Cambridge University Press, 2013) 79.

[35] Drohan, *Brutality in an Age of Human Rights* (n 25) 49.

[36] See Bennett, *Fighting the Mau Mau* (2013) (n 34) 80.

[37] Mantilla, *Lawmaking under Pressure* (n 8) 103.

Protocol II to the 1949 Geneva conventions. One of the historical legacies of the split between Hague law (which regulated the conduct of hostilities) and Geneva law (which provided for the protection of civilians and those no longer able to participate in hostilities) was that the 1949 Geneva conventions did not deal with matters such as proportionality and precautions in attack or the appropriateness of the use of certain types of weapons that have become such a part of the modern debate. After the signing of the 1949 Geneva conventions, though, the ICRC broadened its approach and proposed an extension of the conventions on a number of occasions. At its 1957 conference in New Delhi a new set of 'Draft Rules for the Limitations of the Dangers Incurred by the Civilian Population in Time of War' prepared by a committee of experts was discussed.[38] The Draft Rules were intended to regulate the conduct of hostilities in order to provide better protection to civilians in both international and non-international armed conflicts.[39] They included a ban on nuclear weapons and this, among other things, resulted in opposition from key states, particularly the United States, and the rules were not adopted.[40] The ICRC, nonetheless, continued its efforts and in the 1960s international movements and organizations such as Amnesty International also began to campaign for the protection of human rights in armed conflicts. These culminated in the 1968 Tehran Conference Resolution on 'Human Rights in armed conflicts' which, against the background of the 1967 Arab–Israeli conflict and the Vietnam war, was something of a hybrid measure as the title referred to human rights, but the resolution itself drew the attention of states to the rules of the law of armed conflict.[41]

A process was then begun through the United Nations and the ICRC that led to a series of conferences that culminated in the 1977 additional protocols. Following the Tehran conference, the UN General Assembly passed a resolution that reformulated and affirmed the basic rules contained in articles 22 and 23 of the 1907 Hague regulations which embody the principles of distinction and humanity.[42] Two reports on respect for human rights in armed conflicts were also made by the UN Secretary General at the request of the General Assembly.[43] In 1969 a special report of the XXIst International Conference of the ICRC drew attention to what it saw as a limitation of Common Article 3 where governments had denied the existence of a conflict to which it applied and had claimed that only municipal law applied to the situation.[44] In 1971 the ICRC convened a conference on the reaffirmation and development of

[38] K Suter, *An International Law of Guerrilla Warfare: The Global Politics of Law-Making* (London, Frances Pinter, 1984) 91.

[39] Mantilla, *Lawmaking under Pressure* (n 8) 109.

[40] ibid 110.

[41] UN 'Human Rights in Armed Conflicts', Resolution XXIII adopted by the International Conference on Human Rights, Tehran, 12 May 1968.

[42] L Friedman (ed), *Law of War: A Documentary History* (New York, Random House, 1972) 719 referring to UN General Assembly Resolution 2444.

[43] UN Doc A/7720 and A/8052.

[44] Friedman, *Law of War* (1972) (n 42) 717.

international humanitarian law applicable to armed conflicts which was to include government experts. At the conference, the ICRC initially proposed a separate protocol dealing with guerrilla warfare but this was rejected and political attention was focused on a narrower concept of wars of national liberation. After considerable debate, a compromise was reached that included wars of national liberation within the scope of international armed conflicts for the purposes of what became Additional Protocol I and imposed a composite test for non-international armed conflicts under Additional Protocol II that set a high threshold to its application. It included an explicit threshold by excluding 'situations of internal disturbances and tensions, such as riots, isolated and sporadic acts of violence and other acts of a similar nature'.[45] It then took similar criteria to those that had been discussed at the 1949 conference and established a test that required the participation of state armed forces and, on the insurgents' part, organized armed groups in control of territory with the ability to carry out sustained and concerted operations and to implement the protocol.[46] This was seen at the time as representing in effect a civil war that would have amounted to a belligerency, such as the war that had been fought in Biafra in the 1960s.[47] The additional protocols introduced a number of rules that relate to the conduct of hostilities. They have in common the need to protect the civilian population from the dangers arising from military operations, although the rules applicable to international armed conflicts are more extensive, in particular through the provisions on proportionality and the prohibition on indiscriminate attacks. Additional Protocol I also codified, for the first time, the established rule that civilians must not form the object of attack.[48]

Choosing a Legal Paradigm for the Troubles in Northern Ireland

The threshold test set out in Additional Protocol II has proved difficult to apply in practice. In addition, as Additional Protocol II is expressed to develop and supplement Common Article 3 without modifying its existing conditions of application, it is potentially the case that either Common Article 3 or both of Common Article 3 and Additional Protocol II may apply to a particular armed conflict. A possible example of this can be seen in the British government's concerns during the drafting of the additional protocols over whether they might apply to the Troubles in Northern Ireland. The British Government's position on the violent disturbances in Northern Ireland was, on a political level, straight-forward: the situation was not an armed conflict and would be conducted within the municipal criminal law

[45] 1977 Additional Protocol II to the 1949 Geneva Conventions (AP(II)), Art 1(2).
[46] ibid Art 1(1).
[47] Suter, *An International Law of Guerrilla Warfare* (1984) (n 38) 173.
[48] I Detter de Lupis, *The Law of War* (Farnham, Ashgate Publishing, Ltd, 2013) 243.

as it applied within the United Kingdom. In legal terms, however, the position was not quite as straight-forward. The matter has been open to debate but with no conclusive result beyond the recognition that the British government did not classify the situation as an armed conflict even during the most violent periods of the Troubles and it applied the law-enforcement paradigm throughout for political and practical reasons.[49] This position has also been accepted, rather than decided, by the courts and judgments have been made on that basis. Nevertheless, there was more debate internally within government on the basis of the use of force than its political stance might have indicated.

The British government files are somewhat episodic as issues arose and were dealt with during the Troubles, particularly in 1971 as the violence increased and in 1977 in relation to the negotiation of Additional Protocol II. It might be expected that the deployment of troops to Northern Ireland in 1969 and the increasing violence in 1970–71 would have resulted in some discussion on the basis of operations in the context of Common Article 3 but, subject to what is said below, this does not appear to have been the case. There was, however, some consideration of wider policy options by the government. The first was on the possible creation of special military courts which is referred to in a letter to Sir Philip Allen, the Permanent Under-Secretary of State at the Home Office.[50] The letter also sets out a short but concise account of martial law, including the common law powers to declare martial law in an insurrection, and that the declaration would 'no doubt be followed by an Act of Indemnity'. The second policy option was an act of indemnity.[51] As the violence grew worse in 1971, the government introduced internment and some of the persons arrested for internment were subjected to what were called 'deep interrogation' techniques such as wall-standing, hooding, and subjection to loud noise. The practices quickly became the subject of international and domestic controversy and the case of the detainees was taken up by the Irish government on the basis that their treatment amounted to torture. Most of the government correspondence and notes on the circumstances are not relevant here but there was, among them, consideration of whether Common Article 3 applied to the situation. The Northern Ireland Office was advised by senior counsel on the issue and, in his view, Common Article 3 did apply.[52] Furthermore, the Attorney General of Northern Ireland was called to give evidence to the Parker Committee that was appointed to investigate the allegations of mistreatment of the detainees and he had anticipated that there would be awkward questions on the application of Common Article 3.[53] It appears from the tenor of the note that he had expected that the discussion would not favour

[49] E Wilmshurst, *International Law and the Classification of Conflicts* (Oxford, Oxford University Press, 2012) 479.

[50] TNA, CJ 4/1348, '5 Jul 71–20 Jun 72 Economic and Political Issues. Press Concerns Possible Act of Indemnity', Letter to Sir Philip Allen, dated 6 October [1971]. The writer's name is illegible.

[51] TNA, CJ 4/457 and 4/1348, various notes.

[52] TNA, CJ 4/457, Note from John MacDermott QC to the Crown Solicitor in Belfast, undated, on 'Interrogation of Persons arrested under Special Powers Act'.

[53] TNA, CJ 4/457, Letter from the Attorney-General of Northern Ireland to the Attorney-General, dated 18 January 1972.

the government's position that Common Article 3 did not apply and was relieved that the subject was not raised. There was also a discussion on the possibility of an indemnity bill to cover those who had conducted the interrogations. In the course of that discussion and on other occasions, the government considered whether it might be necessary to include an act of indemnity for those involved in the events that had taken place more generally in the Troubles. A number of factors were raised against doing so, including the propaganda value for the IRA of presenting an indemnity bill, the undesirability of preventing civil claims being brought against the government as opposed to actions against individuals, and the powers of the Attorney General to halt private prosecutions. There had been indemnity legislation passed in colonial conflicts, including Kenya and Cyprus, but part of the justification for it had been the granting of amnesties to insurgents. At one point, a draft bill was prepared in an attempt to direct the discussion but, on each occasion the subject was raised, it was concluded that the then current circumstances did not require an act of indemnity. However, it was felt that this was something that would be required once the Troubles were over.[54] As is now clear from the continuing scrutiny of the actions of British soldiers, this was not something that did occur until the British government introduced a partial stay on proceedings under the Northern Ireland Troubles (Legacy and Reconciliation) Act 2023.

During the process of the negotiation of the additional protocols, departments within the British government conducted their own reviews of the effect of the proposed treaty on the British operations in Northern Ireland and the departmental effort was then coordinated within central government. During the negotiations the Irish Republican Information Service produced a pamphlet in which it claimed that 'Republican forces only operate under responsible command, and exercise such control over certain resources as enables them to carry out concerted and sustained military operation in accordance with Protocol II', and that they were entitled to similar treatment to prisoners of war.[55] This may have been an attempt to influence the negotiations or more generally raise the issue of political status for prisoners, or perhaps just propaganda. It seems to be directed at the test setting out the circumstances in which Additional Protocol II applied although it was not the whole test and there was no specific test for wars of national liberation under Additional Protocol I. As it turned out, Additional Protocol II did not contain provisions for the treatment of prisoners of war. Nonetheless, the question set by the government to its officials was whether the protocols would be applicable 'in the present, or in any foreseeable future situation in Northern Ireland'. A number of notes concluded explicitly that they did not whilst one was more sceptical, not so much on the basis of the actual circumstances as matters of fact but rather questioning why it would be disadvantageous if the protocols did apply.[56]

[54] TNA, CJ 4/457 and 4/1348, various notes.

[55] TNA, DEFE 24/1770, Letter from JD Gutteridge to DS 10, Humanitarian Law – Protocol II to the Geneva Conventions, dated 23 September 1977.

[56] TNA, DEFE 24/1748, 'Disarmament and Arms Control – Humanitarian Law in Armed Conflict – Geneva Diplomatic Conference'. See, eg: Letter to Mr French at the UN Department, FCO from

The British government was opposed to the inclusion of wars of national liberation but, when it became clear that they would be included in Additional Protocol I, they took comfort from the high threshold being set for Additional Protocol II. They thought it would be difficult to argue that a separate lower threshold applied to Additional Protocol I even though there was no threshold actually set out in it.[57] On Additional Protocol II the British government was one of a number of governments that faced serious internal disorder at that time and who were unwilling to accept a low threshold that was being proposed. The British government was then somewhat relieved when the second session of the conference adopted the high threshold that was set out in article 1 of Additional Protocol II without the need for overt British pressure.[58]

The Development of the Laws of War after 1977

There have not been any further conventions on the laws of war governing the conduct of hostilities since the 1977 additional protocols although there has been continuing development of conventions governing other aspects of the laws of war, in particular the means of war, such as the 1997 Ottawa Convention on the Prohibition of Anti-Personnel Landmines, and to a lesser extent wider issues, such as the 2000 Optional Protocol on the Involvement of Children in Armed Conflict.[59] There was also an initiative in the 1990s in the United Nations to draw up a declaration of minimum standards of international humanitarian law that applied in all conflicts but it was not widely adopted.[60] In 2005 the ICRC *Customary Law Study* referred to the additional protocols as having 'brought up to date both the rules governing the conduct of hostilities and those protecting war victims' and in 2011 the ICRC stated that in its view international humanitarian law is an adequate body of law for dealing with the humanitarian problems of armed conflicts but the problem was implementation and observance.[61] This is, however, subject to the objections to the extension of most of the rules of international armed conflicts to non-international

JD Gutteridge at MoD (DS 22), dated 28 April 1977; and Note on the Diplomatic Conference with a hand-written note by JD Gutteridge, dated 26 April 1977. The more sceptical view on the non-application of the Protocols to Northern Ireland is in file DEFE 24/1770, 'Human Rights – Guerrilla Warfare and Humanitarian Law', Letter from BR Galloway, Legal Secretariat to DS 11, 'Humanitarian Law – Applicability of Protocols I and II', dated 2 September 1977.

[57] ibid 'Brief for the UK Delegation', dated 7 April 1977.

[58] ibid.

[59] There is a fuller list of relevant treaties at ICRC, *Customary Law Study*, xvi.

[60] 'Declaration of Minimum Humanitarian Standards', adopted by an expert meeting convened by the Institute for Human Rights, Åbo Akademi University, in Turku/Åbo Finland, 2 December 1990, UN Doc E/CN.4/Sub.2/1991/55 (2 December 1990). See M Happold, 'International Humanitarian Law and Human Rights Law' in ND White and C Henderson (eds), *Research Handbook on International Conflict and Security Law* (Cheltenham, Edward Elgar, 2013) 444.

[61] ICRC, *Customary Law Study*, xv; ICRC, 31st International Conference of the Red Cross and Red Crescent, *Reaffirming and implementing international humanitarian law (Follow-up to Resolution 3 of the 30th International Conference), Report on implementation* (Geneva, 2011) 5.

armed conflicts in the ICRC *Customary Law Study* and its lack of distinction between Additional Protocol II and Common Article 3 conflicts. The ICRC's approach also puts the emphasis on where the threshold for a Common Article 3 conflict lies as it makes an internal armed conflict an all-or-nothing proposition in the sense that, if there is a non-international armed conflict, the laws of war governing the conduct of hostilities apply with its permissive approach to the use of force through the principle of military necessity. If the conflict does not have that legal status, the matter is one of international human rights law. Although a further treaty-based extension of the laws of war seems unlikely, their extension through customary law is less visible, less state-generated and more contested as can be seen through its interaction with international criminal law and the place assumed by military necessity in the laws of war as applied to non-international armed conflicts.

The discussion so far has involved only limited consideration of international criminal law as the modern body of law that contains particular enforcement measures for the laws of war. International criminal law in relation to breaches of the laws of war – war crimes – has something of a separate history and existence from the laws of war. For the purposes of this discussion, it is possible to limit consideration briefly to identifying three aspects of international criminal law that have affected the development of the modern laws of war as they apply to internal armed conflicts beginning with the International Criminal Tribunal for former Yugoslavia (ICTY): the classification of conflicts; the development of war crimes in relation to breaches of the law of non-international armed conflict; and its effect on international customary law.

The case of *The Prosecutor v Tadić* was the first prosecution brought by the ICTY.[62] The ICTY was set up in 1993 by the United Nations Security Council for the 'prosecution of persons responsible for serious violations of international humanitarian law committed in the territory of the former Yugoslavia since 1991'. The definition of armed conflict and the categorisation of war crimes in non-international armed conflict decided by the ICTY were subsequently adopted in the 1998 Rome Statute of the International Criminal Court (ICC) and by the ICRC in its *Customary Law Study*. It has already been described earlier as part of the accepted framework of the laws of war. Although generally accepted now through the affirmation provided by the 1998 Rome Statute, the *Tadić* decision itself caused some controversy at the time, largely due to the judicial development of war crimes made in the decision. Contemporary articles raised particular concerns over whether the judicial recognition of war crimes in non-international armed conflict and the criminalization of violations of Common Article 3 amounted to a breach of the principle of *nullum crimen sine lege* – no crime without law.[63] This principle precludes the prosecution of alleged crimes that were committed before the criminalisation of the particular

[62] *Prosecutor v Tadić* (Decision on Jurisdiction) (1995) Case no IT-94-1-AR72, Appeals Chamber (1996) 35 ILM 32, 2 October 1995.

[63] C Greenwood, 'International Humanitarian Law and the *Tadić* Case' (1996) 7: 2 *European Journal of International Law* 265–83.

behaviour. Subsequently, however, these decisions have been consolidated into works on the laws of war, particularly the ICRC's *Customary Law Study* which made extensive use of the statutes of the international criminal tribunals for Yugoslavia and Rwanda and the International Criminal Court as well as the decisions of the courts as sources.[64] It was also controversial, in part due to methodological concerns over the deduction of customary norms of international law.[65]

After completing the *Customary Law Study*, the ICRC made an attempt to investigate and explain its view of the meaning of one of the fundamental rules of both international and non-international armed conflict that a civilian is protected from direct attack 'unless and for such time as they take a direct part in hostilities'. It published its findings as its 'Interpretive Guidance on the Notion of Direct Participation in Hostilities under International Humanitarian Law' and provoked a fierce debate on its methodology in preparing the guidance as well as the content of it.[66] Put simply, it proposed a test to determine whether a person was taking a direct part in hostilities which required the determination that a person's specific act exceeded a specified threshold of harm and a direct causal link between the act and the likely harm.[67] The *Interpretative Guidance* also considered a related issue of whether the laws of war may now require that participants should be disabled or captured if that is possible rather than killed, a question which had been raised in the conferences it had held and on which it said the experts disagreed.[68] The notion is generally based on a passage by Jean Pictet (1914–2002), a senior lawyer at the ICRC, that '[i]f we can put a soldier out of action by capturing him, we should not wound him; if we can obtain the same result by wounding him, we must not kill him'.[69] Whilst not going so far as this, the ICRC guidance concluded that as a matter of the laws of war 'the kind and degree of force which is permissible against persons not entitled to protection against direct attack must not exceed what is actually necessary to accomplish a legitimate military purpose in the prevailing circumstances' irrespective of whether the conflict was an international or non-international armed conflict.[70] This test will be considered again later in relation to the potential application of right to use lethal force to quell an insurrection under article 2 of the ECHR and controversies over 'shoot-to-kill' policies.

[64] R Cryer, 'Of Custom, Treaties, Scholars and the Gavel: The Influence of the International Criminal Tribunals on the ICRC Customary Law Study' (Summer 2006) 11: 2 *Journal of Conflict and Security Law* 239–263.

[65] D Turns, 'The Law of Armed Conflict (International Humanitarian Law)' in M Evans, *International Law* (Oxford, Oxford University Press, 2014) 846.

[66] N Melzer, 'Interpretive Guidance on the Notion of Direct Participation in Hostilities under International Humanitarian Law' (*ICRC*, May 2009). On the response, see, eg, B Boothby, '"And for Such Time As": The Time Dimension to Direct Participation in Hostilities', (2010) 42 *New York University Journal of Internal Law and Politics* 741–68; W Hays Parks, 'Part IX of the ICRC "Direct Participation in Hostilities" Study: No Mandate, No Expertise, and Legally Incorrect' ibid 769–830; and MN Schmitt, 'Deconstructing Direct Participation in Hostilities: The Constitutive Elements' ibid 697–739.

[67] Melzer, 'Indicative Guidance on the Notion of Direct Participation in Hostilities' ibid 16.

[68] ibid 78 n 212.

[69] ibid 82 n 221.

[70] ibid 82.

The Laws of War in Internal Armed Conflicts

Chapter four described how the current view of Common Article 3 is that when the article applies so do other rules of non-international armed conflict, including those regarding the conduct of hostilities.[71] This is subject to the two thresholds which are set out in Additional Protocol II – the de minimis threshold excluding riots and other sporadic violence and the higher threshold for the protocol to apply which requires the participation of organized armed groups in control of territory and the ability to implement the protocol. The lower threshold at which Common Article 3 applies was itself developed by the International Criminal Tribunal for former Yugoslavia in *Prosecutor v Tadić* such that the law of armed conflict encompassed armed violence by insurgents in circumstances that might traditionally have been described as insurrection or rebellion rather than civil war. The second threshold in Additional Protocol II is then based on a test which is intended to indicate whether the armed conflict has reached a higher intensity at which the provisions of the protocol apply. It has been suggested by a writer present at the conferences that led to the 1977 additional protocols that there was evidently an intention that the Additional Protocol II provisions should subsequently be applied to the lower Common Article 3 threshold.[72] Whilst this has not happened as a treaty, it has in effect been attempted by the ICRC's *Customary Law Study* which does not distinguish between the rules that apply to the different categories of non-international conflicts on the basis, it argues, that states do not apply the distinction in practice.[73] Whether or not the ICRC's approach is justified, one of the consequences of this gradual change is that the principle of military necessity that was developed in the context of war between states, or as it is now termed international armed conflict, was imported into non-international armed conflicts as part of the law governing the conduct of hostilities. As has been seen, military necessity is the principle of the laws of war that permits the destruction of life and property and is seen both in the understanding that the laws of war reflect a balance between military necessity and humanity and its incorporation in specific rules, particularly the rules of proportionality.[74] Military necessity is the feature of the laws of war that distinguishes what has been called the morally exceptional status of armed conflict in permitting killing and injuring people in acts that would otherwise be morally unacceptable.[75] When looking at the literature on the extension of the laws of war to categories of non-international armed conflicts, it

[71] ICRC, *Commentary on the First Geneva Convention: Convention (I) for the Amelioration of the Condition of the Wounded and Sick in Armed Forces in the Field* (Cambridge, Cambridge University Press, 2016) 'Commentary of 2016. Article 3: Conflicts not of an international character' §389.

[72] Suter, *An International Law of Guerrilla Warfare* (n 38) 173.

[73] J Pejić, 'Status of armed conflicts' in E Wilmshurst and S Breau, *Perspectives on the ICRC Study on Customary International Humanitarian Law* (Cambridge, Cambridge University Press, 2007) 85.

[74] The rules of proportionality are set out in AP I but were not included in AP II. Nevertheless, the principle of proportionality is now widely regarded as being customary in nature and applicable to international and non-international armed conflicts.

[75] J Crowe and K Weston-Scheuber, *Principles of International Humanitarian Law* (Cheltenham, Edward Elgar, 2013) 1.

is apparent how the issues of what type of conflict qualified and what rules should apply were debated and decided but it does not appear that the principle of military necessity was considered in relation to the extension. The principle is not specified as such in treaties on the conduct of hostilities or the ICRC *Customary Law Study* but it is set out in various national military manuals. As was explained in chapter one, the origins of military necessity can be traced to *General Order 100*. The drafts of the code before it was published as *General Order 100* show how Lieber had linked his conception of military necessity to the ends of war: the object of war was a renewed state of peace.[76] This was not then changed when section X on internal armed conflicts was added. However, the object was subsequently modified in military manuals through a gradual process that accompanied the development of the laws of war as between states. Most formulations refer to it as 'the complete submission of the enemy', a form that was given judicial approval by the US Military Tribunal sitting in Nuremberg in 1948.[77] In the transition from *General Order 100* to modern military manuals the concept of military necessity has given the ends of war a more Clauswitzian overtone of war – the total submission of the enemy – rather than Lieber's 'renewed state of peace'.[78]

The modern formulation of military necessity was well established at about the time that Common Article 3 extended the laws of war to non-international armed conflicts but the understanding that Common Article 3 brought with it other elements of the conduct of hostilities occurred later, including the principle of military necessity. The principle did not change when the military manuals were up-dated for the 1949 Geneva conventions but there have been small changes to the formulation of the principle in the latest versions of the *British Manual* and *US Manual*.[79] The current *British Manual* refers to 'the complete or partial submission of the enemy' – 'partial' was added after the 1982 Falklands War to reflect British objectives in that conflict and the 1990–91 Gulf War and is intended to show a more modern strategic awareness.[80] In practice, in the 2003 Iraq conflict the military objective for the UK and US was stated as being the removal of Saddam Hussein's regime and it was made the target in targeting decisions.[81] Since the Iraq conflict, the *US Manual* has moderated its form of military necessity too but its meaning has also become more vague, it states that '[m]ilitary necessity may be defined as the

[76] US War Department, *General Order 100*, Arts 14–16.

[77] JD Ohlin and L May, *Necessity in International Law* (Oxford, Oxford University Press, 2016) 110. See *United States v List (Wilhelm) and others (Hostages Case)* Case No 7, (1948) 11 TWC 757, (1948) 15 ILR 632, (United States Military Tribunal, Nuremberg (*NMT*)).

[78] JG Garner, 'General Orders 100 Revisited' 27 (January 1964) *Military Law Review* 1–48, 27.

[79] See, eg, US Department of the Army, *The Law of Land Warfare, FM27-10* (Washington, GPO, 1956) 4.

[80] UK Ministry of Defence, *The Manual of the Law of Armed Conflict* (Oxford, Oxford University Press, 2004) 21 n 2.

[81] The Iraq Inquiry, Geoffrey Hoon, Secretary of State for Defence. Evidence 19 January 2010, 76; and Ian Lee, Director General Operational Policy, from September 2002 to (no date given, possibly May 2004). Evidence 22 June 2010, 25 and Section 6.2 – Military planning for the invasion, January to March 2003, §365.

principle that justifies the use of all measures needed to defeat the enemy as quickly and efficiently as possible that are not prohibited by the law of war' and that it 'has been defined in military publications, judicial decisions and scholarly works'.[82] The footnotes to the section then illustrate this with various citations including *General Order 100*. It is clear then that the situating of military necessity in the context of war between states remains and it is reasonable to ask whether, after the 1949 Geneva conventions or the 1977 additional protocols or at least when the current *UK Manual* and the *US Manual* were produced, they should have reconsidered both the basis of constructing military necessity as the test of means and the permissiveness of the use of force as expressed through the principle of proportionality for non-international armed conflicts?

Conclusion

The debate over the British position on applying the laws of war in its colonial conflicts and Northern Ireland demonstrates the differences in view between the formal legal position governing the different types of conflict and, in any given circumstances, the British government's view of what type of conflict it was involved in. Professor Stephen Neff has summed-up the types of conflict into five categories of civil disturbance in international law: 'isolated and sporadic acts of violence' governed by municipal law and international human rights law – ie as being within the law-enforcement paradigm; internal armed conflict to which Common Article 3 of the 1949 Geneva conventions applies; Additional Protocol (II) conflicts where rebels have de facto control over part of the territory of a state to which AP(II) and possibly customary law apply; conflicts of 'national liberation' to which Additional Protocol (I) applies without any requirement for the insurgents to have control over any territory; and 'full-blown belligerency' to be treated on a par with an interstate war including applying the law of neutrality and the belligerent rights outside the state's territory.[83] In practical terms, the ICRC have argued that customary rules apply to Common Article 3 and Additional Protocol II conflicts and that those rules are the same that apply to international armed conflicts, with a few exceptions that are not relevant to non-international armed conflicts. This remains a contested approach. Against this, British practice up to 2001 can be seen as a three-part scheme:[84]

(1) internal disturbances within the United Kingdom to which municipal law applied and, in relation to disturbances after 1978, there may have been a right to bring a case before the ECtHR on the basis of the ECHR as reflected

[82] US Department of Defense, *Law of War Manual* (Washington, Department of Defence, 2015) 52.
[83] SC Neff, *War and the Law of Nations, A General History* (Cambridge, Cambridge University Press, 2005) 375.
[84] 2001 is a representative date preceding British involvement in Afghanistan and Iraq and the publication of the UK Ministry of Defence, *Manual of the Law of Armed Conflict* (n 80) in 2004.

in English/Northern Irish law. This was the category applied to Northern Ireland throughout the Troubles;[85]

(2) insurrections or rebellions in Ireland (up to partition in 1922), British colonies, or other territories outside of the United Kingdom in which British forces were deployed in an internal security role, to which municipal law (as amended by emergency legislation including forms of 'statutory martial law') and the rules on the use of lethal force under the laws of war applied; and

(3) a civil war to which the law of non-international armed conflict applied.

The British approach to classification has had three implications for the issue of the use of lethal force against insurgents. The first is that if, as has been argued, the standards of protection provided by Common Article 3 were actually those of what Pictet called 'civilised countries' in the commentaries on the 1949 Geneva conventions, then, provided the rights are respected and maintained, the level of protection offered by relying on municipal law in states with developed human rights systems will have been the same or better than that provided by Common Article 3. In that case, this provides a qualification to the argument that there was a loss of protection where one of those states such as the UK denied the application of Common Article 3, except perhaps for the loss of the official influence that the ICRC could assert through its humanitarian role and the ability to derogate through emergency legislation. Where rights were abused, it was as much a breach of municipal law as international law. Furthermore, human rights are now part of both municipal law and international law for many states, including the UK, and the forums provided by international human rights law, particularly the right of application to the ECtHR, may provide a more available means of obtaining a remedy.

Second, it highlights the role of the modern view that Common Article 3 includes rules on the conduct of hostilities, in particular rules deriving from the principles of distinction, military necessity and proportionality, which may be more permissive of the use of force than would be the case under municipal law. This point is hinted at obliquely in the 2016 updated Commentary on the First Geneva Convention in which the passage by Pictet quoted above on applying Common Article 3 as widely as possible has been replaced by a note that cautions:

> Thus, while there may be no apparent need to discern possible limits to the scope of application of common Article 3, it is important that the rules applicable in armed conflicts apply only in the situations for which they were created. The existence of a situation that has crossed the threshold of an 'armed conflict not of an international character occurring in the territory of one of the High Contracting Parties' must

[85] For these purposes, 1978 is also a representative date chosen to include the ECtHR judgment in *Ireland v the United Kingdom* App no 5310/71, A no 25 (1978) ECHR 1 on the treatment of detainees in Northern Ireland although it has not been possible to identify a particular date that this extension to the ECtHR came to be accepted.

> therefore be neither lightly asserted nor denied. Humanitarian law standards must be applied only in the situation – armed conflict – for which they were intended and developed, carefully balancing considerations of military necessity and humanity.[86]

This passage is a significant departure from the 1952 commentary's approach of advocating the application of Common Article 3 as widely as possible and the perception that in practice the ICRC sought to lower the threshold of Common Article 3 as a protective step. It also contains a change in legal argument as it suggests that the test of whether Common Article 3 applies is not based solely on the objective criteria now used covering geographical and temporal scope (as the ICRC footnote suggests), the organization of the armed group and the intensity of the fighting. There is now something more – a judgment of whether the situation was one in which it was intended that the rules should apply. This in turn raises additional questions on how that is to be determined and whether it creates legal uncertainty for international criminal law, for example, where the determination of a Common Article 3 armed conflict is a necessary condition for establishing a war crime under article 8.2(c) of the 1998 Rome Statute.[87] It may suggest a revival of the issue as to whether armed conflicts are in part distinguishable from other forms of violence by their purpose and the debate over the deletion of references to types of internal armed conflicts from the 1948 Stockholm drafts of the Geneva conventions on the basis that, among other reasons, 'the character of a situation is independent of its motives'.[88] This has been noticed in another context in the contrasting examples of the conflict in Kosovo and Mexican drug wars, where it has been suggested that the classification of an armed conflict 'seems to apply in practice not so much based on a threshold of violence but on whether the violence is framed in political terms'.[89] The ICRC's latest view on the application of Common Article 3 also has implications for human rights law, whether municipal or international, as it suggests that it is more appropriate in circumstances where it was not intended that international humanitarian law should apply, which may impact the situations in which a derogation may be made.

[86] ICRC, 'Commentary of 2016. Article 3' (n 71) §389–90. The paragraphs also refer to passages of the Commentary giving details on the geographic and temporal scope of application of Common Article 3.

[87] The lists of war crimes relating to non-international armed conflicts are set out in Article 8.2 of the 1998 Rome Statute and appear to create separate categories of non-international armed conflict for the purposes of specifying war crimes. Under Art 8.2(c), there are war crimes arising from serious violations of Common Article 3 and, under Art 8.2(e), other serious violations of the laws and customs applicable to non-international armed conflicts. However, it would appear that in practice the International Criminal Court has not made a distinction between the types of non-international armed conflict, see N Quénivet, 'Article 8(2)(c)' in M Klamberg and J Nilsson (eds), *Commentary on the Law of the International Criminal Court – The Rome Statute* (Brussels, Torkel Opsahl Academic EPublisher, 2020).

[88] ICRC, 'Commentary of 2016. Article 3' (n 71) §373.

[89] C Chinkin and M Kaldor, *International Law and New Wars* (Cambridge, Cambridge University Press, 2017) 283.

Finally, the British approach has consistently denied the political dimension of the use of armed violence against the British state or its colonies. By taking a high threshold to the laws of war, in effect a civil war, it sought to take lesser intensities of organized armed violence out of the laws of war. In doing so, it relied on the municipal law to legitimate its operations through the courts upholding the right to repel force with force and the common law right to use reasonable force to prevent a crime. In colonial conflicts, the common law rights were supplemented by the use of emergency powers to create the 'special' and 'prohibited' areas and authorize the use of lethal force in them. The 'prohibited' areas in Kenya where lethal force could be used where necessary to prevent anyone entering or remaining in the area were used to support military operations which were thought to be effective but, although 'danger' areas were created in Cyprus with equivalent regulations, the authority to open fire without challenge was not used as it was thought to carry too great a risk of mistakenly killing a civilian. In Northern Ireland, the British government then treated the position as solely one of law-enforcement and did not recognize an insurrection for the purpose of justifying military operations under the ECHR. This was perhaps seen as having the best of both worlds from the British policy perspective at the time but it resulted in the government having to justify its use of lethal force in self-defence within the narrow parameters set out in *McCann*. By the time that the development of human rights law reached that position, the level of violence in Northern Ireland was far lower and the British government could feasibly maintain its position but, faced with very different levels of violence in Iraq in 2004, its policy failed to cope with the circumstances and, at the same time, left itself open to human rights challenges on self-defence.

7

Overlapping Paradigms: The Extension of Human Rights Law to War-time

The paradigms of armed conflict and law-enforcement have each developed in a number of ways since 1945. The new paradigm of armed conflict included non-international armed conflicts which were previously in the sphere of municipal law but the paradigms were still seen as separate until an overlap was created through the recognition that human rights apply in war as well as in peace. As the previous chapters have shown, this view overlooks an area of overlap in which the British army adopted some provisions of the laws of war whilst operating generally within the sphere of municipal law in internal armed conflicts. The use of military force in this situation was based on the sovereign right to repel force with force, the prevention of crime and necessity. The justification of necessity for the use of lethal force was then incorporated into international human rights law through the European Convention on Human Rights (ECHR). In their book, *Necessity in International Law*, Jens Ohlin and Larry May argued that different meanings are given to 'necessity' under *jus ad bellum*, the laws of war, international human rights law and international criminal law.[1] The separate meanings of necessity will, they suggest, result in a difference in legal outcome in situations where the laws of war and international human rights law are applied to the same circumstances.[2] I agree with that general analysis but think that it requires further examination. Their consideration of international human rights law is focused on the European Court of Human Rights (ECtHR) and, although they mention all of the exceptions to the right to life in article 2 of the ECHR, they do not examine insurrection or derogation for lawful killing in war.[3] This chapter examines how modern military operations have been viewed in the area of overlap where human rights law applied, or may have applied, in each paradigm. Through an examination of cases decided by the ECtHR that involve military operations with war-like applications of lethal force, this chapter argues that states maintained the idea of separate paradigms by continuing to justify their actions as self-defence and the ECtHR has avoided making judgments by reference to the laws of war even though it implicitly acknowledged particular circumstances as armed conflict. It also looks at the

[1] JD Ohlin and L May, *Necessity in International Law* (Oxford, Oxford University Press, 2016) 273.
[2] ibid 128.
[3] ibid 132.

principles of necessity and proportionality in human rights law and how the court has avoided addressing some essential questions on the use of lethal force in military operations, in particular questions on the interpretation of the exceptions and how it should assess necessity and proportionality in cases of the use of lethal force other than in personal self-defence. It has instead concentrated on the basis for the lawful use of lethal force in municipal law. As a matter of English law, this may be provided by the defences of public or private necessity for homicide. However, the defence of necessity has a long and complex history which has left it uncertain and the English courts reluctant to develop it. In considering an alternative approach through the exception to the right of life in quelling an insurrection, it will be seen that there has been very little consideration of it and, apart from some insurance cases that shed some light on its meaning, there is considerable uncertainty over the correct judicial approach to deciding what is insurrection and what constitutes necessity for the purposes of deciding whether a killing was necessary to suppress an insurrection.

Jurisdiction Over the Right to Life

As was seen in chapter five, the ECHR sets out the right to life with specific exceptions where the killing was intentional but absolutely necessary for a prescribed purpose. In addition, there is provision in article 15 for derogation in respect of deaths resulting from lawful acts of war although no state has used it.[4] There is some debate on what is meant by 'war' in this context.[5] Derogations are permitted for other rights in time of war or other public emergency threatening the life of the nation and there are differing views held as to whether war is to be interpreted as being only an international armed conflict or would include a Common Article 3 or an Additional Protocol II type of non-international armed conflict.[6] In the light of the drafting history of the Geneva conventions, there is a strong argument that it was intended to mean only a war as understood at that time as a contention between states or a state of belligerency that had been recognized by a state. The ECtHR has implied that Russia might have derogated in respect of the situation in Chechnya in 1999–2000 but did not expand on whether they considered it a war

[4] D Murray (ed), *Practitioner's Guide to Human Rights Law in Armed Conflict* (Oxford, Oxford University Press, 2016) 105. The ECtHR, however, has now applied it to international armed conflicts.

[5] See, eg, N Melzer, *Targeted Killing in International Law* (Oxford, Oxford University Press, 2008) 121; L Doswald-Beck, *Human Rights in Times of Conflict and Terrorism* (Oxford, Oxford University Press, 2011) 174.

[6] See, eg, Doswald-Beck, *Human Rights in Times of Conflict* ibid 192 who argues that derogation should apply only to international armed conflicts; Murray and Park leave open the possibility that it applies to non-international armed conflicts: Murray, *The Practitioner's Guide to Human Rights Law in Armed Conflict* (2016) (n 4) 104 and I Park, *The Right to Life in Armed Conflict* (Oxford, Oxford University Press, 2018) 199; and S Aughey and A Sari, 'Targeting and Detention in Non-International Armed Conflict: Serdar Mohammed and the Limits of Human Rights Convergence' (2015) 91 *International Legal Studies* 115 state that it applies to all three types of armed conflict.

or another type of public emergency.[7] In *Hassan*, a detention case relating to the Iraq conflict, the ECtHR accepted that the principle of derogation under article 15 applied to detention in an international armed conflict,[8] and subsequently the UK Supreme Court interpreted it as also including a non-international armed conflict.[9] Most recently, in *Georgia v Russia (II)*, the ECtHR decided that article 2 did not apply to an international armed conflict during the conduct of hostilities even without derogation.[10] By contrast, the International Covenant developed in a different way and provides that no derogation is permitted from the right to life. The United Nations Human Rights Committee updated its guidance on the right to life under article 6 of the International Covenant in 2018 and adopted a binary approach that distinguishes between the armed conflict and law-enforcement paradigms.[11] In armed conflict, the legality of the use of lethal force will depend on that use not being in breach of the laws of war. In law-enforcement, the use of force by state agents will be subject to the 'Basic Principles on the Use of Force and Firearms by Law Enforcement Officials' (1990) which embody narrow rules of self-defence against an imminent threat of death or serious injury, to prevent a serious crime involving a grave threat to life, or the making of an arrest or the preventing escape where there is the same danger. They also require the use of 'less-lethal' means to avoid the use of lethal force unless they would be insufficient to achieve one of the prescribed objectives. The Human Rights Committee does not make reference to the judgments of the ECtHR in the context of military operations. Given the extent of the case law on article 2 and paucity of other international judgments as well as the relevance of the ECHR, this chapter will focus on the judgments of the ECtHR.

The legal methodology for analysing the case law under the ECHR is a complex area but can be seen, generally, as having a number of steps which involve establishing the applicable law and then applying the law to the facts of an individual case. The starting point for determining whether an allegation of a particular killing by state agents would be in breach of the right to life is that the killing must have occurred within the jurisdiction of a state for the purposes of article 1 of the ECHR. If it is, then, unless the state has made a derogation for war, the state must demonstrate that the deprivation of life was 'absolutely necessary' and was 'lawful' for one of the purposes set out in articles 2.2 (a), (b) or (c). This requires the state to show three things: (i) that the killing fell within one of the exceptions, which involves the issue of what is the meaning of the terms used in them, in particular whether the terms 'self-defence', 'riot' and 'insurrection' have a particular legal meaning; (ii) that it was 'lawful' – meaning that there was a legal basis for the use of force in the circumstances of the exception; and (iii) that it was 'absolutely

[7] *Isayeva v Russia* App no 57950/00 (2005) ECHR 128, §133.
[8] *Hassan v United Kingdom* App no 29750/09 (2014) ECHR 936, §110.
[9] *Abd Ali Hameed Al-Waheed v Ministry of Defence* (2017) UKSC 2, SC, §158 and §163.
[10] *Georgia v Russia (II)* App no 38263/08 (2021) ECHR 58, §144.
[11] UN HRC, 'General comment No 36: Article 6, Right to Life (2018)' §10–14 and 64.

necessary' and 'proportionate' for achieving the purpose of the exception, that is defending a person from unlawful violence, making an arrest or preventing an escape, or quelling a riot or insurrection. A failure to establish any one these elements will mean that the killing is in breach of the convention and each of them will be considered below.

Under the ECHR, states undertake to 'secure to everyone within their jurisdiction the rights and freedoms' set out in the convention.[12] The ECtHR initially took a territorial approach to the application of the right to life other than in 'exceptional circumstances', such as whilst a person was under the physical control of a state's agents.[13] In a leading judgment the court decided that the persons killed in the bombing of a radio tower in Belgrade by NATO aircraft did not fall within the jurisdiction of the court.[14] The established view at the time of military operations in Afghanistan and Iraq between 2001 and 2009 was, therefore, that operational shooting incidents and other battlefield killings outside of a convention state would not fall within the ECHR.[15] However, the issue was raised again in relation to Iraq in the *Al-Skeini* case as the judgment extended the jurisdiction of the UK to Iraq during the occupation in 2003–04 for the purposes of establishing the right to an investigation of a killing by state-agents under article 2.[16] It was unclear to what extent the judgment had extended the extra-territorial application of the substantive right to life as the court set out a number of grounds that might apply. However, following the *Al-Skeini* case, the English courts adopted a process designed to bundle together similar cases so that the principles on which they should be conducted or settled could be decided. The litigation was grouped under a test case under the name *Al-Saadoon* and was to be heard by the same judge, Leggatt J.[17] In the first case (sometimes referred to as 'AS1'), the court sought to settle questions of jurisdiction under article 1 of the ECHR and set out an approach that was based on what the judge understood as the principles that underlay the ECtHR's decision in *Al–Skeini*.[18] He took the view that persons shot during the course of British military operations in Iraq during the occupation were within the scope of article 1 'both (a) because such shootings occurred in the course of security operations in which British forces were exercising public powers that would normally be exercised by the government of Iraq and (b) because shooting

[12] ECHR, art 1.

[13] *Issa v Turkey* App no 31821/96 (2004) ECHR 629, §68.

[14] *Banković v Belgium* App no 52207/99 (2001) ECHR 890, §82.

[15] There is a related issue of the right to an effective investigation of a killing under the ECHR which is outside of the scope of this book. There is an extensive literature on this subject, eg: H Russell, *The Use of Force and Article 2 of the ECHR in Light of European Conflicts* (London, Hart Publishing, 2017); M Lattimer, 'The Duty in International Law to Investigate Civilian Deaths in Armed Conflict' in M Lattimer and P Sands (eds), *The Grey Zone: Civilian Protection between Human Rights and the Laws of War* (London, Hart, 2018); and N Quénivet, 'The Obligation to Investigate after a Potential Breach of Article 2 ECHR in an Extra-Territorial Context: Mission Impossible for the Armed Forces?', (2019) 37: 2 *Netherlands Quarterly of Human Rights*, 119–38.

[16] *Al-Skeini v United Kingdom* App no 55721/07 (2011) ECHR 1093, §177.

[17] Now Lord Justice Leggatt, he was appointed to the Supreme Court in 2020.

[18] *R (Al-Saadoon and ors) v Secretary of State for Defence* [2015] EWHC 715 (Admin), QBD, §95–118.

someone involves the exercise of physical power over that person'.[19] This finding was, however, overturned on appeal and the Court of Appeal held that the English courts should not extend the scope of application of article 1 beyond what the ECtHR had 'clearly showed it to reach'. It said that the current position from the ECtHR cases was that article 2 would apply only 'where there was an element of control of the individual prior to the use of lethal force'.[20]

In a second procedural application (here referred to as 'AS2') the High Court was asked to determine the extent of the British government's obligation to investigate claims of mistreatment or unlawful killing in Iraq.[21] During the course of the hearing, the judge, again Leggatt J, made some wide-ranging observations on the circumstances in which lethal force could be used and the criteria by which it would be assessed. He held that 'the use of armed force to suppress riots and other forms of civil unrest, prevent looting, or otherwise maintain law and order in a conflict area during a period of occupation could not be classified as part of the hostilities'. He reached this conclusion after considering a variety of sources on the applicable law of occupation and, on the facts, he held that the extensive violence was 'endemic' but not the work of organized armed groups and, in such circumstances, the situation was governed not by the laws of war but by human rights law.[22] He based the decision on a number of grounds including the findings in *Al-Skeini* and *AS1* and the decision of the ECtHR in the *Makaratzis* case that police officers should not be left in a vacuum when exercising their duties to maintain public order in a riot.[23] Although much of the case is not relevant here as it concerned the belligerent occupation of another state (which falls under the law of international armed conflict) and the judgment insofar as it related to the extension of jurisdiction to cover shootings by British forces during events that the judge characterized as riots or other disorder was overturned by the Court of Appeal, the case is noteworthy for the emphasis that the judge placed on the violence, although extensive and prolonged, not being part of the conduct of hostilities as it was not the doing of organized armed groups. The decision also reinforced the requirement for there to be a clear basis for the exercise of powers to use force to maintain public order in a riot which would, by extension, apply equally to insurrection. The judge went on to make two further points.[24] First, he said that the British rules of engagement set out in Card Alpha were not based on the laws of war but were consistent with the United Nations' 'Basic Principles on the Use of Force and Firearms by Law Enforcement Officials'. As has been seen, these are based on self-defence and this raises once again the problem of the lawful basis for the use of force to quell an insurrection as permitted under article 2 of the ECHR if the use of force is limited to self-defence. Second, he said that, in applying

[19] ibid §294.
[20] *R (Al-Saadoon and ors) v Secretary of State for Defence* [2016] EWCA (Civ) 811, CA, §69–70.
[21] *R (Al-Saadoon and ors) v Secretary of State for Defence (No 2)* [2016] EWHC 773 (Admin), QBD.
[22] ibid §73–88.
[23] *Makaratzis v Greece* App no 50385/99 (2005) ECHR 694, §49.
[24] *R (Al-Saadoon) v Secretary of State for Defence (No 2)* (n 21) §89–91.

the rules of engagement, 'in terms of the duty to protect civilian life, there is in any case little difference between the standards applicable under article 2 and those applicable to the conduct of military operations under the laws of war'. He based this on the ECtHR's decision in the *Finogenev* case – this followed the approach it had taken in *Ergi v Turkey* in referring to precautions in attack under the laws of war.[25] The judge's conclusion is a highly contested interpretation of the laws of war and, among other things, overlooks that precautions in attack are linked to the principle of proportionality under the laws of war and the assessment of the lawfulness of the incidental loss of life in the attack does not include combatants or civilians who directly participate in hostilities. He also seemed to conceive of the rules of engagement being part of the legal framework for operations by security forces but, as has been seen, the legal status of them as a basis for founding liability is not clear. These additional points are also, I think, obiter and, therefore, not binding on another court.

The approaches that the ECtHR took to extra-territorial jurisdiction in Iraq have been subject to some gradual development since *Al-Skeini*, initially in relation to the subsidiary right to an effective investigation of a killing by state agents but subsequently in relation to the substantive right.[26] In *Georgia v Russia (II)*, the ECtHR decided for the first time that extra-territorial jurisdiction did not extend to the 'active phase of hostilities' in an international armed conflict.[27] It then reiterated that it may apply to a situation in which a state had 'effective control' over part of another state's territory – a concept akin to military occupation under the laws of war – and also where a person was within the authority and control of state agents. The difference in application between having 'effective control' over an area and state agent authority and control over an individual being that, in the former, all the substantive rights under the ECHR would apply whereas, in the latter, the rights may be 'divided and tailored' so that only those relevant to individual concerned apply.[28] State agent authority and control could be established in a number of ways. In Iraq the court found that it was through the UK taking on 'public powers' under the coalition that would normally have been exercised by Iraq or through the person being in the physical power and control of state agents. However, in *Georgia v Russia (II)*, the court also noted a line of cases in which it

[25] *Finogenov v Russia* App nos 18299/03 and 27311/03 (2011) ECHR 2234, §208.

[26] In another case on operations in Iraq, the court found that jurisdiction was established for the purposes of the right to an investigation for a person who was shot whilst in a vehicle passing through a checkpoint during the occupation of Iraq (*Jaloud v the Netherlands* App no 47708/08 (2014) ECHR 1292, §152) but the breach of the substantive right not to be deprived of one's life was not included in the application. The Netherlands had argued that the use of a weapon did not of itself bring the target within a state's control (ibid §119) citing *Banković* but the point was undecided. In another recent case, *Hanan v Germany* App no 4871/16 (2021) ECHR 131 which concerned deaths resulting from an air-strike by NATO aircraft in Afghanistan, the applicants' claims were limited to the breach of the procedural obligations under article 2 to investigate the deaths and the court did not decide on the extra-territorial application of substantive right to life.

[27] *Georgia v Russia (II)* (n 10) §138.

[28] ibid §200.

had applied the concept of 'State agent authority and control' to circumstances that went beyond the exercise of physical power and control in the context of an arrest or detention and concerned 'isolated and specific acts involving an element of proximity'.[29] What was meant by 'proximity' was not entirely clear, it seemed to suggest physical proximity but the cases that it cited also arose either from border incidents in which it was unclear whether the incident arose within the actual territory of Turkey (which was the state concerned) or from an incident within the United Nations' buffer zone in Cyprus. The court then cited this in its judgment in *Carter v Russia*, a case about the poisoning of Aleksandr Litvinenko in London by what it found to be state agents of Russia, and said that the element of proximity also applied 'in cases of extrajudicial targeted killings by State agents acting in the territory of another Contracting State outside of the context of a military operation'.[30] This is then, in general terms, the current position on jurisdiction over the use of lethal force in British military operations.

Grounds for Killing in Self-defence, Making an Arrest, Riot and Insurrection

Self-defence

Where jurisdiction has been established, the *McCann* case has been the starting point for the ECtHR's jurisprudence on the use of lethal force. As was explained in chapter five, it was treated as one of soldiers acting in a law-enforcement context. The UK government justified the killing of the three members of the IRA under article 2.2(a) as the use of force by the soldiers on the basis of self-defence under Gibraltar law. It was accepted to be in practice the same as under English law, and article 2 and the rules of engagement were found to be consistent with that approach. There are, however, a number of cases in which people have been killed in British military operations in Northern Ireland, Turkish military operations in south-east Turkey and Russian military operations in Chechnya that were not so obviously within the law-enforcement paradigm and yet were justified as self-defence. In relation to these, the UK had, like the Gibraltar case, argued that its operations were conducted under strict rules of engagement consistent with the Northern Irish law standard of self-defence (again, a standard argued to be in practice the same as English law) and consistent with article 2. This is what I refer to as the narrow definition of self-defence based on an immediate threat of death or serious injury and a response limited to the use of firearms with aimed shots at an individual who is identified as posing the threat. There are, though, some British cases in Northern

[29] ibid §131–32.
[30] *Carter v Russia* App no 20914/07 (2021) ECHR 766, §130.

Ireland that challenge this definition. In particular, in perhaps the most prominent incident of this type, British special forces killed eight members of the IRA when they attacked a police station at Loughgall in 1987. A passer-by was also killed by mistake. However, the ECtHR has not examined the case or other similar ones in relation to the loss of life itself but only in relation to a breach of the right to an investigation and, as such, the British cases are not considered further.[31]

In *Ergi v Turkey*, a judgment set down three years after *McCann*, there was an escalation in violence from the *McCann* law-enforcement scenario. The case concerned a Turkish security forces' operation in which a woman, Havva Ergi, was killed by a stray shot that went into her village. The court noted 'that, on the Government's own account, the security forces had carried out an ambush operation and had engaged in an armed clash with the PKK [a Kurdish armed group] in the vicinity of the village'.[32] The court also used terminology taken from article 57 of Additional Protocol I when it referred to taking 'all feasible precautions in the choice of means and methods of a security operation mounted against an opposing group with a view to avoiding, and in any event, minimizing, incidental loss of civilian life'.[33] This had the effect of moving the exception away from the narrow definition of self-defence as an ambush is a premeditated attack, not an act of self-defence. The court, nonetheless, applied the framework that it had established in *McCann* even though the court in *McCann* had seemed to regard premeditated killings as not falling within self-defence. It referred to the exceptions in article 2.2(a), (b) and (c) but avoided examining them and concentrated instead on the (in)adequacy of the planning and conduct of the ambush. In effect, the court turned what it had explained as a war-like military operation into a poorly-executed law-enforcement operation. This case marks the point at which the ECtHR made a significant step away from the meaning of self-defence in municipal criminal law as, by not excluding ambush as an act of self-defence, the court allowed parties to offer a different meaning of self-defence. One that in *Ergi* overlaps with the laws of war and in the Chechen cases is closer to the sense of state self-defence used in *jus ad bellum*.

The Chechen cases marked a considerable escalation in the use of force which placed them further outside of the setting of law-enforcement operations. One of the first and leading cases, *Isayeva v Russia*, involved a military operation in 1999 to clear a village of insurgents who had arrived there as the result of using a supposed safe route but was actually part of a ruse to induce the insurgents away from Grozny.[34] Although the case report refers to a village, it had some 18,000 to 25,000 inhabitants and, once the insurgents had arrived there, the Russian

[31] *Kelly v United Kingdom* App no 30054/96 (2001) ECHR 328, §99–110; and Interim Resolution CM/ResDH(2007)73, Action of the Security Forces in Northern Ireland (Case of McKerr against the United Kingdom and five similar cases) adopted by the Committee of Ministers on 6 June 2007.

[32] *Ergi v Turkey* App No 40/1993/435/514, (ECHR, 28 July 1998) §79.

[33] ibid.

[34] *Isayeva v Russia* (n 7). The other leading case is *Isayeva, Yusupova, Bazayeva v Russia* App nos 57947/00, 57948/00 and 57949/00 (2005) ECHR 129. The cases are consistent in relation to the points made here.

forces blocked off the exit routes and launched artillery and aircraft attacks on the rebels trapped inside the village. This operation can be seen as part of a situation that was within the scope of the laws of war.[35] It would be at least a Common Article 3 armed conflict due to the numbers and organisation of the armed insurgents and the intensity of the fighting and may even have amounted to an armed conflict within the scope of Additional Protocol II.[36] However, the Russian government pleaded that its forces had acted in self-defence under article 2.2(a). The court in its judgment set out its framework from *McCann* that '[a]ny use of force must be no more than "absolutely necessary" for one or more of the purposes set out in sub-paragraphs (a) to (c) [of article 2]' and gave the interpretation of 'absolute necessity' that it had used before.[37] However, it also referred to the situation in Chechnya as justifying 'exceptional measures by the State in order to regain control over the Republic and suppress the illegal armed insurgency'.[38] It then held that the use by the Russian forces of unguided bombs with a damage radius exceeding 1,000m

> in a populated area, outside wartime and without prior evacuation of the civilians, is impossible to reconcile with the degree of caution expected from a law-enforcement body in a democratic society. No martial law and no state of emergency has been declared in Chechnya, and no derogation has been made under Article 15 of the Convention. The operation in question therefore has to be judged against a normal legal background.[39]

The Russian government appeared to be trying to interpret self-defence in the broader sense applied in *jus ad bellum* to justify the use of force by a state. It does seem that it did not try to justify itself under article 2.2(c) in order to avoid admitting to an insurrection.[40] The court in my opinion correctly resisted this but was unclear in its reference to articles 2.2(a) to (c) and to derogation as to how the convention might have applied. A court is expected to determine a case as presented by the parties and not to make arguments for them but in this case the judgment is flawed and mismatches the provisions and circumstances. First, the judgment referred to articles 2.2(a) to (c) and to armed insurgents but it also noted that Russia had not derogated under article 15, so by implication accepting that it could have done so in relation to what was in effect a non-international armed conflict. In those circumstances the operation was justiciable on the basis of the laws of war by operation of law and was not dependent on the Russian position. Second, the court referred to the operations as being in pursuit of a legitimate aim – the suppression of an illegal armed insurgency – and that they 'could presumably

[35] See, eg, W Schabas, 'The Right to Life' in A Clapham and P Gaeta (eds), *The Oxford Handbook of International Law in Armed Conflict* (Oxford, Oxford University Press, 2014) 383–84.

[36] N Quénivet, 'The Moscow Hostage Crisis in the Light of the Armed Conflict in Chechnya', (2001) 4 *Yearbook of International Humanitarian Law* 355 discusses this position in more detail.

[37] *Isayeva v Russia* (n 7) §173.

[38] ibid §180.

[39] ibid §191.

[40] Doswald-Beck, *Human Rights in Times of Conflict* (2011) (n 5) 173.

include the deployment of army units equipped with combat weapons, including military aviation and artillery' and yet made them subject to the standards set for the use of lethal force in self-defence in law-enforcement operations.[41] This pattern was subsequently repeated in a number of other cases where the Russian forces used heavy weapons such as aircraft with unguided bombs and rockets, attack helicopters and artillery.[42] In particular, it can be seen in the court's finding that the use of force was indiscriminate. By contrast in *Zalov and Khakulova v Russia*, the court found that a Russian operation in the Republic of Kabardino Balkaria which resulted in the deaths of 95 insurgents was not in breach of article 2 but did not specify which exception it had applied.[43] There has also been a development of the court's thinking on the scope of protection as it found that the operations had not been prepared 'in such a way as to avoid or minimize, to the greatest extent possible, the risk of a loss of life, *both for persons at whom the measures were directed and for civilians*' (emphasis added) and again referred to *McCann*.[44] By contrast, in *Isayeva* it had referred to minimizing incidental loss of civilian life and referred to *Ergi*.[45] This is a significant development and brings out an essential difference between military necessity under the laws of war and necessity in self-defence under international human rights law.

In a more recent case, *Cangöz v Turkey*, there is the beginning of an argument by a state on the right to life which combines articles 2.2(a), (b) and (c).[46] It concerned the killing in 2005 of 17 members of the Maoist Communist Party (MCP), whom the Turkish government described as an armed terrorist group, by an armed attack helicopter. It sought to justify the operation on the grounds of article 2.2(a), (b), and (c) but the court found that there was a breach of the substantive right to life as the government had not proved its case as to the necessity of the killings. It did not address the argument on paragraph (c) directly.

Killing in an Attempt to Arrest

The case to which the court usually refers to support of its judgment in relation to a case involving a claim of the use of force in arrest is *Nachova v Bulgaria*.[47] The case concerned the attempted arrest of two deserters from the Bulgarian security forces

[41] *Isayeva v Russia* (n 7) §180.

[42] See *Isayeva, Yusupova, Bazayeva v Russia* (n 34); *Khamzayev v Russia* App No 1503/02 (ECHR, 3 May 2011); *Khatsiyeva and ors v Russia* App no 5108/02 [2008] ECHR 46; *Esmukhambetov v Russia* App no 23445/03 (2011) ECHR 532.

[43] *Zalov and Khakulova v Russia* App no 7988/09 (2014) ECHR 54. The case was actually brought under art 3 in relation to the treatment of the bodies of the applicants' relatives.

[44] *Esmukhambetov v Russia* (n 42) §146; *Khamzayev v Russia* (n 42) §172.

[45] *Isayeva v Russia* (n 7) §196.

[46] *Cangöz v Turkey* App no 7469/06 (2016) ECHR 377.

[47] *Nachova v Bulgaria* App nos 43577/98 and 43579/98 (2005) ECHR 465.

who were subsequently shot and killed whilst trying to run away. In the judgment, the court held that

> [l]ethal force might be justified when strictly proportionate to circumstances which needed to be strictly construed. The legitimate aim of effecting a lawful arrest only justified putting life at risk when 'absolutely necessary'. In principle there could be no such necessity when the person to be arrested was known not to pose a serious threat and was not suspected of having committed a violent offence.[48]

The latter part has become the court's usual definition of necessity in arrest operations and in effect makes arrest a variant of self-defence in the sense that the person poses a threat to the person attempting to make an arrest or to others if left at large. The difference between it and narrow self-defence is the immediacy of the threat. It is notable that here the court is developing a legal meaning of absolute necessity by setting parameters around the circumstances in which it may apply – not just treating it as a matter of fact.

Riot

There are few cases on riot but the ones there are make four main points.[49] First, on the basis that there may be differences in law and practice between states, 'riot' is to be given an autonomous meaning.[50] This was the approach of the court in *Kathleen Stewart v UK* – the case of the boy accidentally killed by a baton round in Northern Ireland considered in chapter five – and creates the situation that there could be a serious inconsistency between state law and practice and the convention. Here, the conception of human rights is again becoming separated from its original context of riot as understood under municipal law, at least in the United Kingdom. After reviewing the court's case law, Russell found that the court had identified a number of elements in various cases, such as that in *Stewart* the violence had to cause serious injury to the security forces, but the overall meaning remained unclear and she called for the court to clarify the definition.[51] However, although the commission's approach was established some 40 years ago and has been followed in the few cases on riot, it is not the only approach the court could take and is different to the approach that it took to the question of whether the meaning of absolute necessity in article 2 is the same as the common law standard of being 'reasonably necessary'. In *McCann* and since, the court has emphasized that it is not its role 'to examine *in abstracto* the compatibility of national legislative or constitutional provisions with

[48] ibid §94–95.

[49] *Güleç v Turkey* App no 21593/93 (1998) ECHR 58; *Giuliani and Gaggio v Italy* App no 23458/02 (2011) ECHR 513; *Şimşek v Turkey* App no 35072/97 (2005) ECHR 546.

[50] *Stewart v United Kingdom* App no 10044/82 (1984) EHRR 453; 39 Eur Comm'n HR Dec & Rep 162 (1984) §25.

[51] Russell, *The Use of Force* (2017) (n 15) 37–38.

the requirements of the Convention.'[52] However, the court then held that 'the difference between the two standards is not sufficiently great that a violation of Article 2 para 1 (art 2–1) could be found on this ground alone.'[53] It would be consistent with that approach, therefore, for the court to examine a state's municipal definition of 'riot' and determine whether the difference was of itself enough to ground liability.[54] Although this would not be as useful as setting out a definition of riot, it would be a positive step. The same argument would apply to 'insurrection' if it were to be considered by the court. Second, the authorities are expected to have access to non-lethal means of quelling a riot, at least in circumstances in which violent disturbances could be expected, but it is still possible that lethal weapons may lawfully be used.[55] This point has arisen in two rather different cases. In *Güleç v Turkey* the Turkish authorities had opened fire with a machine gun on what they described as armed protestors but the court found that they should have anticipated violence at the protest march and had non-lethal weapons available, as well as being unconvinced about the presence of armed protestors. In *Giuliani and Gaggio v Italy* the Italian authorities were policing an environmental protest rally which became violent and an injured policeman, who was in a police car that was overturned by the protestors, shot one of the protestors. The court found that he was acting in self-defence. The court's approach is linked to its view that absolute necessity 'for the purposes of the Convention requires that, where different means are available to achieve the same aim, the means which entails the least danger to the lives of others must be chosen.'[56] Third, that when their lives are threatened, the actions of security force personnel in a riot may be based on self-defence – as occurred in *Giuliani and Gaggio v Italy*.[57] Finally, the European Commission also specifically acknowledged '[t]he right of the authorities to take action to quell a riot without imposing any requirement of retreat or avoiding action in the face of mounting violence.'[58] This statement relates back to an English law concern that there was a duty to retreat but this has since been held not to be the case. What then of insurrection?

Insurrection

The application of the exception for insurrection has hardly been addressed by the ECtHR or academic literature. Where article 2.2(c) is mentioned, such divergent

[52] *McCann v United Kingdom* App no 18984/91 (1995) ECHR 31, §153.

[53] ibid §155.

[54] The modern definition of riot in English law is set out in the Public Order Act 1986. It provides: 'Where twelve or more persons who are present together use or threaten unlawful violence for a common purpose and the conduct of them (taken together) is such as would cause a person of reasonable firmness present at the scene to fear for his personal safety, each of the persons using unlawful violence for the common purpose is guilty of riot.' The Act also abolished the common law definition of riot (Public Order Act 1986, ss 1(1) and 9(1)).

[55] *Güleç v Turkey* (n 49) §71.

[56] *Giuliani and Gaggio v Italy* (n 49) §214.

[57] ibid §216; the issue was also raised in *Stewart v UK* (n 50) §30 but the Commission found it unnecessary to decide it as it had found that the killing was justified in the course of the suppression of a riot.

[58] *Stewart v United Kingdom* (n 50) §27.

opinions have been given as that 'it is very unlikely that lethal force to quell a riot or insurrection can be justified under the Convention at all' and that article 2 contains 'plainly necessary limitations' but without giving any additional consideration or authority beyond the few cases of riot described above.[59] It has been suggested that 'insurrection' should be given an autonomous meaning, again based on the *Stewart* case on riot but without further argument.[60] Russell, on the other hand, concluded that the court should define 'insurrection' and that it might start from a dictionary definition that insurrection is 'a violent uprising against an authority or government'.[61] It is a recent development for paragraph (c) to be raised by the Turkish government in *Cangöz v Turkey* and the most common approach of states involved in internal armed conflicts has been to plead self-defence or the attempt to make an arrest or, as the Turkish Government did in *Benzer v Turkey*, to deny any involvement in a situation at all, even though the court subsequently found that Turkish aircraft had bombed two villages killing 33 people.[62] The court's general approach is difficult to reconcile with its statements that proportionality is to be determined by reference to the aims set out in articles 2.2 (a) to (c) so including killing to quell an insurrection. If one were to generalize the facts of the cases argued before the court by states in cases such as *Ergi* and *Isayeva* as operations mounted by security forces against identified, armed insurgents, once the security forces are threatened on the ground, they may legitimately use lethal force in self-defence. They may also use lethal force in the attempt to arrest as the insurgents would pose a serious threat and/or be suspected of having committed a violent offence. In this scenario, force used to attack the insurgents might also be said to be an attempt to quell an insurrection and that might fall within what the commission meant in the passage used in the court's judgments that dates back to *Stewart* that implies that there is a part of article 2.2 that does extend to intentional killing. The intentional killing must then be 'absolutely necessary' and 'strictly proportionate'. What is proportionate must be determined against the purpose – the killing of the insurgents to quell the insurrection – and not as a balance between the number of the non-insurgents that may be expected to be injured or killed against the military advantage of the killing of the insurgents as it would be under the principle of proportionality in the laws of war. In practice, the court has not been asked to follow its own logic in this way as states have not made their argument in these terms. When the circumstances have clearly been beyond the scope of narrow self-defence, the court has not examined the purpose, for example, in *Isayeva* the ECtHR turned the purpose of the operation from the attempt to defeat the insurgents into being to protect the civilian population in the village. In *Tagayeva*, in a very difficult case, it followed *Isayeva* in finding that indiscriminate weapons had been used in breach of article 2, although on this

[59] R Otto, *Targeted Killings* (Heidelberg, Springer, 2012) 178; and G Marston, 'The United Kingdom's Part in the Preparation of The European Convention on Human Rights, 1950', (1993) 42: 4 *International and Comparative Law Quarterly* 811, respectively.

[60] D Harris and M O'Boyle (eds), *Harris, O'Boyle & Warbrick: the Law of the European Convention on Human Rights* (Oxford, Oxford University Press, 2014) 232.

[61] Russell, *The Use of Force* (n 15) 38–39.

[62] *Benzer v Turkey* App no 23502/06 (2013) ECHR 1116.

occasion they were infantry weapons.[63] The case concerned a siege that followed the taking over of a school in Beslan, North Ossetia, Russia by heavily armed insurgents in 2004 and the subsequent storming of the school by Russian security forces in which over 330 people were killed. At other times, it has found that there was a violation of article 2 through indiscriminate aerial bombing and referred to this also being in breach of treaty or customary rules of the laws of war as it did in *Ergi* and the two *Isayeva* cases, and more recently in *Benzer v Turkey*.[64] Whilst these judgments can properly be seen as holding the state accountable for indiscriminate attacks, they reflect an inconsistent and incoherent approach. The standard section that the court now includes in its judgments based on *McCann* was founded on the narrow conception of self-defence in law-enforcement operations. Nevertheless, the framework it created could on its own terms be applied to a case such as *Isayeva*. If it were, the court would have to decide what use of lethal force is strictly proportionate to quelling an insurrection. Instead, the court has gone along with the expansion of self-defence to include military combat operations and made references to rules of the laws of war but not tried to reconcile the two bodies of law. Perhaps the nearest that the court has come to this was in *Özkan v Turkey*, a case about an operation by Turkish security forces to clear a village of suspected PKK insurgents in 1993. The evidence given about the operation was very contradictory but the court found that, as the troops approached the village, shots were fired at them and they responded with intense 'tactical' fire to suppress the insurgents. No civilians were killed by the gun-fire but a soldier was later shot dead and two children were subsequently injured and died as the troops carried out a search of the village in circumstances which left the court unable to determine responsibility. On the initial firing by the security forces, however, the court concluded that, having been fired upon, it was 'absolutely necessary' to lay down intense fire, whilst emphasizing that no civilians were injured or killed by the firing. The court referred both to the 'absolute necessity' of the use of force under article 2.2(a) to (c) as established in *McCann* and the 'choice of means and methods' for the operation from *Ergi*, but was not clear about whether it regarded the firing as justified under paragraph (a) in self-defence or (c) suppressing the insurgents.[65] However, since then, the court has seemed to be approaching something of a decisive point in the Chechin cases as it is difficult to see how the approach that the court took in *Esmukhanbetov* and *Khamzayev*, that operations have to be planned in such a way as to avoid or minimize the risk of a loss of life both of the insurgents who are being targeted and of civilians and to minimize the recourse to lethal force, is reconcilable with the laws of war.[66]

As has already been mentioned in relation to the cases on the issue of jurisdiction in Iraq, Leggatt J considered whether the violence in Basra during

[63] *Tagayeva v Russia* App no 26562/07 (2017) ECHR 354, §609–11.
[64] *Benzer v Turkey* (n 62) §184.
[65] *Ahmet Özkan v Turkey* App no 21689/93 (2004) ECHR 133, §305.
[66] *Esmukhambetov v Russia* (n 42) §146; *Khamzayev v Russia* (n 42) §172.

the occupation period could amount to an insurrection. He held that, even if it could be said to be an insurrection,

> [86] … it was nevertheless civil disorder.
>
> 87 These descriptions are significant, not only because they are inconsistent with the conduct of hostilities, but also because the use of lethal force in a situation of this kind … is specifically covered by article 2 of the Convention … In these circumstances it seems to me neither necessary nor possible to interpret article 2 as permitting the use of force which, although not absolutely necessary for any of the purposes specified in article 2.2 including sub-paragraph (c), would be permitted in conducting hostilities under IHL.[67]

This passage is significant because it is the first modern consideration of the possible application of the exception for insurrection. What the judge sems to be saying is that the ECHR would coexist or take priority over the laws of war in occupation. Although I do not agree with the decision insofar as it relates to the law of occupation, this does I think amount to judicial support for the argument that there is an overlap between the paradigms and they have different standards. In such a case, the security forces would have to comply with both bodies of law and recognize that the limits on the use of force are more restrictive under the ECHR than the laws of war when applied to the same circumstances.

The difficulty that courts and academic writers have had in deciding what is an insurrection for the purposes of the English criminal law and the ECHR has not been shared by the commercial courts in England. The issue has arisen as a matter of insurance law in cases that reflect the changing character of war over more than a century. In these cases, the courts are clear, and sometimes expressly state, that they are dealing with matters of insurance law and that they take no position on matters of public law but they nonetheless reflect similar issues that change over time.

In the Boer War, when the courts were dealing with what was war as a matter of public law, the issue was also relevant in commercial law as war could in certain circumstances nullify an insurance contract.[68] In order to decide whether the seizure of gold from a train on the orders of the Transvaal government occurred during a war, the High Court took a definition from a leading international law textbook, *Hall on International Law*,[69] 4th edn, that characterized war as an armed conflict between states or an act of violence by one state that another took to be a breach of the peace.[70] It then decided that a war did exist with the Transvaal but not at the time that the gold was seized and not as a result of it. However, during the Easter Rising in 1916 in Ireland, the court found in *Curtis & Sons v Mathews*

[67] *R (Al-Saadoon) v Secretary of State for Defence (No 2)* (n 21) §86–87.

[68] *Driefontein Consolidated Gold Mines v Janson* [1900] 2 QB 339, CA; [1901] 2 KB 419, HL, [1902] AC 484 at 493.

[69] WH Hall, *A Treatise on International Law* (Oxford, Clarendon Press, 1895).

[70] *Driefontein Consolidated Gold Mines v Janson* (n 68) 343.

that 'Easter week in Dublin was a week not of mere riot but of civil strife amounting to warfare waged between the military and usurped powers and involving bombardment'.[71] This is 'the only illustration in the English cases of the type of situation which is capable of amounting to a civil war'.[72] Particular findings often turned on long-established but arcane phrases, in this case what was 'usurped power' as it would constitute a ground for the insurance company avoiding liability. A few years later in the Irish War of Independence, a police witness gave evidence that there was a state of 'guerrilla warfare' in parts of County Cork which the Lord Chancellor, giving judgment, described as 'something amounting to civil commotion, perhaps, indeed, to rebellion' within the area prior to the declaration of martial law.[73] Cases were sometimes argued at length and appealed where necessary to facilitate a judgment that could be used to settle other cases arising from similar circumstances. For example, a case was heard by the House of Lords in June 1923 that was one of the last to be heard by it before the separation of the Irish courts following partition but unusually the successful insurance company did not seek costs from the insured as it regarded it as a test case with over three hundred other cases depending on the outcome.[74] Two relatively recent cases have also taken this approach. In *Spinney's* case, the case concerned the damage to and looting of the plaintiffs' shop in Beirut in 1976, the insurance policy contained a special condition setting out an exclusion for '(a) … civil war; (b) … civil commotion assuming the proportions of or amounting to a popular rising … insurrection, rebellion, revolution military or usurped power'. The court found the wording was an issue of insurance law and the insurance policy rather than public international law. It decided that there was not a civil war in Lebanon at the time and neither did the situation constitute a rebellion, an insurrection or riots, but it was a 'popular rising' and so the exclusion applied.[75] In a very well thought-out judgment, the judge, Mustill J, noted that definitions may be different between public and business law and may change as circumstances change. Precedents were, therefore, a guide but not more. He considered the definition of rebellion by starting with the *Oxford English Dictionary* definition as 'organised resistance to the ruler or government of one's country; insurrection, revolt', to which he said that he would add that 'the purpose of the resistance must be to supplant the existing rulers or at least to deprive them of authority over part of their territory'. He noted that the dictionary 'defines 'insurrections' in a similar manner, but also suggests the notion of an incipient or limited rebellion', which he thought was the sense used in the policy but 'that a lesser degree of organisation may also mark off an insurrection from a rebellion'. However, both rebellion and insurrection required there to 'be action against the government with a view to supplanting it'.[76] *Spinney's* case

[71] *Curtis & Sons v Mathews* [1918] 2 KB 825, KBD at 825.
[72] *Spinney's (1948) Ltd v Royal Insurance Co. Ltd* [1980] 1 Lloyd's Rep 406, QBD (Com Ct) at 427.
[73] *Cooper v General Accident, Fire and Life Assurance Corp* [1922] 13 Ll L Rep 219, HL at 220.
[74] *Motor Union Insurance Co v Boggan* [1923] 1 IR 136, HL at 142.
[75] *Spinney's (1948) Ltd v Royal Insurance Co Ltd* (n 72) 406 and 411.
[76] ibid 436–37.

was considered in *National Oil Co of Zimbabwe (Private) Ltd v Sturge*.[77] The case concerned loss resulting from an explosion at an oil tank farm in Mozambique caused by the Mozambique National Resistance (Renamo) in 1982 and the insurance policy contained an exclusion for loss caused by 'war civil war revolution rebellion insurrection, or civil strife arising therefrom'. After considering the decision in *Spinney's* case and deciding that the words of the policy were to be given their business meaning, the court found that

> 'civil war' meant a war with the special characteristic of being civil, ie being internal rather than external; 'rebellion' and 'insurrection' had similar meanings to each other and meant an organised and violent internal uprising in a country with as a main purpose the object of trying to overthrow or supplant the government of that country although insurrection denoted a lesser degree of organization and size than rebellion.[78]

The judge then then found that the circumstances in Mozambique at that time amounted to an insurrection. He also noted that 'Underwriters accept that if they cannot establish insurrection then they must necessarily fail on rebellion',[79] which again implies that rebellion is a more violent form of insurrection.

Self-defence and Necessity in English law

In situations of armed conflict, the lawfulness of the use of lethal force is addressed through the permissive aspect of the principle of military necessity, subject to the individual rules that restrict it. However, each of the exceptions in article 2.2 of the ECHR has a separate requirement for lawfulness. In a situation where both the laws of war and international human rights law applied, the 'lawful' element required by both could be supplied under the approach that, as a matter of customary law, Common Article 3 implies the principle of military necessity. However, as has been seen, the ECtHR has not taken this approach, for example in *Isayeva v Russia* it looked at Russian constitutional and anti-terrorist laws for the basis of Russian combat operations as it noted that martial law had not been declared.[80] This raises questions of what the court thought martial law would involve and why the laws of war were not invoked as a matter of law but the court did not explore those issues except to note that there had been no derogation under the ECHR. However, it has explained its approach in relation to police officers:

> The use of lethal force by police officers may be justified in certain circumstances. Nonetheless, art 2 does not grant a carte blanche. Unregulated and arbitrary action by state agents is incompatible with effective respect for human rights. This means that policing operations must be sufficiently regulated by national law, within the

[77] *National Oil Co of Zimbabwe (Private) Ltd v Sturge* [1991] 2 Lloyd's Rep 281, QBD (Com Ct).
[78] ibid 281.
[79] ibid 282.
[80] *Isayeva v Russia* (n 7) §191 and 199.

framework of a system of adequate and effective safeguards against arbitrariness and abuse of force.[81]

This would also apply to soldiers engaged in military operations in a public order role, such as in *McCann* and operations in Northern Ireland, but this leaves open the issue in relation to military combat operations of the type seen in Turkey and Chechnya. The lawful use of lethal force by military forces became an issue of some constitutional debate in Australia after 9/11 after the Australian government deployed the Australian Defence Forces (ADF) in a precautionary public order role. In two works on the Australian position by serving or former legal officers in the ADF, the authors set out the general position under English case law before considering relevant Australian statutes and case law and they provide a well argued case that doubts that there is a defence to the use of lethal force in law-enforcement outside of self-defence.[82] This is a significant conclusion in this area of debate but it would be of little value to repeat their arguments in full here as they depend in part on specific Australian legislation. However, it is instructive to deconstruct them in so far as they considered English case law and use them as a starting point to consider the position from a wider perspective.

In the first study Rob McLaughlin focuses the issue on whether there is a 'non self-defence based "reasonable and necessary force" excuse for the use of lethal force by a member of the military on a law-enforcement operation'.[83] He identifies the principle case of relevance as *Attorney-General for Northern Ireland's Reference (No 1 of 1975)* (*A-G's Reference (1975)*) and contrasts it with two cases from the Second World War in which a soldier shot an individual who was trying to escape from his custody but was acquitted of murder at trial.[84] His starting point is Dicey's theory that the position of a soldier in law-enforcement operations is subject to all the liabilities of an ordinary citizen. *A-G's Reference (1975)* was an application to obtain the House of Lords' opinion on a hypothetical scenario of a soldier shooting a fleeing man who is believed to be a member of the IRA in the context of the Troubles in Northern Ireland at that time but it was based on a case that had actually come before the courts in Northern Ireland. One of the central issues in the case arose from the English law definition of murder. Murder is a common law offence in English law, meaning that it has been developed by the courts over hundreds of years rather than being introduced or defined only by statute. Its modern definition can be reduced to three essential features, it is whether an act 'would be (1) an unlawful (2) killing of a person (3) with intent to kill or cause

[81] *Giuliani and Gaggio v Italy* (n 49) §249.

[82] McLaughlin, 'The Use of Lethal Force by Military Forces on Law Enforcement Operations – Is There a "Lawful Authority"?' (2009) 37: 3 *Federal Law Review* 441–469; C Moore, *Crown and Sword: Executive Power and the Use of Force by the Australian Defence Force* (Canberra, ANU Press, 2017).

[83] McLaughlin, 'The Use of Lethal Force' ibid 444.

[84] *Attorney-General for Northern Ireland's Reference (No 1 of 1975)* [1977] AC 105, HL; *HM Advocate v Sheppard* [1941] JC 67, HCJ; and *Hajdamovitz v Attorney General* [1944] 11 Palestine Law Reports 140.

grievous bodily harm'.[85] The difficulty here is the particular meaning that English law has developed of what acts can be said to be done with 'intent'. After a series of difficult cases which were said to have resulted in the law being in disarray, the House of Lords established the test as being whether death or serious harm will be virtually certain, barring some unforeseen intervention, to result from a person's act.[86] In the context of military operations, a soldier who deliberately fires his or her firearm at a person will, therefore, have the intent to murder. In both *A-G's Reference (1975)* and a later case *R v Clegg*, the court confirmed that, due to having the necessary intent, a soldier who fired in these circumstances (other than while on military operations abroad to which the laws of wars apply) would be guilty of murder, and so subject to the mandatory sentence of life imprisonment, rather than the lesser charge of manslaughter.[87] These cases show the reluctance of the courts to intervene in the issue despite the recognition that the law placed the soldier in a very different position to a civilian and that the Diceyian analogy was very misleading. A soldier, unlike a civilian, is subject to a duty enforceable by military law to carry out operations that may put his or her life in danger and is armed with a lethal weapon that may put him or her in the position of having to use it or lose it. Despite this recognition, the response of the courts has been to say that it is a matter for parliament and yet, in other matters, the courts have been willing to entertain the possibility of a defence of necessity.

Discussion of the defence of necessity almost always leads to a reference to the infamous English case of *R v Dudley and Stephens* in 1884.[88] Dudley and Stephens were shipwrecked in a storm and cast away in an open boat with two others including a cabin boy, Richard Parker. Seeing no other prospect of survival and that the boy was ailing, they killed him and ate his body. Four days later they were rescued and, on being brought to England, tried and convicted of murder. The court considered their defence of necessity but ruled it out on several grounds, including the immorality of permitting it in the circumstances. This case is the basis for the often repeated restriction that the defence of necessity is not available for murder.[89] However, this view is subject to two qualifications: first, in *R v Dudley and Stephens*, Lord Coleridge giving the judgment of the court said that 'the necessity which justifies homicide is of two kinds: (1) the necessity which is of a private nature; (2) the necessity which relates to the public justice and safety'.[90] He then went on to consider only private necessity. The nature of the defence as it relates to public safety seems not to have been considered by the courts although it was said to cover, as an example, the destruction of a house to provide a fire-break

[85] *Re A (Children) (Conjoined Twins: Surgical Separation)* [2001] Fam 149, CA at 198 (*Re A (Children)*).

[86] ibid 199.

[87] *R v Clegg* [1995] 1 AC 482, HL at 496.

[88] *R v Dudley and Stephens* [1884] 14 QBD 273, QBD.

[89] See, eg, *R v Sasikaran Selvaratnam* [2006] EWCA Crim 1321, CA Criminal Division, §35. The case bases this on a precedent that leads back through other cases to *R v Dudley and Stephens* (n 88).

[90] *R v Dudley and Stephens* (n 88) 282.

in a burning city as happened in the Great Fire of London in 1666.[91] There is also a reference in *Dudley and Stevens* to Hale's *The History of the Pleas of the Crown* as a source for the defence of necessity and in it Hale makes the distinction between necessity by compulsion and fear, and other necessity.[92] Within the former is self-defence and, in relation to the latter, he refers to the arrest of felons and the putting down of a riot. *Hale's* deals with insurrection in a separate chapter on levying war against the King, which is treason. Second, although the modern judgments do not establish a clear line of authority, there have been cases where necessity formed the basis of the defence of an act that would otherwise have been murder.[93]

Like the law on martial law, the defence of necessity has a long and confused history. The leading modern English case on the subject is *Re A (Children) (Conjoined Twins: Surgical Separation)* which was considered by the Court of Appeal in 2001.[94] As the name indicates, the case concerned the separation of conjoined twins, Mary and Jodie, who would both die without surgery. The operation would preserve the life of Jodie who could survive on her own but would result in the death of Mary, who could not. Among the issues it raised was the use of lethal force, for that is what the operation would be, and the potential liability of the doctors for murder if they took action to save a life and in doing so took another. The point in contention arose from the peculiar definition of intent in English law that the courts had struggled with in the shooting cases in Northern Ireland. The Court of Appeal took the test to be whether death or serious harm will be virtually certain, barring some unforeseen intervention, to result from the person's act.[95] The three judges unanimously rejected the appeal against an order permitting the operation but gave separate judgments that covered the issues, including murder and the defence of necessity, in their own terms which are somewhat different. One judge applied what he called the 'quasi-self-defence [of Jodie], modified to meet the quite exceptional circumstances of the case'.[96] Another considered the defence of necessity and concluded that '[i]n the absence of parliamentary intervention the law as to the defence of necessity is going to have to develop on a case by case basis … I would extend it, if it needs to be extended, to cover this case'.[97] Brooke LJ, however, went into the defence of necessity in considerably more depth and gave a full discussion of its history though case law, Royal Commissions and both nineteenth century and modern academic writing. As he drew the arguments together he rejected the need for necessity to be grounded in emergency: 'The

[91] *Re A (Children)* (n 85) at 220 citing Lord Goff in *Re F (Mental Patient: Sterilisation)* [1990] 2 AC 1, HL at 74.

[92] Sir M Hale, *The History of the Pleas of the Crown*, Vol 1 (London, T Payne, 1778). There are several editions of the work available including versions published in 1736 and 1800 in which the chapter on necessity appears.

[93] See in particular *Re A (Children)* (n 85). The argument was also made but rejected in *R (Nicklinson) v Ministry of Justice (CNK Alliance Ltd intervening)* [2015] 1 AC 657, SC, §130.

[94] *Re A (Children)* (n 85) at 147.

[95] ibid, Ward LJ at 199 describing the test from *R v Woollin* [1999] 1 AC 82, HL.

[96] ibid, Ward LJ at 204.

[97] ibid, Robert Walker LJ at 255.

principle is one of necessity, not emergency'.[98] He also rejected the need for 'unjust aggression' which it had been argued was required as it would be in self-defence. He said '[n]one of the formulations of the doctrine of necessity which I have noted in this judgment make any such requirement: in this respect it is different from the doctrine of private defence'.[99] He, then, arrived at a defence of necessity based on a nineteenth century textbook definition:

> there are three necessary requirements for the application of the doctrine of necessity: (i) the act is needed to avoid inevitable and irreparable evil; (ii) no more should be done than is reasonably necessary for the purpose to be achieved; (iii) the evil inflicted must not be disproportionate to the evil avoided.[100]

Brooke LJ attributed the definition to Sir James Stephen who was a judge and leading author in the late nineteenth century.[101] He was also a cousin of AV Dicey. The choice of language is archaic but the judge seems to be seeking to justify his argument on the basis that there is a long-established precedent for a defence of necessity. All three judges also considered the right to life under the ECHR that was shortly to become directly applicable in English law under the Human Rights Act 1998. They agreed that Mary would not be unlawfully deprived of her right to life on the basis that the act would not be intentional and 'intentionally' should be given its natural and ordinary meaning in the ECHR and not the wider meaning it has under English criminal law. The courts have since warned against using *Re A (Children)* as a precedent. In *Nicklinson*, the Court of Appeal said that, in relation to assisted suicide, it was 'too slender a thread on which to hang such a far-reaching development of the common law'.[102]

The difference in policy terms between 'self-defence' and 'necessity as a defence to homicide' is said to be that in necessity '[t]he policy of the law is to prevent A being judge in his own cause of the value of his life over B's life or his loved one C's life, and then being executioner as well'.[103] Self-defence is a separate legal defence that allows this decision and action in the face of an imminent threat of death or serious injury, subject to necessity and proportionality. In trying to decide whether there is an existing defence of necessity for the use of lethal force in military operations, one is then broadly left with three possibilities, first, and it seems to me that this is compelling, that the line of judgments relying on *Dudley and Stevens* that necessity is no defence to murder is not good authority in this context as the court specifically distinguished between public and private necessity and there is no modern authority on public necessity. Second, that Brooke LJ's formulation evidences a general defence but one which the courts are very wary of

[98] ibid Brooke LJ at 239.
[99] ibid at 240.
[100] ibid.
[101] Sir James Stephen and his works were mentioned in *Dudley and Stephens* as Stephen's *Digest of Criminal Law* (London, Macmillan and Co, 1883) and *History of the Criminal Law* (London, Macmillan and Co, 1883). Lord Coleridge also acknowledged the source in the case.
[102] *R (Nicklinson) v A Primary Care Trust* [2013] EWCA Civ 961, CA, §63.
[103] *Re A (Children)* (n 85) at 200.

extending. This is perhaps the more common view among leading textbooks but I think subject to the issue of use of force to quell an insurrection properly being seen as one of public not private necessity. Third, if those suggestions are incorrect, the main distinction between killing in self-defence of others and a more general defence of killing out of necessity is imminence. Of course, the less imminent an event is, the greater the possibility that there could be an intervening event which might render the proposed action unnecessary. In the case of the twins, the medical evidence was that it was only a matter of time.

Finally, necessity was the subject of some debate in relation to the use of lethal force against an attack of the type carried out on 9/11. The UK government's position was understood to be that 'it would be lawful to shoot down a plane, killing all the innocent passengers and crew if this were the only way to prevent a much greater impending disaster'.[104] Furthermore, according to the Parliamentary Select Committee on Defence, the policy was said to have been decided after legal advice and was based on the application of a necessity principle.[105] The test of necessity set out in the Select Committee's Report was the same as the one given by Brooke LJ in *Re A (Children)* from the nineteenth century work by Stephen.[106] It is also said that the justification could be based in the extended meaning of self-defence where a person acts to defend others who are being threatened.[107] Cameron Moore edges towards this view too but sees it as being characterized as a use of lethal force in the defence of others and notes that others have doubted this is correct.[108] Nonetheless, this does suggest that the British government have, and the select committee is willing to accept, a wider understanding of necessity as a defence to homicide than has previously been the case on the basis of the particular circumstances contemplated.[109]

Conclusion

The modern framework for the use of lethal force in military operations has been dominated by the approach of the courts and the question of how the laws of

[104] D Ormerod and K Laird, *Smith and Hogan's Criminal Law* (Oxford, Oxford University Press, 2016) 421.

[105] ibid – referring to the House of Commons Select Committee's Sixth Report, *Defence and Security in the UK 2001–2002* HC 518–1 (2002) para 8.

[106] The test used in the Select Committee Report is set out in Ormerod and Laird, *Smith and Hogan's Criminal Law* (2016) (n 104) 422.

[107] A right to intervene on behalf of others is recognized at common law and is confirmed by the Criminal Justice and Immigration Act 2008, s 76(10) which states that 'references to self-defence include acting in defence of another person' (AP Simester, JR Spencer, F Stark GR Sullivan and GJ Virgo, *Simester and Sullivan's Criminal Law: Theory and Doctrine* (London, Bloomsbury, 2016) 819.

[108] Moore, *Crown and Sword* (2017) (n 82) 200 and citing S Bronitt and D Stephens, '"Flying Under the Radar" – The Use of Lethal Force Against Hijacked Aircraft: Recent Australian Developments' (2007) 7: 2 *Oxford University Commonwealth Law Journal* 267–9.

[109] See Ormerod and Laird, *Smith and Hogan's Criminal Law* (n 104) 421.

war and international human rights law interact. In particular, states party to the ECHR have been called to account for their use of lethal force in military operations in internal armed conflicts and have sought to justify their actions as self-defence. This constitutes an expansion of the criminal law defence on which the necessity of self-defence was originally based and the avoidance of any recognition of the political nature of the armed groups which they oppose. The ECtHR has accepted the nomenclature of self-defence and based its jurisprudence on its existing methodology for assessing the necessity of self-defence that was first set out in *McCann*. In doing so, it has sought to apply the right to life in military operations but without addressing some essential questions: on a technical level on how to interpret the exceptions; and, on a policy level, on how it should assess necessity and proportionality in cases of the use of lethal force other than in narrow self-defence. It has also interpreted article 2 as requiring that the use of force is lawful under municipal law. This eschews the lawfulness that may be provided by operation of law through the laws of war and also produces a problem of category for human rights law as, in municipal law, necessity is grounded in criminal law and the two concepts are not the same. Furthermore, in English law they are underdeveloped and uncertain as matters of public law if not insurance law: underdeveloped from a nineteenth century concept of public necessity and uncertain in the application of private necessity as a defence to homicide. The differences then that exist between the laws of war and international human rights law undermine attempts to reconcile the different bodies of law and say that they reach more-or-less the same result. As the law stands, the portrayal of them as separated by a threshold of violence is well-established as a matter of the laws of war through the test of what is an armed conflict set down in the *Tadić* case[110] but the application of the right to life under international human rights law in armed conflict is less settled. However, a better understanding of it and the relationship between the two paradigms can be gained through the recognition of an overlap between international human rights law and the laws of war in circumstances of insurrection.

[110] *Prosecutor v Tadić*, (Decision on Jurisdiction) (1995) Case no IT-94-1-AR72, Appeals Chamber (1996) 35 ILM 32, 2 October 1995.

8

Re-aligning the Paradigms?

The British military experience in Iraq and the litigation that followed provided a rare insight into the application of the two legal paradigms of the laws of war and law-enforcement in a modern conflict and the problems that this can create. There was genuine uncertainty on some aspects of the law, particularly over the application of human rights law but, added to that, it can be seen that the British government chose to treat the paradigms as separate which created an artificial distinction that does not reflect how force is used in military operations in practice nor in all circumstances as a matter of law. Rather than seeing the paradigms as separated by a threshold of violence, they should be seen as overlapping so as to accommodate different levels of violence, such as was seen in Basra in 2004. The need to see the paradigms as overlapping is in part a matter of how to set the rules of engagement for military operations to maintain public order against organized armed groups when the conflict does not fit neatly into legal conceptions of the use of force as being in either law-enforcement or armed conflict. More fundamentally, however, it is about the appropriate type and level of force that may be used in internal armed conflicts that fall short of what was traditionally regarded as civil war. Looking back now, it is possible to see how the legal basis for regulating the use of force in these types of conflict moved from municipal law to the international laws of war due to particular circumstances at the time. Extending the laws of war to internal armed conflicts was intended to provide humanitarian relief but it also brought with it more permissive rules on the use of force. At the same time, international human rights law was also conceived to apply in circumstances of insurrection, although not in the way that it is now as war and peace were still seen as separate. This can be seen most clearly in the drafting of the European Convention on Human Rights (ECHR)[1] as it provides a mechanism for internal armed conflicts whereby a state could either treat the situation as insurrection and operate within the limitations that the municipal law and international law allow, or it could derogate from the convention on the basis that there is a war and operate under the laws of war.

[1] Convention for the Protection of Human Rights and Fundamental Freedoms (Rome, 4 November 1950).

Reassessing the Use of Force in the Paradigm of Law-enforcement

As a matter of legal theory and argument, the existence of two bodies of international law that may both apply in armed conflict raises an important question of how international humanitarian law and international human rights law interact. Both bodies of law justify the use of force through necessity but different meanings are given to 'military necessity' under the laws of war and 'necessity' under international human rights law. In practice, however, the bodies of law have remained largely separate with separate courts that ground their decisions in their particular area of legal competence. There are several arguments which seek to account for the potential area of overlap between human rights law and the laws of war in relation to lawful killing in internal armed conflicts. The first is to reject the overlap by arguing either that human rights do not apply on the battlefield or, conversely, that human rights are paramount. As was seen, the majority view, at least in Europe, is that these are too extreme, particularly in relation to states subject to the ECHR. The second is to argue that there is no breach of the right to life under human rights law if a person is killed in an armed conflict in accordance with the laws of war as the *lex specialis* in situations of armed conflict. The starting point is the International Court of Justice's views as stated in the *Nuclear Weapons* advisory opinion that under article 6 of the International Covenant a killing in accordance with the laws of war would not be 'arbitrary'. The reasoning is more difficult to apply to the ECHR given that it has specific exceptions although it is more generally consistent with the regime for derogating from the right to life in war. This indicates one way forward for member states, subject to reconciling the reference to 'war' with 'armed conflict'. In the cases on Russian operations in Chechnya, the European Court of Human Rights (ECtHR) could have treated the matter as one of derogation where it was clear that an armed conflict existed but perhaps it did not do so not only as it was not raised as a defence by Russia but also as to do so would have suggested its own irrelevance. This issue has now arisen in the more recent case of *Georgia v Russia (II)* as the court decided that the rights recognized under article 2 of the ECHR did not apply during the conduct of hostilities phase of the conflict but it has been criticized for doing so. However, making a more coherent argument on the ECHR then leads back to issues on the International Covenant and how it applies in situations that would fail to satisfy the legal definition of an armed conflict such that the deprivation of life was not 'arbitrary'. The third approach is to apply the principle that the ECHR should as far as possible be interpreted in harmony with other provisions of international law so as to interpret the obligations under article 2 consistently with the laws of war.[2] This goes a step

[2] In *Hassan v United Kingdom* App no 29750/09 (2014) ECHR 936, the ECtHR said that it would take into account the context and the provisions of the 1949 Geneva conventions in relation to the right to detain persons in international armed conflicts when interpreting and applying the provisions of

further than the argument that the court is applying the laws of war *sub silentio*,[3] and goes too far. It is possible to see the influence of the laws of war in case law, such as the references to methods and means of war, and in the similarity of result, especially in relation to indiscriminate attacks. This may imply a common approach. However, in other cases the court seems to be on different ground, and creating its own approach, when it has referred to a duty to avoid or minimize the risk of a loss of life of both insurgents and civilians. Finally, the fourth approach is to take the view that in armed conflict the two regimes 'mostly lead to the same results'.[4] This argument is based on an interpretation of certain of the rules of the laws of war in such a way as to bring them closer to human rights law, and in particular a judgment by the ECtHR in which it said that, in relation to the principle of proportionality, that there is little difference between the standards applicable under article 2 and those applicable to the conduct of military operations under the laws of war.[5] The problem with this is that it misunderstands the test of proportionality under the laws of war because under the laws of war the test excludes the lawful target. It has also been argued that this overlooks the differences between necessity and military necessity as, under the laws of war, the principles of distinction and military necessity allow status-based targeting – that is targeting a person on the basis that he or she is a combatant – and that it is difficult to see how human rights law would permit it as currently interpreted.[6] There is a point here but the perceived difference arises because the current interpretation of human rights law is limited to self-defence and has a narrow view of necessity. If insurrection is included, it may allow the status-based targeting of insurgents on the basis of the necessity of meeting armed insurgents with lethal force rather than acting only in self-defence. In my view all the attempts to argue equivalence between the two bodies of law are too stretched and they should be treated separately, which means acknowledging that they may have different results. Furthermore, they should

art 5 of the ECHR to the detention of persons by British forces during the military occupation of Iraq. It accepted that the principle of derogation under art 15 applied to detention in an international armed conflict even though no notification of a derogation had been made for Iraq (*Hassan v UK* at §103–04). The court has also since noted that, as a matter of practice, states have not made derogations in relation to international armed conflicts outside of their own territory, *Georgia v Russia (II)* App no 38263/08 (2021) ECHR 58 at §139.

[3] N Quénivet, 'The History of the Relationship between International Humanitarian Law and Human Rights Law' in R Arnold and N Quénivet (eds), *International Humanitarian Law and Human Rights Law: Towards a New Merger in International Law* (Leiden, Martinus Nijhoff Publishers, 2008) 332.

[4] M Lattimer and P Sands (eds), *The Grey Zone: Civilian Protection between Human Rights and the Laws of War* (London, Hart, 2018) 5 quoting M Sassòli and L Olsen, 'The Relationship between International Humanitarian Law and Human Rights Law Where It Matters: Admissible Killing and Internment of Fighters in Non-International Armed Conflicts' (2008) 90: 871 *International Review of the Red Cross* 600.

[5] *Finogenov v Russia* App no 18299/03 (2011) ECHR 2234, §208.

[6] M Milanovic, 'A Norm Conflict Perspective on the Relationship between International Humanitarian Law and Human Rights Law' (2010) 14: 3 *Journal of Conflict and Security Law*, 478. The argument is also repeated in the final chapter of M Milanovic, *Extraterritorial Application of Human Rights Treaties: Law, Principles, and Policy* (Oxford, Oxford University Press, 2011).

have different results where they address different circumstances of insurrection and a civil war-like intensity of armed conflict.

Refining the Meaning of the Exception for Insurrection

As has been argued, the examination of the drafting of the International Covenant and the ECHR shows that the exception for insurrection in the right to life in the ECHR was intended to represent the final level in a hierarchy of defences grounded in the criminal law for the use of force in the face of increasing violence. From the perspective of the British government and English law, the exceptions were mixed matters of law and fact, rather than merely fact, as each of the terms has elements that go beyond the ordinary meaning of the words. For example, in English law, the circumstances are considered from the perspective of what the person acting in self-defence believed them to be and whether the force used was reasonable in those circumstances. In the case of the other exceptions, there would have to be an arrestable offence to justify the use of force in arrest and there were statutory and common law definitions of riot. All of these are matters of law but there is no modern case law to provide a definition of insurrection. In general terms, as a matter of law, insurrection means something more than its ordinary dictionary definition of 'a violent uprising against authority' but, in public law at least, its further elaboration is contained in old cases that are unclear as to the distinctions between insurrection and treason. The most prominent case is *R v Frost*, which concerned the Chartist uprising in 1839, in which the judge directed the jury that for the charge of treason to be made out 'there must be an insurrection, that there must be force accompanying such insurrection, and the object of it must be of a general nature'.[7] The pre–ECHR understanding of insurrection was based partly on this case and set out by the Parliamentary Counsel, Sir Henry Thring, in the first *Manual of Military Law* when it was published in 1884 and continued through revised editions until the Second World War. It defined insurrection by contrasting it with riot and the essence of insurrection was its 'general and public nature' and 'an intention to "levy war against the King" … or otherwise act in general defiance of the government of the country'.[8] This is consistent with the eighteenth century authority that there was an offence of 'a constructive levying of war in peace-time if three or more persons "arose" to effect some public purpose'.[9] There is also nineteenth century authority that it is the treasonable purpose that distinguishes treason, which would include levying war against the king, from riot.[10] It also makes a link to an additional

[7] *R v Frost and Eleven Others* [1839] 173 ER 771 at 785.

[8] War Office, *Manual of Military Law* (London, HMSO, 1884), 280–92.

[9] J Baker, *An Introduction to English Legal History* (Oxford, Oxford University Press, 2019), citing *R v Damaree* (1709) Foster 213, 15 State Tr 521.

[10] D Ormerod (ed), *Halsbury's Laws* (5th edn, 2020) Vol 26, 'Criminal Law', para 553 citing *Hardie's Case* (1820) 1 State Tr NS 609 at 765.

element that those perpetrating insurrection have to use force.[11] This can be seen in Thring's explanation of the authority to use force to suppress an insurrection and the limitation he placed on it that '[t]he existence of an armed insurrection would justify the use of any degree of force necessary effectually to meet and cope with insurrection' whilst 'care being taken to avoid any unnecessary bloodshed or injury'.[12] The Privy Council has since then explicitly upheld 'the right to administer force against force in actual war' and confirmed that it did not depend upon the proclamation of martial law.[13] It is certainly arguable that the reference to 'war' should be taken to mean a state of belligerency but the courts did recognize during the Boer War and the Irish War of Independence that insurrection and rebellion could amount to actual war. The Irish courts (prior to independence) also accepted that what was variously described as insurrection and rebellion amounted to actual war of a guerrilla character. In addition, there was a notion of going 'armed in a war-like manner' that the courts had used in a sense of a persons armed with weapons of some sort acting as part of a group rather than a narrow sense of war as being fought between armies with firearms and other modern weapons.

For states other than the UK which are party to the ECHR, it is, of course, irrelevant what English law provides and the ECtHR has insisted that states are able to demonstrate the lawfulness of the use of force under their municipal law as well as compliance with the convention. This has led to consideration of whether the English, Northern Irish and Gibraltarian law of self-defence is consistent with the provisions of article 2, which they were each found to be, as well as wider consideration of the municipal law applicable in states of emergency. Although there is no evidence in the *travaux préparatoires* of the convention, states other than the UK were presumably satisfied that they were capable of complying with the provisions of paragraph (c) of article 2 concerning insurrection or they did not think that it was an issue that would affect them. It does though seem consistent with the idea that other European states have a concept of 'a state of siege' or some other form of emergency law which would provide the authority under municipal law for the use of force to quell an insurrection.

The meaning of necessity in relation to article 2 is simpler to state in so far as the ECtHR has developed an approach out of the framework set out in *McCann* that has three main elements: (i) any use of force must be no more than absolutely necessary for one or more of the purposes set out in sub-paragraphs 2(a), (b) and (c) of article 2; (ii) 'absolute necessity' is a stricter and more compelling test of necessity; and (iii) that the force used must also be 'strictly proportionate' to the achievement of the aims set out in those sub-paragraphs. The court has not, however, considered what amount of force might be considered absolutely necessary and proportionate against insurgents in circumstances that may be

[11] J Curwood, *A Treatise on the Pleas of the Crown by William Hawkins*, Vol I of Criminal Offences (London, S Sweet, 1824), 11 citing 1 Hale, 131 and other sources.

[12] War Office, *Manual of Military Law* (1884) 280–92.

[13] *Tilonko v Attorney-General of Natal* [1907] AC 93, PC at 94.

seen as insurrection. In its judgments it has focused instead on the indiscriminate nature of the weapons used by the military forces rather than the purposes for which they were used. An indication of what the British military thought was justifiable can be seen in the approach it developed prior to the Second World War that identified different but overlapping levels of force that could be used: in firing on rioting crowds the policy was 'broadly stated as the use of the minimum force necessary' in the immediate circumstances and it should not be used for deterrent effect.[14] As such, riot stood somewhere between self-defence and insurrection. The use of force in a riot could be based on the immediate necessity of protecting the lives of soldiers or civilians and their property or, under the terms of the Riot Act 1714, it could be pre-meditated once the prescribed form of notice had been given. In both cases, the force used had to be limited to that amount of force necessary to disperse the rioters and it could not be punitive. However, there were no legal restrictions on the amount of force that could be used against armed rebels, unless and until they were captured or otherwise *hors de combat*. This can be seen as a modification of the principles of distinction and military necessity in that it limits the use of lethal force to armed rebels. This is, I would argue, the difference between the use of force in self-defence and in insurrection as it was understood at the time of the ECHR. Once soldiers confront armed rebels, the use of force is likely to be justified in self-defence but if self-defence is understood narrowly to exclude attack or pre-meditated violence, as it is in English criminal law, the difference between it and the use of lethal force in military operations against insurgents becomes clearer. The use of lethal force against insurgents may be pre-meditated and planned but it must also be discriminating. The emergency regulations used in colonial conflicts could then be seen as lessening the degree of discrimination in treating persons found in 'prohibited areas' as insurgents and reducing the protection of persons in 'special areas' who failed to stop when challenged. Nevertheless, the difficulty of finding the balance of what is necessary remains from the pre-convention British courts approach that treated necessity as a matter of fact and avoided developing any further rules. The courts have been reluctant to expand the common law except on a very limited, case-by-case basis, such as was seen in the conjoined twins case (*Re A (Children)*), as the judges say that is a matter for parliament.[15] Parliament has, however, been equally reluctant to act, for reasons perhaps expressed by Lord Haldane, as a lawyer and government minister, as the difficulty of specifying what its parameters might be. The drafters of the ECHR took the approach that it was more desirable to have legal certainty by specifying the exceptions to the right to life, but there is little certainty in the legal literature over the meaning of the exception for insurrection. Nevertheless, the British military–legal framework that was developed in the first half of the twentieth

[14] War Office, Army Pamphlet, 'Notes on Imperial Policing' (1934) 41.
[15] *Re A (Children) (Conjoined Twins: Surgical Separation)* [2001] Fam 147, CA at 255.

century provides a better understanding of it. The drafters of the ECHR also continued the English law approach that the use of force in riot and insurrection is to be justified as a matter of 'necessity' or 'absolute necessity'. This approach was considered by Professor William Holdsworth (1871–1944) in one of the leading texts on the historical development of martial law when it became an issue at the time of the Boer War and in it he explained how necessity had been viewed differently in the English cases depending on the level of violence. The approach in riot was exemplified in *Pinney's* case – the case of riot in Bristol in 1832 – in which the judge, Littledale J., held that the magistrate or military officer ordering the use of force 'is bound to hit the exact line between an excess and doing what is sufficient'. However, Holdsworth submitted, whilst this applied to riot, as 'riot approaches rebellion, when it practically amounts to a state of war, as the necessity is greater, so the discretion of those whose duty it is to restore order is more free'.[16] Professor Frederick Pollock (1845–1937), another eminent professor of law and editor of the *Law Quarterly Review*, also argued at that time that, when called to account for acts taken in exercising that discretion, 'the existence of a reasonable and probable cause for the act complained of, having regard to the public danger, is necessary and sufficient to justify it'.[17] The issue of accountability and discretion was considered again by the authors of one of the most authoritative books on constitutional law in the 1970s and 80s prior to the development of the ECtHR's jurisprudence on the right to life.[18] They argued that Dicey's approach that 'absolute necessity' requires there to be an immediate necessity for each use of force could be seen as being too hard because, unlike self-defence or riot, the use of force in quelling an insurrection is not confined to a single incident which can be judged in isolation but part of an organized military campaign in which the uses of force contribute collectively to the suppression of the insurrection. On the other hand, leaving the use of force to the discretion of the military commander, even one acting in good faith, left too great a risk of unaccountability for reckless violence. In order to address these conflicting concerns, rather than being looked at individually as cases of immediate necessity, the instances where force was used should be seen in the context of their contribution to the successful quelling of the rebellion. Nevertheless, it would still be very difficult for a defendant to prove, and for a court to determine, whether or not each separate use of force was necessary to achieve the purpose. Instead, in a reworking of Pollock's views, they suggested that it should be for the applicant who alleged wrong-doing to show either that the defendant acted in bad faith or that no reasonable person would deem the particular use of force as absolutely necessary to quell the rebellion.[19] They admitted that although, as Dicey had said, there was no authority in English law

[16] WS Holdsworth, 'Martial Law Historically Considered' (1902) 18 *Law Quarterly Review*, 130.
[17] F Pollock, 'What is Martial Law?' (1902) 18 *Law Quarterly Review*, 154.
[18] DL Keir and FH Lawson, *Cases in Constitutional Law* (Oxford, Clarendon Press, 1979).
[19] ibid 224.

for that proposition, 'it was nothing but a development and extension of his doctrine of immediate necessity, to cover the case where the act is not isolated but part of an interconnected plan of campaign'.[20] Alternatively, one might say that Dicey's own argument on the position of a soldier in using force to quell a riot or insurrection being the same as a citizen's was probably ill-founded insofar as it concerned insurrection. As has been seen, the ECtHR has developed the concept of 'absolute necessity' in self-defence in *McCann* and has followed it in subsequent cases where it has referred to the necessity and proportionality of the use of force being related to the purpose for which it is used. If that is then applied to insurrection, the 'absolute necessity' of the use of force should be seen as being different to an isolated incident of self-defence or riot and as an issue of whether it contributed to the purpose of quelling the insurrection. In terms of the test suggested by Keir and Lawson as the basis for proving wrongdoing, it is a question of whether it can be shown that no reasonable person would have deemed the particular use of force absolutely necessary to quell the insurrection.

The Potential Consequences of Making Use of the Exception for Insurrection

One of the issues raised by the argument that there should be more recognition of the exception for insurrection and its potential application is whether it would provide legal protection for so-called 'shoot-to-kill' policies or targeted killings that would not otherwise exist except in circumstances that amounted to a non-international armed conflict. Controversies over the existence of a shoot-to-kill policy being sanctioned by the British government have been most apparent in relation to the Troubles in Northern Ireland but have also been raised by recent histories of Britain's withdrawal from empire. There are two distinct aspects to this which reflect the military–legal framework for law-enforcement operations in Northern Ireland on the one hand, and operations in colonial conflicts and more recently in Iraq and Afghanistan on the other.

The journalist and author Mark Urban tried to encapsulate what was meant by 'shoot-to-kill' in the context of Northern Ireland as being a combination of three different dimensions based on the context of the shooting: last resort – could the terrorist attack have been avoided by other means; necessity – was it necessary to shoot and was a challenge made first; and intent – were the shots intended to kill?[21] He then discards the third dimension on the basis that it describes how the British security forces are taught to use firearms by aiming at the centre of the body. It

[20] ibid 225.

[21] M Urban, *Big Boys' Rules: The SAS and the Secret Struggle Against the IRA* (London, Faber & Faber, 1992) 70.

may seem unrealistic to suggest that it is possible to do anything else in an engagement but the idea that it may be possible to shoot to wound was raised in the *McCann* case and left undecided due to a lack of evidence.[22] The question is more accurately, then, whether there was a policy of 'shoot-on-sight'.[23] After weighing the evidence on the other two dimensions, Urban comes to the conclusion that there was no shoot-to-kill policy as such but that there were operations that were planned and executed in a such a way that, in practice, soldiers were confronted by armed men and left with no choice but to open fire in self-defence and kill them. On other occasions, however, it appeared that operations were planned and carried out as arrest operations. From the evidence available it is difficult to conclude whether the different types of operations and outcomes were the product of different circumstances rather than being open to the making of a policy choice and the issue remains contested. John Stalker, a former chief constable who was leading one of the main inquiries into some of the allegations of shoot-to-kill before he was controversially removed from it, also thought that there was no policy as such to be found but there was an understanding among those involved as to what was the expected outcome.[24] Several attempts to raise the issue with the ECtHR have since been rejected on procedural grounds, including the lack of admissible evidence that had been submitted in support of the applications. These issues have been raised again recently in an inquest into the killing of four IRA men by SAS soldiers at Clonoe in County Tyrone in 1992 after they had attacked a nearby police station with a machine gun. The coroner found that the use of force had been unjustified and unreasonable and, echoing the words of the ECtHR, that the operation 'was not planned and controlled in such a way as to minimize to the greatest extent possible the need for recourse to lethal force'.[25] I think, however, that it is also possible to approach the controversy over 'shoot-to-kill' from a different viewpoint based on the overlap of the paradigms of law-enforcement and armed conflict.

As a matter of the law-enforcement paradigm, the core issue for allegations of a shoot-to-kill policy in the Troubles was the application of the self-defence rules of engagement set out in the Yellow Card. The card was revised from its original form early in the Troubles by the addition of a provision on opening fire without having given a warning. Under it, a soldier could open fire without warning 'if there is no other way to protect yourself or those whom it is your duty to protect from the danger of being killed or seriously injured'.[26] This then became a matter of the municipal law of self-defence as to the soldier's subjective belief in

[22] *McCann v United Kingdom* App no 18984/91 (1995) ECHR 31, §212 and Joint Dissenting Opinion, §21–22.

[23] TR Mockaitis, *British Counterinsurgency in the Post-imperial Era* (Manchester, Manchester University Press, 1998) 123.

[24] H Russell, *The Use of Force and Article 2 of the ECHR in Light of European Conflicts* (London, Hart Publishing, 2017) 214–15.

[25] J O'Neill, 'SAS "not justified" in 1992 shooting of four IRA men', *BBC News*, 6 February 2025.

[26] R Fisk, 'British Army Instructions on Opening Fire (1973)', *The Times*, 6 March 1973.

the threat and then the taking of reasonable steps in response to that threat. The limits of this defence were tested in a number of cases where soldiers were waiting for members of the IRA to arrive and the operation could be viewed as either a pre-planned ambush, which would not be within the traditional understanding of self-defence, or a reactive response to the threat once presented, which could be. There is then a further issue that moves from the interpretation of the law and evidence into whether there was any alternative to the operation which might have prevented the recourse to lethal force. As previously discussed, this was one of the points decided by the ECtHR in the *McCann* case and marks a point of departure from self-defence as a matter of the criminal law into a separate body of human rights law.

In armed conflict, the targeting of specific individuals is an area of some controversy in the laws of war as there has been a long-standing aversion to the personalization of killing which has led to some difficult distinctions being drawn as to what is permissible and what is not. The rules on targeting are generally classified although NATO publishes its targeting doctrine and there is a discrete literature on targeting.[27] In Iraq in the period of hostilities prior to the occupation, the British authorities approached the issue of targeting individuals on the basis that the individuals had either to be members of the Iraqi armed forces within the definition of armed forces set out in article 43 of the Additional Protocol I or civilians 'for such time as they take a direct part in the hostilities' under article 51(3) of the protocol. The British approach was that the determination was 'a question of fact to be made on the basis of the actual status, functions and activities of the person concerned' and that, in relation to Iraqi leaders, the 'individual's constitutional position was not in itself sufficient to justify the conclusion that he was a member of the armed forces'.[28] This approach is consistent with the interpretation provided in the subsequent 2004 UK Ministry of Defence, *Manual of the Law of Armed Conflict* but appears to contrast with the approach of the US, at least as evidenced by the 2015 US Department of Defense, *Law of War Manual* published after the conflict. It seems to put more emphasis on the position or office held by the individual leader although it is not entirely clear.[29] In addition, the issue of targeting individuals and shoot-to-kill relates to an earlier discussion as to whether there is a principle under the laws of war that requires a combatant to disable or capture, if possible, rather than kill another combatant or civilian directly participating in hostilities (capture–kill). As has been argued, the correct view of the current

[27] D Turns, 'Targets', in ND White and C Henderson (eds), *Research Handbook on International Conflict and Security Law* (Cheltenham, Edward Elgar, 2013) 372. Turns cites a book by an Australian officer who had completed a PhD on targeting: I Henderson, *The Contemporary Law of Targeting: Military Objectives, Proportionality and Precautions in Attack under Additional Protocol I* (Leiden, Martinus Nijhoff Publishers, 2009). The main textbook on the subject is W Boothby, *The Law of Targeting* (Oxford, Oxford University Press, 2012).

[28] The Iraq Inquiry, Section 6.2 (Military planning for the invasion, January to March 2003) §749.

[29] See the UK Ministry of Defence, *The Manual of the Law of Armed Conflict* (Oxford, Oxford University Press, 2004) §5.3.3 and the US Department of Defense, *Law of War Manual* (Washington, Department of Defense, 2015) §5.8.4.

law is that combatants have the right to kill other combatants or civilians directly participating in hostilities without warning or stay unless or until they are *hors de combat*. This would also apply to combatants in non-international armed conflicts (if, like the ICRC, one takes the view that under customary international law there is combatant status for fighters in non-international armed conflicts) and to civilians who take a direct part in hostilities. Notwithstanding the concern about targeting civilian leaders and the need to determine their status as seen in Iraq, the implication, if there is one, that there was something illegitimate about shoot-to-kill policies which target civilians who are taking a direct part in a non-international armed conflict is, to that extent, somewhat off-point.[30] However, in internal armed conflicts that do not pass the threshold of a non-international armed conflict, the issue is how the court should approach the requirement that it is absolutely necessary to use lethal force to quell an insurrection. In trying to examine that, there are a range of views that could be taken to the issue of shoot-to-kill in an insurrection which would overlap with the judgments in existing cases on self-defence and the ethical arguments made by writers in relation to capture-kill or the extent to which soldiers should risk their lives to make a positive identification of a person on the battlefield as an enemy combatant.[31] The ECtHR, as has been seen, took different approaches to the interpretation of self-defence in the *McCann*, *Ergi* and *Esmukhambetov* cases. In *McCann*, the emphasis was on whether the State took appropriate steps to minimize the recourse to lethal force in the context of an arrest operation, whereas in *Ergi* the emphasis was whether the State took all feasible precautions to avoid or minimize the loss of civilian life in an ambush of armed insurgents. In the *Esmukhambetov* case, the court blurred the difference in applying the general test in *McCann* and criticized operations against armed insurgents which had not been prepared 'in such a way as to avoid or minimize, to the greatest extent possible, the risk of a loss of life, both for persons at whom the measures were directed and for civilians'. The formulation of this test may be based on the principle that the right to life is universal but it is also deceptively simple and incomplete in that an operation to avoid or minimize the risk to life in an armed arrest operation on the streets of Gibraltar is very different from one which is confronting a group or groups of heavily armed insurgents and the test as stated does not take into account the risk to the lives of the security forces. The difficulty is partly due to the wide meaning given by the court to self-defence as it makes it difficult to express the difference between the different exceptions. It has been noted that the ECtHR's references to the duty to minimize the recourse to lethal force under articles 2.2(a), (b) and (c) have led to an interpretation of the use of lethal force to make an arrest which has come very close in effect to the meaning of killing in self-defence for the protection

[30] Milanovic, 'A Norm Conflict Perspective' (2010) (n 6) 478. Milanovic refers to there being 'temporal limitations' in relating to engaging civilians who take a direct part in hostilities which may imply a development of the test but not so far as the ICRC's framework in its *Interpretative Guidance*. I take the view that time is an integral part of the test as to whether they are taking a direct (or active) part in hostilities.

[31] See JD Ohlin and L May, *Necessity in International Law* (Oxford, Oxford University Press, 2016) Ch 9 'Disabling versus Killing in War', 207–33 for a good summary of the debate.

of others and the extension of the duty to insurrection would, in effect, equate it with capture/kill and the broader notions of self-defence. The essential difference between the exception for self-defence and insurrection in this context is the purpose for which lethal force is used and in *Ergi* the court implicitly accepted the necessity of using armed force against armed insurgents rather than examining it from the perspective of capture–kill as it would in a case of arrest in a law-enforcement operation. In this sense, *Ergi* is better seen as a case of insurrection and the necessity of using lethal force against armed rebels. The difference is in the purpose of the operation, in the case of *Ergi* an ambush of armed insurgents. More generally, it would allow offensive operations subject to maintaining proportionality in relation to the purpose and the balance between the lives, on the one hand, of civilians and the security forces and, on the other, the armed insurgents. This can also be seen in a different way in the *Özkan* case where, once the soldiers had been fired upon, the court accepted the 'absolute necessity' of the soldiers returning intense, tactical fire. Put more conceptually on the basis of the hierarchy of violence underlying the exceptions to the right to life in the ECHR, the difference is that in self-defence the law has to determine how to balance the right to life of the attacker and the defender and it weighs more heavily on the defender's side, whereas in insurrection civilian lives are counted equally with the security forces and their joint protection in the quelling of the insurrection and restoration of public order weighs more heavily than the lives of armed insurgents. By contrast, once the threshold to armed conflict is crossed, under the balance created by the laws of war, the lives of the opposing combatants are weighed equally and civilian lives are outweighed by military advantage to the extent that their loss is proportionate. In practice, as in the *Ergi* and *Özkan* cases, this weighting would recognize both that engaging armed rebels as such with lethal force may be absolutely necessary and that there is a need to provide greater protection to civilians than they would receive under the laws of war. If that is correct, it may also be that 'absolute necessity' in insurrection becomes a matter of law, and not only a matter of fact.

This understanding of the distinction between self-defence and insurrection can be illustrated by looking again at the circumstances in the *Cangöz* case which was argued by the Turkish government as being a use of lethal force within article 2.2(a), (b) or (c) of the ECHR without the actual grounds being specified. It could be argued from the government's version of the events that those killed were engaged in an act of insurrection.[32] The government's argument has the elements which, if true, could satisfy the meaning of insurrection which was argued earlier – its troops were targeting armed members of a proscribed communist group attending a meeting to plan attacks in Turkey. The facts were contested and the court found only that they were going to attend a meeting and that any further purpose was not substantiated. However, as a matter of human rights law, as the court found, it was still necessary to show that the shootings were absolutely necessary and proportionate to their purpose, whether it be acting in self-defence,

[32] *Cangöz v Turkey* App no 7469/06 (2016) ECHR 377.

making an arrest or quelling the insurrection. So, to take a different and hypothetical example, what if there were an end to the international armed conflict in Ukraine but armed violence continued and there was an incident between the Ukrainian army and an armed, separatist group? Ukraine is a signatory of the ECHR and the circumstances might then be more widely seen as the legitimate suppression of an insurrection. It would still be for Ukraine to show that any killings by the Ukrainian army in such circumstances were absolutely necessary and proportionate as understood under the ECHR. As has been discussed, the meaning of absolute necessity and proportionality under the ECHR would require development and would in many ways be an issue of policy rather than law but the potential difference in the rules that would apply does seem to offer a meaningful application of the exception for insurrection in the ECHR and provide greater protection to the right to life of those involved than would be given by the laws of war in similar circumstances.

Revisiting the Use of Lethal Force against Insurgents

The legal methodology adopted here to investigate the applicable law required it to distinguish the law as it is (*lex latis*) from the law as it was in the past (*lex prior*) or is desired to be in the future (*lex ferenda*). In assessing the argument that the military operations and the use of lethal force do not occur in separate paradigms of law-enforcement and the law of armed conflict and that they should rather be seen as overlapping, it must be recognized that the test of what is an armed conflict set down in the *Tadić* case[33] is firmly established in the laws of war and international criminal law. It requires that in order for there to be an armed conflict there must be organized armed groups engaged in protracted violence, and the rule was subsequently developed by the understanding that protracted violence required a certain degree of intensity. The test in effect created a threshold of violence that is required for there to be an armed conflict. The overlapping nature of the use of lethal force between the two paradigms is then limited as a matter of *lex latis* in that once the test is satisfied the laws of war apply, or, to put it the other way round, the laws of war do not apply until the threshold of violence is passed, however difficult that may be to establish as a matter of fact and notwithstanding that the judgment will be retrospective. The overlap between the paradigms exists, therefore, in a sense only on one side such that the armed conflict paradigm does not extend below the threshold but the law-enforcement paradigm may extend above it and continue to apply. The analogy of a Venn diagram is, therefore, not quite correct. The common area of overlap brings the paradigm of law-enforcement into the paradigm of armed

[33] *Prosecutor v Tadić*, (Decision on Jurisdiction) (1995) Case no IT-94-1-AR72, Appeals Chamber (1996) 35 ILM 32, 2 October 1995.

conflict but it does not overlay the paradigm of law-enforcement with the paradigm of armed conflict.

Although this overlap is set in the existing law, there is room to challenge how it has come to be applied and to provide a legal basis on which to influence the legal approach to the use of lethal force in future military operations in insurrections. First, it has been argued that, properly understood, Common Article 3 provided a level of humanitarian protection and it was the attempt to apply Common Article 3 as widely as possible which brought the laws of war on the conduct of hostilities into non-international armed conflicts at lower levels of violence. In particular, it brought with it the principle of military necessity, a principle conceived for war as understood as a conflict between states and itself changed over time to a more belligerent form. In a sense, this change completed Lieber's conception of a monolithic class of wars of insurrection, rebellion and civil war under the laws of war and hid the European tradition of separating insurrection and rebellion, on the one hand, from civil war and belligerency, on the other. This unacknowledged change was then carried into the ICRC's *Customary Law Study* which applied almost all of the rules of the laws of war to non-international armed conflicts, including the rule of proportionality which incorporates the principle of military necessity. Nonetheless, the concept of 'armed conflicts not of an international character' was contested and deliberately left undefined which makes it possible for courts to apply a stricter factual test within the existing law and set a higher threshold of violence for the transition from law-enforcement to armed conflict. Moving the threshold towards civil war could mean that the activities of the ICRC and national Red Cross societies were made more difficult as governments might again argue that they have no role in internal conflicts. More tangentially, it would also mean that the ICC or other tribunals would lack the jurisdiction for war crimes that they might otherwise have had as there would be no 'armed conflict'. This could result in a loss of the protection that the ICRC may provide and the accountability that the ICC may bring, or it could place more reliance on human rights groups and bodies such as the UN Human Rights Committee which were either not conceived or active in the period when the threshold was lowered. These are policy matters which would have to be considered but it would also be a reflection of the change away from the assessment of the use of force under the laws of war and the focus on the protection of human rights in and outside of armed conflict.

Second, the meaning of self-defence in cases brought under article 2 of the ECHR has become distorted by arguments which introduce the concept of self-defence as a state act, as it is in *jus ad bellum*. This has the effect of making the exception for the use of force to quell an insurrection and the ability of states to derogate for acts of killing in war redundant in practice and weakens the protection afforded by the convention in circumstances short of insurrection and war. It could be argued that giving effect to the exception for insurrection would lessen the protection of the convention and permit justifications for targeted killings and 'shoot-to-kill' policies. However, given the uncertainty of the current law and the move away from the use of acts of indemnity, it is unlikely that the security forces, who are well aware of the legal risks of military operations, would be prepared to take the risk of conducting 'shoot-to-kill' operations outside of a conflict in which it could be argued that they were acting lawfully under the laws of war in targeting the insurgents as civilians directly participating in the conflict. If the laws of war could not be argued to apply or if both the laws of war and international human rights law applied, a move towards narrowing the concept of self-defence to return it to its original limits would mean that these policies, if they were carried out, would have to be justified by policy-makers and military commanders as the use of force in quelling an insurrection rather than putting the onus on soldiers to show that they were acting in self-defence. Each killing would have to be defended on the basis of the absolute necessity of using lethal force against the insurgents, which is a stricter test than military necessity under the laws of war. It also does not carry with it the allowance for lawful civilian casualties that falls within the concept of proportionality under the laws of war. This would then leave a clearer line between the paradigms of armed conflict and law-enforcement drawn at a level of Additional Protocol II which requires greater levels of state-like organisation and the possession of territory, in effect what was understood as civil war. Killings in civil war would be subject to derogation under the ECHR and would properly fall into the *lex specialis* of the laws of war under the International Covenant. It might be that governments would see little incentive to change and be reluctant to admit to an insurrection or to lose the additional latitude that they have under the laws of war to use military force, but governments have a variety of institutions and interests as was seen in the case of British government counter-insurgency policies or the negotiation of international conventions. Some institutions, particularly foreign ministries and state departments, may see some advantage in criticising the amount of force used by other governments in quelling insurrections and have to reflect this in their policy and defend their own use of force when criticized by others.

Third, the legal interpretation of the exception for insurrection is underdeveloped but there are sources which may contribute to its understanding. One is the case law on insurance cases and the other is the chapter on riot and insurrection in the 1884 *Manual of Military Law* written by Sir Henry Thring. The concepts of necessity and proportionality would require judicial development but there is existing authority that distinguished public and private necessity. Public necessity has not been used for some two centuries but it should be seen as separate from private necessity as developed by the courts over the past century. By looking back at authoritative academic opinion on what constituted public 'absolute necessity' under English law, it is possible to reconstruct an understanding of how it was perceived as looking at an act in the wider context of its contribution to quelling an insurrection and how it differed from the more immanent 'absolute necessity' in self-defence or quelling a riot. There is no direct authority for the concept of proportionality for the use of force in an insurrection but the examples of the Lieber Code and British practice suggest that it extends only to armed rebels whilst, at the same time, excluding civilians killed by accident or mistake. This is not to say that there is no uncertainty in this but it would allow a debate on what are the acceptable limits of the use of force in internal armed conflicts. This should include a debate over what being an 'insurgent' means; for example, is it limited to those who are actually armed or does it include a bomb-maker or the driver of a vehicle containing rebels carrying weapons, much as there is a debate on whether such roles fall within the definition of a combatant or a civilian directly participating in hostilities under the laws of war. There would also be an issue over collateral killings and whether any civilian causalities, including bomb–makers or drivers of vehicles if they are not regarded as being armed insurgents, were within a proportionate use of force but it would allow a more restrictive approach than currently applies to proportionality under the laws of war. In practice, a major difference between operations under the laws of war and human rights law would be the restriction of fire support provided by aircraft or artillery where there was a risk of incidental civilian casualties. This is a very difficult area as the laws of war already contain an obligation to avoid or at least minimize civilian casualties and, if, as a matter of policy, there is to be a difference, it is arguable that operations below the threshold of armed conflict would have to be planned to avoid civilian casualties. Any that did occur would then have to have been the result of a mistake – the test might be drawn as requiring that the casualties were unforeseen or, if it were more strictly drawn, unforeseeable – or, perhaps in cases such as the use of civilians as human-shields, unavoidable, but proportionate to the purpose.

Fourth, the separation of martial law and the right to repel force with force developed in the first half of the twentieth century has not been overturned by the courts but British government practice in colonial conflicts and then Northern Ireland avoided reliance on it. The government placed more weight on the common law duty to prevent crime which was supplemented by the Criminal Law Act 1967 and its Northern Irish equivalent that '[a] person may use such force as is reasonable in the circumstances in the prevention of crime, or in effecting or assisting in the lawful arrest of offenders or suspected offenders or of persons unlawfully at large'.[34] Although they appear in some respects to be quite different, this common basis can be seen in the rules of engagement set out in the Red Card in Cyprus and the Yellow Card in Northern Ireland. The Red Card directed troops to open fire when being attacked whereas the Yellow Card permitted troops to open fire in self-defence and it is difficult to see a substantial difference between the two when the right in the Yellow Card extended to opening fire without issuing a challenge if not to do so would increase the risk to the lives of the soldiers or civilians. The same approach was then taken in Iraq under Card Alpha which limited the use of lethal force in self-defence to preventing loss of life on the part of coalition forces or Iraqi civilians.[35] The various cards also show how difficult it is to set rules of engagement within the law-enforcement paradigm against more intense levels of violence. The British army has been aware of the risks and limitations of relying on the common law and sought additional emergency powers on which they could rely as the basis for offensive operations as well as acts of indemnity. The acts of indemnity passed at the end of the colonial conflicts such as Kenya and Cyprus were sometimes part of a process of offering amnesties to

[34] Criminal Law Act 1967, s 3(1).
[35] Iraq Inquiry Report, Section 9.2 (May 2003 to June 2004) §1145.

insurgents and political detainees but the British government subsequently moved away from exonerating security force actions through acts of indemnity. There was no act of indemnity at the time of the Good Friday Agreement in 1998 and the attempt to prevent further proceedings under the Northern Ireland Troubles (Legacy and Reconciliation) Act 2023 has been subject to successful challenges in the Northern Irish courts in relation to provisions that are incompatible with the ECHR and it is to be amended or repealed by the British government. Similarly, the Overseas Operations (Service Personnel and Veterans) Act 2021 which restricts prosecutions of service personnel after five years (except for sexual offences) was an attempt to draw a line under the litigation resulting from the operations in Afghanistan and Iraq but was very controversial and may be challenged. If the public order situation required the deployment of British armed forces within the United Kingdom, there are statutory powers to make emergency regulations under the Civil Contingency Act 2004 and the Emergency Powers Act 1964 and, to the extent they still exist, residual common law or prerogative powers. If a government did decide to invoke the authority of the exception to the right to life in insurrection, the main difficulty would be shaping emergency powers to accommodate the requirements of the ECHR but it is conceivable that additional powers might be necessary to meet a particular threat to public order. This is unlikely within the UK but if, for example, British troops were deployed to assist another government in Europe faced with border incursions by heavily-armed insurgents, it would be possible that the host country could provide the municipal law basis for offensive operations against the insurgents that were wider than self-defence but more limited than would be possible in an international or non-international armed conflict.

Taken together, these possibilities, together with the fact that the exception to the right for life in insurrection already exists in the ECHR, mean that, for so long as there is overlap, it would be possible to interpret the convention as setting a more restrictive standard for the conduct of military operations in insurrection. This approach was alluded to by Leggat J in *AS2* in the different circumstances of belligerent occupation but it provides an alternative to the existing approaches to resolving the conflict between the two bodies of law in the areas of overlap, such as harmonization or *lex specialis*. The argument that recognizing the exception may be more permissive of 'shoot-to-kill' policies and targeted killings cuts both ways in that it may be more permissive of the use of force against armed insurgents but, in the area of overlap between the paradigms, the exceptions to the right to life may act to impose stricter standards of protection than the laws of war would provide. Once there is an armed conflict by virtue of the circumstances satisfying the test set out in *Tadić*, the laws of war will apply but international human rights law may also apply, directly in the terms of the ECHR unless or until a state derogates on the basis that there is a war. This could be said to be a peculiarly European position as there is no derogation in relation to the right to life under the International Covenant and, in the opinion of the ICJ in the *Nuclear Weapons* advisory opinion and the Human Rights Committee, once there is an armed conflict, the laws of war apply as the *lex specialis*. Nevertheless, it would be possible for bodies such as the HRC to address the issue by making a distinction in the case of an armed conflict that is also an insurrection through the interpretation of what is, or is not, an arbitrary killing in a non-international armed conflict. The human rights approach generally could then be developed to provide greater protection by imposing restrictions on self-defence that exclude pre-meditated killings, developing the concepts of necessity and proportionality in insurrection and then requiring acts to be held to those standards irrespective of what the laws of war permit through military necessity and the test of proportionality.

Finally, none of these arguments should be taken as suggesting that accepting that it is lawful to use lethal force other than in self-defence to suppress an insurrection does not raise some very difficult issues or that the arguments made here can provide a neat solution to them. It has been seen how governments have not, and perhaps will not, admit to there being an insurrection but that would seem to overlook the past and how things continue to change. In future operations, the British government would be likely either to have to derogate from the ECHR (or have denounced the convention) or it would have to develop a legal strategy better suited to the conditions that it might face than it did for Iraq. When negotiating the International Covenant and the ECHR there was a wide consensus amongst states that there could be circumstances in which a state would have to use armed force to quell an insurrection or rebellion or, to use more modern language, to maintain or restore public order against the challenge provided by armed insurgents. The law that has been explored here has been shaped by how internal armed conflict has changed over the period from wars between traditional armies to guerrilla wars with insurgents operating covertly with more powerful weapons. Faced with new circumstances, the law had to adapt and it did in different ways that were in part by design and in part contingent. Changes to the laws of war have meant that the use of force in non-international armed conflicts may be more permissive than the drafters of the various conventions and subsequent practitioners allowed for and was the case prior to their development. As a result, the laws of war which were designed for war between states can fail to strike an acceptable balance for the protection of civilians in internal armed conflicts short of civil war. At the same time, international human rights law has become more restrictive and seen as permitting the use of force only in accordance with rules and legal judgments based in law-enforcement and self-defence rather than the wider issues of the maintenance of public order which can leave the security forces unable to challenge effectively organized armed groups with modern military weapons. The application of the law to quelling insurrections, therefore, requires reconsideration of the existing law so that it provides a better balance for the protection of civilians and the security forces in the face of armed violence and is more suited to the conditions of modern internal armed conflicts. As Pollock wrote of the law's application when the character of war was changing, '[b]y recognizing this fact we do not alter the law, but apply it to the facts as they exist'.[36]

[36] Pollock, 'What is Martial Law?' (1902) (n 17) 156.

BIBLIOGRAPHY

Akande, Dapo and Hill-Cawthorne, Lawrence, 'The Lieber Code and the Regulation of Civil War in International Law' *Columbia, Lieber Series* (2015)

Alexander, Amanda, 'A Short History of International Humanitarian Law' (2015) 26: 1 *European Journal of International Law* 109–38

Andler, Charles, *'Frightfulness' in Theory and Practice as Compared with Franco-British Usages* (London, T Fisher Unwin, 1916)

Armitage, David, 'Cosmopolitanism and Civil War' (2016) – published in 'Cosmopolitanism and Civil War' in Joan-Pau Rubiés and Neil Safier (eds), *Cosmopolitanism and the Enlightenment* (Cambridge, Cambridge University Press, 2023)

Armitage, David, *Civil Wars: A History in Ideas* (New Haven, Yale University Press, 2017)

Arnold, Roberta and Quénivet, Noëlle (eds), *International Humanitarian Law and Human Rights Law: Towards a New Merger in International Law* (Leiden, Martinus Nijhoff Publishers, 2008)

Aughey, Sean and Sari, Aurel, 'Targeting and Detention in Non-International Armed Conflict: Serdar Mohammed and the Limits of Human Rights Convergence' (2005) 91: 60 *International Legal Studies* 61–116.

Baker, Sir John, *An Introduction to English Legal History* (Oxford, Oxford University Press, 2019)

Baxter, Richard, R 'First Codification of the Law of War: Francis Lieber and General Orders No 100' (April 1963) 3: 25–26 *International Review of the Red Cross* 170–89 and 234–50

Becket, Ian, *Modern Insurgencies and Counter-Insurgencies: Guerrillas and their Opponents since 1750* (London, Routledge, 2001)

Bennett, Geoffrey and Ryan, Christopher, 'Armed Forces, Public Order and the law in the United Kingdom' in Peter Rowe and Chris Whelan (eds), *Military Intervention in Democratic Societies* (London, Croom Helm, 1985)

Bennett, Huw, *Fighting the Mau Mau: The British Army and Counter-Insurgency in the Kenya Emergency* (Cambridge, Cambridge University Press, 2013)

Best, Geoffrey, *Humanity in Warfare, The Modern History of the International Law of Armed Conflict* (London, Weidenfeld and Nicholson, 1980)

Best, Geoffrey, *War and Law since 1945* (Oxford, Clarendon Press, 1997)

Bluntschli, Johan C, 'The Service of Francis Lieber to Political Science and International Law' (1880) Vol XIII *International Review* 50–55

Bluntschli, Johan C, *Das Moderne Kriegsrecht der Civilisirten Staten* (Nördlingen, CH Beck, 1866)

Bluntschli, Johan C, *Le Droit International Codifié* (Paris, Guillaumin, 1870)

Boothby, William, '"And for Such Time As": The Time Dimension to Direct Participation in Hostilities' (2010) 42 *New York University Journal of International Law and Politics* 741–68

Boothby, William, *The Law of Targeting* (Oxford, Oxford University Press, 2012)

Bossuyt, Marc J, *Guide to the 'Travaux Préparatoires' of the International Covenant of Civil and Political Rights* (Dordrecht, Martinus Nijhoff, 1987)

Boynton, Lindsay, 'Martial Law and the Petition of Right' (April 1964) 79: 311 *The English Historical Review* 255–84

Bronitt, Simon and Stephens, Dale, '"Flying Under the Radar" – The Use of Lethal Force Against Hijacked Aircraft: Recent Australian Developments' (2007) 7: 2 *Oxford University Commonwealth Law Journal* 265–78

Callwell, Charles E, *Small Wars: Their Principles and Practice* (London, HMSO, 1906 – republished by Endeavour Press Ltd, 2016)

Campbell, Colm, *Emergency Laws in Ireland 1918–25* (Oxford, Clarendon Press, 1994)
Cann, John P, 'Low-intensity Conflict, Insurgency, Terrorism and Revolutionary War' in Matthew Hughes and William J Philpott, *Modern Military History* (London, Palgrave Macmillan, 2006)
Carnahan, Burrus M, 'Lincoln, Lieber and the Laws of War: The Origins and Limits of the Principle of Military Necessity' (1998) 92: 2 *American Journal of International Law* 213–31
Cassese, Antonio, *International Law* (Oxford, Oxford University Press, 2005)
Castrén, Erik, *Civil War* (Helsinki, Suómalainen Tiedeakatemia, 1966)
Childress, James F, 'Francis Lieber's Interpretation of the Laws of War: General Orders No 100 in the Context of His Life and Thought' (1976) 21: 1 *American Journal of Jurisprudence* 34–70
Chinkin, Christine and Kaldor, Mary, *International Law and New Wars* (Cambridge, Cambridge University Press, 2017)
Clapham, Andrew and Gaeta, Paula (eds), *The Oxford Handbook of International Law in Armed Conflict* (Oxford, Oxford University Press, 2014)
von Clausewitz, Carl, *On War*, edited and translated by Michael Howard and Peter Paret (Princeton, Princeton University Press, 1976)
Clode, Charles, *The Administration of Justice Under Military and Martial Law* (London, John Murray, 1872)
Coker, Christopher, *Rebooting Clausewitz: On War in the 21st Century* (London, Hurst & Company, 2017)
Crowe, Jonathan and Weston-Scheuber, Kylie, *Principles of International Humanitarian Law* (Cheltenham, Edward Elgar, 2013)
Cryer, Robert, 'Of Custom, Treaties, Scholars and the Gavel: The Influence of the International Criminal Tribunals on the ICRC Customary Law Study' (Summer 2006) 11: 2 *Journal of Conflict and Security Law*, 239–263.
Cullen, Anthony, 'Key Developments Affecting the Scope of Internal Armed Conflict in International Humanitarian Law' (2005) 183 *Military Law Review* 66–109
Curwood, John, *A Treatise on the Pleas of the Crown, by William Hawkins*, Vol I of Criminal Offences (London, S Sweet, 1824)
Detter de Lupis, Ingrid, *The Law of War* (Farnham, Ashgate Publishing Ltd, 2013)
Dicey, Albert V, *An Introduction to the Study of the Law of the Constitution* (London, MacMillan, 1915) republished by LibertyClassics (1982)
van Dijk, Boyd, 'Human Rights in War: On the Entangled Foundations of the 1949 Geneva Conventions' (2018) 112: 4 *American Journal of International Law* 553–82
van Dijk, Boyd, *Preparing for War: The Making of the Geneva Conventions* (Oxford, Oxford University Press, 2022)
Dinstein, Yoram, *War, Aggression and Self-Defence* (Cambridge, Cambridge University Press, 2017)
Dinstein, Yoram, *Non-international Armed Conflicts in International Law* (Cambridge, Cambridge University Press, 2014)
Dinstein, Yoram, *The Conduct of Hostilities under the Law of International Armed Conflict* (Cambridge, Cambridge University Press, 2016)
Dixon, Paul, 'Hearts and Minds? British Counter-Insurgency from Malaya to Iraq' (2009) 32: 3 *Journal of Strategic Studies* 353–81
Doswald-Beck, Louise, *Human Rights in Times of Conflict and Terrorism* (Oxford, Oxford University Press, 2011)
Dowdeswell, Tracey, 'The Brussels Peace Conference of 1874 and the Modern Laws of Belligerent Qualification' (2017) 54: 3 *Osgoode Hall Law Journal* 805–50
Droege, Cordula, 'The Interplay between International Humanitarian Law and International Human Rights Law in Situations of Armed Conflict' (2007) 40: 2 *Israel Law Review* 310–55
Drohan, Brian, *Brutality in an Age of Human Rights: Activism and Counterinsurgency at the End of the British Empire* (Ithaca, Cornell University Press, 2017)
Dyzenhaus, David, 'The Puzzle of Martial Law' (2009) 59: 1 *University of Toronto Law Journal* 1–64
Edmonds, Colonel James and Oppenheim, Lassa, *An Exposition of the Laws and Usages of War on Land for the Guidance of Officers of His Majesty's Army* (London, HMSO, 1912)

Edwards, Aaron, 'Misapplying Lessons Learned? Analysing the utility of British counterinsurgency strategy in Northern Ireland, 1971–76' (2010) 21:2 *Small Wars & Insurgencies* 303–30

Edwards, Aaron, *Defending the Realm? The Politics of Britain's Small Wars Since 1945* (Manchester, Manchester University Press, 2012)

Elkins, Caroline, *Legacy of Violence: A History of the British Empire* (New York, Alfred A Knopf, 2022)

Finlason, William F, *A Treatise on Martial Law as Allowed by the Law of England in Time of Rebellion; with Practical Illustrations drawn from the Official Documents in the Jamaica Case, and the Evidence taken by The Royal Commission of Enquiry* (London, Stevens & Sons, 1866)

Fleck, Dieter (ed), *The Handbook of International Humanitarian Law* (Oxford, Oxford University Press, 2013)

Forsyth, William, *Cases and Opinions on Constitutional Law, And Various Points of English Jurisprudence, Collected and Digested from Official Documents and Other Sources*; with Notes (London, Stevens and Haynes, 1869)

French, David, *The British Way in Counter-insurgency, 1945–1967* (Oxford, Oxford University Press, 2011)

Friedman, Leon (ed), *Law of War: A Documentary History* (New York, Random House, 1972)

Garner, James G, 'General Orders 100 Revisited' (January 1964) 27 *Military Law Review* 1–48

Garrod, Matthew, 'The British Influence on the Development of the Laws of War and the Punishment of War Criminals: From the Grotius Society to the United Nations War Crimes Commission' in Robert McCorquodale and Jean-Pierre Gauci (eds), *British Influences on International Law* (Leiden, Brill Nijhoff, 2016)

Greenwood, Christopher, 'International Humanitarian Law and the *Tadić* Case' (1996) 7: 2 *European Journal of International Law* 265–28

Greenwood, Christopher, 'International Law and the "War on Terrorism"' (2002) 78 *International Affairs* 301–17

Greenwood, Christopher, *Essays on War in International Law* (London, Cameron May, 2006)

Greenwood, Christopher, 'Human Rights and Humanitarian Law – Conflict or Convergence' (2010–11) 43: 1 *Case Western Reserve Journal of International Law* 491–512

Gwynne, Sir Charles, *Imperial Policing* (London, MacMillan & Co. Ltd, 1934)

Hale, Sir Matthew, *The History of the Pleas of the Crown, Vol 1* (London, T Payne, 1778) (also published by Google Books)

Halleck, Henry, *International Law: Or, Rules Regulating the Intercourse of States in Peace* (New York, D Van Nostrand, 1861)

Happold, Matthew, 'International Humanitarian Law and Human Rights Law' in Nigel D White and Christian Henderson (eds), *Research Handbook on International Conflict and Security Law* (Cheltenham, Edward Elgar, 2013)

Harris, David and O'Boyle, Michael (eds), *Harris, O'Boyle & Warbrick: The Law of the European Convention on Human Rights* (Oxford, Oxford University Press, 2014)

Hartigan, Richard Shelly, *Lieber's Code and the Law of War* (Chicago, Precedent, 1983)

Hathaway, Oona A and Shapiro, Scott J, *The Internationalists: How a Radical Plan to Outlaw War Remade the World* (New York, Simon & Schuster, 2017)

Hays Parks, William, 'Part IX of the ICRC "Direct Participation in Hostilities" Study: No Mandate, No Expertise, and Legally Incorrect' (2010) 42 *New York University Journal of International Law and Politics* 767–830

Henckaerts, Jean-Marie and Doswald-Beck, Louise, *Customary International Humanitarian Law*, Vols I and II (Cambridge, Cambridge University Press, 2005)

Henderson, Ian, *The Contemporary Law of Targeting: Military Objectives, Proportionality and Precautions in Attack under Additional Protocol I* (Leiden, Martinus Nijhoff Publishers, 2009)

Holland, Sir Thomas E, *The Laws and Customs of War on Land, as defined by the Hague Convention of 1899* (London, Harrison and Sons, 1904)

Holland, Sir Thomas E, *The Laws of War on Land* (Oxford, Clarendon Press, 1908)

Holdsworth, Sir William, 'Martial Law Historically Considered' (1902) 18 *LQR* 117–32

Horder, Jeremy, *Ashworth's Principles of Criminal Law* (Oxford, Oxford University Press, 2016)

Hughes, Matthew and Philpott, William J, *Modern Military History* (London, Palgrave Macmillan, 2006)

Hughes, Matthew, 'Introduction: British Ways of Counter-insurgency' (2012) 23: 4–5 *Small Wars & Insurgencies* 580–90

Hussain, Nasser, *The Jurisprudence of Emergency: Colonialism and the Rule of Law* (Ann Arbor, The University of Michigan Press, 2003)

ICRC, *Commentary on the First Geneva Convention: Convention (I) for the Amelioration of the Condition of the Wounded and Sick in Armed Forces in the Field* (ICRC, 1952)

ICRC, *Commentary on the First Geneva Convention: Convention (I) for the Amelioration of the Condition of the Wounded and Sick in Armed Forces in the Field* (Cambridge, Cambridge University Press, 2016)

Jessup, Philip C, 'Should International Law Recognize an Intermediate Status between Peace and War?' (January 1954) 48: 1 *American Journal of International Law* 98–103

Johnson, Robert, 'Command of the Army, Charles Gwynn and *Imperial Policing*: The British Doctrinal Approach to Internal Security in Palestine 1919–29' (2015) 43: 4 *The Journal of Imperial and Commonwealth History* 570–89

Joseph, Sarah and Castan, Melissa, *The International Covenant on Civil and Political Rights: Cases, Materials and Commentary* (Oxford, Oxford University Press, 2013)

Keir, Sir David and Lawson, Frederick, *Cases in Constitutional Law* (Oxford, Clarendon Press, 1979)

Kitson, Frank, *Low Intensity Operations: Subversion, Insurgency, Peacekeeping* (London, Faber and Faber, 1971)

Klamberg, Mark and Nilsson, Jonas (eds), *Commentary on the Law of the International Criminal Court – The Rome Statute* (Brussels, Torkel Opsahl Academic EPublisher, 2020)

Kolb, Robert, 'The Relationship between International Humanitarian Law and Human Rights Law: A Brief History of the 1948 Universal Declaration of Human Rights and the 1949 Geneva Conventions' (1998) 38: 324 *International Review of the Red Cross* 409–19

Kostal, Rande W, *A Jurisprudence of Power: Victorian Empire and the Rule of Law* (Oxford, Oxford University Press, 2005)

Kretzmer, David, 'Targeted Killing of Suspected Terrorists: Extra-Judicial Executions or Legitimate Means of Defence' (2005) 16: 2 *The European Journal of International Law* 171–212

Lattimer, Mark and Sands, Philippe (eds), *The Grey Zone: Civilian Protection between Human Rights and the Laws of War* (London, Hart, 2018)

Lattimer, Mark, 'The Duty in International Law to Investigate Civilian Deaths in Armed Conflict' in Mark Lattimer and Philippe Sands (eds), *The Grey Zone: Civilian Protection between Human Rights and the Laws of War* (London, Hart, 2018)

Lauterpacht, Sir Hersch (ed), *International Law, A Treatise by L Oppenheim*, Vol II, (London, Longmans, Green & Co, 1940)

Lauterpacht, Sir Hersch, *Recognition in International Law* (Cambridge, Cambridge University Press, 1947)

Lieber, Francis, *Political Ethics* (Boston, CC Little and J Brown, 1839)

Lieber, Francis, 'Guerrilla Parties Considered in Reference to the Laws and Usages of War', 17 August 1862. A copy is published in Richard Shelly Hartigan, *Lieber's Code and the Law of War* (Chicago, Precedent, 1983)

Lieber, Francis, 'The Civil Status of Paroled Rebels' (27 May 1865, New York) *Army and Navy Journal*

Lino, Dylan, 'The Rule of Law and the Rule of Empire: AV Dicey in Imperial Context' (September 2018) 81: 5 *Modern Law Review* 739–64

Liivoja, Rain, 'Technological Change and the Evolution of the Law of War', *International Review of the Red Cross* (Winter 2015) 97: 900, 'The Evolution of Warfare', 1157–78

Lovat, Henry, *Negotiating Civil War* (Cambridge, Cambridge University Press, 2020)

Mackay, Lord James (ed), *Halsbury's Laws* (5th edn, 2011) Vol 3, 'Armed Conflict and Emergency'

Mackinlay, John, *The Insurgent Archipelago* (London, Hurst, 2009)

Macready, General The Rt Hon Sir Nevil, *Annals of an Active Life*, Vol 1 (London, Hutchinson & Co 1924)

Mantilla, Giovanni, *Lawmaking Under Pressure: International Humanitarian Law and Internal Armed Conflict* (New York, Cornell University Press, 2020)

Marsala, Vincent, *Sir John Peter Grant, Governor of Jamaica, 1866–1874: An Administrative History* (Louisiana State University, LSU Historical Dissertations and Theses, 1967)

Marston, David and Malkasian, Carter (eds), *Counterinsurgency in Modern Warfare* (Oxford, Osprey Publishing, 2008)
Marston, Geoffrey, 'The United Kingdom's Part in the Preparation of The European Convention on Human Rights, 1950' (1993) 42: 4 *International and Comparative Law Quarterly* 796–826
McCorquodale, Robert and Gauci, Jean-Pierre, *British Influences on International Law* (Leiden, Brill Nijhoff, 2016)
McCurry, Stephanie, 'Enemy Women and the Laws of War in the American Civil War' (August 2017) 35: 3 *Law and History Journal* 667–710
McLaughlin, Robert, 'The Use of Lethal Force by Military Forces on Law Enforcement Operations – Is There a "Lawful Authority"?' (2009) 37: 3 *Federal Law Review* 441–69
McNair, Sir Arnold D, *Collective Security, An Inaugural Lecture* (Cambridge, Cambridge University Press, 1936)
Melzer, Nils, *Targeted Killing in International Law* (Oxford, Oxford University Press, 2008)
Melzer, Nils, 'Interpretative Guidance on the Notion of Direct Participation in Hostilities under International Humanitarian Law', *ICRC*, May 2009
Meron, Theodor, 'Francis Lieber's Code and the Principles of Humanity' (1997) 36 *Columbia Journal of Transnational Law* 269–81
Milanovic, Marko, 'A Norm Conflict Perspective on the Relationship between International Humanitarian Law and Human Rights Law' (2010) 14: 3 *Journal of Conflict & Security Law* 459–83
Milanovic, Marko, *Extraterritorial Application of Human Rights Treaties: Law, Principles, and Policy* (Oxford, Oxford University Press, 2011)
Milanovic, Marko and Hadzi-Vidanovic, Vidan, 'A Taxonomy of Armed Conflict' in Nigel D White and Christian Henderson (eds), *Research Handbook on International Conflict and Security Law* (Cheltenham, Edward Elgar, 2013)
Mockaitis, Thomas R, *British Counterinsurgency, 1919–60* (Basingstoke, MacMillan, 1990)
Mockaitis, Thomas R, *British Counterinsurgency in the Post-imperial Era* (Manchester, Manchester University Press, 1995)
Moir, Lindsay, 'The Historical Development of the Application of Humanitarian Law in Non-International Armed Conflicts to 1949' (1998) 47: 2 *International and Comparative Law Quarterly* 337–61
Moore, Cameron, *Crown and Sword: Executive Power and the Use of Force by the Australian Defence Force* (Canberra, ANU Press, 2017)
Murray, Daragh (ed), *Practitioners' Guide to Human Rights Law in Armed Conflict* (Oxford, Oxford University Press, 2016)
Nabulsi, Karma, *Traditions of War, Occupation, Resistance and the Law* (Oxford, Oxford University Press, 1999)
Neff, Stephen C, 'The Prerogatives of Violence – In Search of the Conceptual Foundations of Belligerents' Rights' (1995) 38 *German Yearbook of International Law* 41–72
Neff, Stephen C, *War and the Law of Nations, A General History* (Cambridge, Cambridge University Press, 2005)
Neff, Stephen C, *Justice in Blue and Gray: A Legal History of The Civil War* (Harvard, Harvard University Press, 2010)
Nowak, Manfred, *UN Covenant on Civil and Political Rights, CCPR Commentary* (Kekl, Germany, NP Engel, 2005)
O'Connell, Mary Ellen, 'Historical Development and Legal Basis' in Dieter Fleck (ed), *The Handbook of International Humanitarian Law* (Oxford, Oxford University Press, 2013)
O'Connell, Mary Ellen, 'The Prohibition on the Use of Force' in Nigel D White and Christian Henderson, *Research Handbook on International Conflict and Security Law* (Cheltenham, Edward Elgar, 2013)
Odello, Marco, 'Fundamental Standards of Humanity: A Common Language of International Humanitarian Law and Human Rights Law' in Roberta Arnold and Noëlle Quénivet (eds), *International Humanitarian Law and Human Rights Law: Towards a New Merger in International Law* (Leiden, Martinus Nijhoff Publishers, 2008)

Ohlin, Jens David and May, Larry, *Necessity in International Law* (Oxford, Oxford University Press, 2016)
Oppenheim, Lassa, *International Law, A Treatise, Vol II War and Neutrality* (London, Longmans, Green, and Co, 1912)
Ormerod, David and Laird, Karl, *Smith and Hogan's Criminal Law* (Oxford, Oxford University Press, 2015)
Ormerod, David (ed), *Halsbury's Laws* (5th edn, 2020) Vol 26, 'Criminal Law'
Otto, Roland, *Targeted Killings and International Law* (Heidelberg, Springer, 2012)
Park, Ian, *The Right to Life in Armed Conflict* (Oxford, Oxford University Press, 2018)
Pejić, Jelena, 'Status of Armed Conflicts' in Elizabeth Wilmshurst and Susan Breau (eds), *Perspectives on the ICRC Study on Customary International Humanitarian Law* (Cambridge, Cambridge University Press, 2007)
Pejić, Jelena, 'The Protective Scope of Common Article 3: More than Meets the Eye' (2011) 93: 881 *International Review of the Red* Cross 1–37
Perry, Thomas Sergeant (ed), *The Life and Letters of Francis Lieber* (Boston, James Osgood and Company, 1882)
Pollock, Sir Frederick, 'What is Martial Law?' (1902) 18 *LQR* 152–58
Quénivet, Noëlle, 'The Moscow Hostage Crisis in the Light of the Armed Conflict in Chechnya' (2001) 4 *Yearbook of International Humanitarian Law* 348–72
Quénivet, Noëlle, 'The History of the Relationship between International Humanitarian Law and Human Rights Law' in Roberta Arnold and Noëlle Quénivet (eds), *International Humanitarian Law and Human Rights Law: Towards a New Merger in International Law* (Leiden, Martinus Nijhoff Publishers, 2008)
Quénivet, Noëlle, 'The Obligation to Investigate after a Potential Breach of Article 2 ECHR in an Extra-Territorial Context: Mission Impossible for the Armed Forces?' (2019) 37: 2 *Netherlands Quarterly of Human Rights* 119–38
Quénivet, Noëlle, 'Article 8(2)(c)' in Mark Klamberg and Jonas Nilsson (eds), *Commentary on the Law of the International Criminal Court – The Rome Statute* (Brussels, Torkel Opsahl Academic EPublisher, 2020)
Roberts, Sir Adam, 'Counter-terrorism, Armed Force and the Laws of War' (2002) 44 *Survival* 7–32
Rodenhäuser Tilman, *Organizing Rebellion: Non-State Armed Groups under International Law* (Oxford, Oxford University Press, 2018)
Rogers, Maj Gen AVP, *Law on the Battlefield* (Manchester, Manchester University Press, 2004)
Root, Elihu, 'Francis Lieber' (July 1913) 7: 3 *American Journal of International Law* 453–69
Rubin, Gerry R, 'The Legal Education of British Army Officers, 1860–1923' (1994) 15 *Journal of Legal History* 223–51
Rubin, Gerry R, 'Book review of *Emergency Law in Ireland, 1918–25* by Colm Campbell' (Oxford, Clarendon Press, 1994)' (1995) 111 *LQR* 520–30
Russell, Hannah, *The Use of Force and Article 2 of the ECHR in Light of European Conflicts* (London, Hart Publishing, 2017)
Sassòli, Marco and Olsen, Laura, 'The Relationship between International Humanitarian Law and Human Rights Law Where It Matters: Admissible Killing and Internment of Fighters in Non-International Armed Conflicts' (2008) 90: 871 *International Review of the Red Cross* 599–627
Schabas, William, 'The Right to Life' in Andrew Clapham and Paula Gaeta (eds), *The Oxford Handbook of International Law in Armed Conflict* (Oxford, Oxford University Press, 2014)
Schabas, William, *The Trial of the Kaiser* (Oxford, Oxford University Press 2018)
Schmitt, Michael N, 'Deconstructing Direct Participation in Hostilities: The Constitutive Elements' (2010) 42 *New York University Journal of International Law and Politics* 697–739
Simester, Andrew P, Spencer, John R, Stark, Findlay, Sullivan, Bob and Virgo, Graham J, *Simester and Sullivan's Criminal Law: Theory and Doctrine* (London, Bloomsbury, 2016)
Simpson, AWB, *Human Rights and the End of Empire: Britain and the Genesis of the European Convention* (Oxford, Oxford University Press, 2001)
Simson, Col HJ, *British Rule and Rebellion* (London, William Blackwood & Sons Ltd, 1937)

Sivakumaran, Sandesh, *The Law of Non-International Armed Conflict* (Oxford, Oxford University Press, 2012)
Skinner, Stephen, 'Citizens in Uniform: Public Defence, Reasonableness and Human Rights' (2000) *Public Law* 266–81
Solis, Gary, *The Law of Armed Conflict: International Humanitarian Law in War* (Cambridge, Cambridge University Press, 2016)
Spaight, James M, *War Rights on Land* (London, Macmillan and Co Ltd, 1911)
Stephen, Sir James, *Digest of Criminal Law* (London, Macmillan and Co, 1883)
Stephen, Sir James, *History of the Criminal Law* (London, Macmillan and Co, 1883)
Strachan, Hew and Scheipers, Sibylle (eds), *The Changing Character of War* (Oxford, Oxford University Press, 2011)
Stubbs, Richard, 'From Search and Destroy to Hearts and Minds: The Evolution of British Strategy in Malaya 1948–60' in Daniel Marston and Carter Malkasian (eds), *Counterinsurgency in Modern Warfare* (Oxford, Osprey Publishing, 2008)
Suter, Keith, *An International Law of Guerrilla Warfare: The Global Politics of Law-Making* (London, Frances Pinter, 1984)
Taggart Michael, Book Review: 'Ruled by Law?: A Jurisprudence of Power: Victorian Empire and the Rule of Law by R W Kostal' (November 2006) 69: 6 *The Modern Law Review* 1006–25
Teitel, Ruth, *Humanity's Law* (Oxford, Oxford University Press, 2011)
Thayer, Martin Russell, *Life, Character and Writings of Francis Lieber* (Philadelphia, Collins, 1873)
Thompson, Sir Robert, *Defeating Communist Insurgency: Experiences from Malaya and Vietnam* (London, Chatto & Windus, 1966)
Thornton, Rod, 'The British Army and the Origins of the Minimum Force Philosophy' (2004) 15: 1 *Small Wars & Insurgencies* 83–106
Townshend, Charles, 'Martial Law: Legal and Administrative Problems of Civil Emergency in Britain and the Empire, 1800–1940' (1982) 25: 1 *The Historical Journal* 167–95
Townshend, Charles, *Britain's Civil Wars: Counterinsurgency in the Twentieth Century* (London, Faber and Faber, 1986)
Turns, David, 'Targets', in Nigel D White and Christian Henderson (eds), *Research Handbook on International Conflict and Security Law* (Cheltenham, Edward Elgar, 2013)
Turns, David, 'The Law of Armed Conflict (International Humanitarian Law)' in Malcolm Evans (ed), *International Law* (Oxford, Oxford University Press, 2014)
Urban, Mark, *Big Boys' Rules: The SAS and the Secret Struggle against the IRA* (London, Faber & Faber, 1992)
UK Ministry of Defence, *The Manual of the Law of Armed Conflict* (Oxford, Oxford University Press, 2004)
US War Department, Adjutant General's Office, *General Orders, No 100: Instructions for the Government of Armies of the United States in the Field* (Washington, GPO, 1863)
US War Department, Adjutant General's Office, *General Orders, No 100: Instructions for the Government of Armies of the United States in the Field* (reprint by D van Norstrand (New York), 1863) – also available as a facsimile book published by Leopold Classic Library
US Government Printing Office, *Instructions for the Government of Armies of the United States in the Field, prepared by Francis Lieber, LL.D, Originally Issued as General Orders No 100, Adjutant General's Office, 1863* (Washington, 1898)
US War Department, *Rules of Land Warfare* (Washington, GPO, 1914)
US War Department, *Rules of Land Warfare, FM27-10* (Washington, GPO, 1940)
US Department of the Army, *The Law of Land Warfare, FM27-10* (Washington, GPO, 1956)
US Department of Defense, *Law of War Manual* (Washington, Department of Defense, 2015)
de Vattel, Emer, *The Law of Nations; or Principles of the Law of Nature, Applied to the Conduct and Affairs of Nations and Sovereigns*. From the French of Monsieur de Vattel. Sixth American edition, from a new edition, by Joseph Chitty (Philadelphia, T & JW Johnson, 1844)
War Office, *Manual of Military Law* (London, HMSO, 1884)
War Office, *Manual of Military Law*, 5th edn (London, HMSO, 1907)

War Office, *Manual of Military Law*, 6th edn (London, HMSO, 1914)
War Office, *Manual of Military Law*, 7th edn (London, HMSO, 1929)
Walker, Clive, 'Book Review: Emergency Law in Ireland 1918–25 by Colm Campbell' (Oxford, Clarendon Press, 1994) (1995) 15(2) *Legal Studies* 311–22
Whewell, Sir William, *The Elements of Morality, Including Polity*, Vol I (New York, Harper & Brothers, 1845)
White, Nigel D and Henderson, Christian (eds), *Research Handbook on International Conflict and Security Law* (Cheltenham, Edward Elgar, 2013)
Wilson, Heather, *International Law and the Use of Force by National Liberation Movements* (Oxford, Clarendon Press, 1988)
Wilmshurst, Elizabeth, 'The Chatham House Principles of International Law on the Use of Force in Self-Defence' (2006) 55: 4 *International and Comparative Law Quarterly* 963–72
Wilmshurst, Elizabeth and Susan Breau, *Perspectives on the ICRC Study on Customary International Humanitarian Law* (Cambridge, Cambridge University Press, 2007)
Wilmshurst, Elizabeth (ed), *International Law and the Classification of Conflicts* (Oxford, Oxford University Press, 2012)
Witt, John Fabian, 'Anglo-American Empire and the Crisis of the Legal Frame (Will the Real British Empire Please Stand Up?)' (2007) 120: 3 *Harvard Law Review* 754–96
Witt, John Fabian, *Lincoln's Code: The Laws of War in American History* (New York, Free Press, 2012)
Zamir, Noam, *Classification of Conflicts in International Humanitarian Law: The Legal Impact of Foreign Intervention in Civil Wars* (Cheltenham, Edward Elgar, 2017)

INDEX

www.ingramcontent.com/pod-product-compliance
Ingram Content Group UK Ltd.
Pitfield, Milton Keynes, MK11 3LW, UK
UKHW020814290926
15470UKWH00003B/1150

9 781509 992225